History

for the IB Diploma

Rights and Protest

Jean Bottaro and John Stanley
Series Editor: Allan Todd

Cambridge University Press's mission is to advance learning, knowledge and research worldwide.

Our IB Diploma resources aim to:

- encourage learners to explore concepts, ideas and topics that have local and global significance

- help students develop a positive attitude to learning in preparation for higher education

- assist students in approaching complex questions, applying critical-thinking skills and forming reasoned answers.

CAMBRIDGE
UNIVERSITY PRESS

CAMBRIDGE
UNIVERSITY PRESS

University Printing House, Cambridge CB2 8BS, United Kingdom

Cambridge University Press is part of the University of Cambridge.

It furthers the University's mission by disseminating knowledge in the pursuit of education, learning and research at the highest international levels of excellence.

Information on this title: education.cambridge.org

© Cambridge University Press 2015

First published 2011
Second edition 2015

Printed in the United Kingdom by Latimer Trend

A catalogue record for this publication is available from the British Library

ISBN 978-1-107-55638-6 Paperback

Contents

Contents

Introduction

This book is designed to prepare students taking the Paper 1 topic *Rights and Protest* (Prescribed Subject 4) in the IB History examination. It focuses on the struggles for rights and freedom in the mid–20th century by looking at two case studies taken from two different regions of the world. Both of these case studies must be studied. The first case study explores the Civil Rights Movement in the United States between 1956 and 1965; the second case study explores the protests against apartheid in South Africa between 1948 and 1964. Each case study will examine three main aspects relating to these two examples of rights and protest: the nature and characteristics of discrimination based on race in the United States and South Africa; the protests (both non-violent and violent) and actions taken by those opposed to this discrimination; and the role and significance of individuals, political parties and groups in these struggles for rights and freedom.

Figure 1.1   Racial unity in a demonstration against the imprisonment of civil rights activist Wally Nelson, in 1946

Overview

Themes

To help you prepare for your IB History exams, this book will cover the main themes and aspects relating to Rights and Protest as set out in the IB *History Guide*. In particular, it will examine the protests against segregation and discrimination based on race in the United States and South Africa after the Second World War. The focus of the two case studies is on the major areas shown below:

- The social and economic position of African Americans by the mid-1950s, following many years of racism, segregation and intimidation due to the 'Jim Crow laws' disenfranchisement and the activities of the Ku Klux Klan.

- Growing unhappiness with racial segregation in education, and a decision by the Civil Rights Movement to test this system with the *Brown v. Topeka Board of Education* case in 1954 and at Little Rock, Arkansas in 1957.

- The gradual shift from non-violent to violent protest that took place over the decade between the Montgomery Bus Boycott of 1956 and the Watts Riots in Los Angeles in 1965.

- The introduction of the Civil Rights Act of 1964 and the Voting Rights Act of 1965 and their significance as major pieces of legislation.

- The role and significance of the different civil rights organisations, together with the importance of Martin Luther King Jnr. and the black churches.

- How developing technology in the 1960s enabled television to become the predominant medium of communication, and the extent to which TV and the Civil Rights Movement were mutually useful and beneficial during this period of protest.

- The implementation of apartheid in South Africa after 1948, which involved the classification of the population into different race groups and a rigid system of political and social segregation.

- The suppression of resistance to apartheid and opposition labelled as 'communist'.

- The decade of non-violent protest against apartheid during the 1950s, ending in the shooting by police of 69 people in a peaceful protest at Sharpeville in 1960.

- International protests against apartheid by the United Nations and the Anti-Apartheid Movement.

- The switch to violent forms of protest against apartheid, the arrest of leaders of the underground movement, and their sentences to life imprisonment in the Rivonia Trial.

- The role of the National Party in implementing apartheid and suppressing opposition; and the roles played by the ANC, PAC, Communist Party, MK, Nelson Mandela and Albert Luthuli in different forms of protest against it.

Each chapter will help you focus on the main issues and to compare the main developments relating to the two case studies.

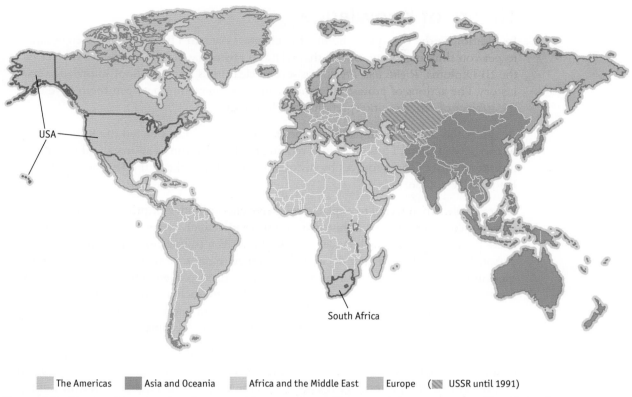

The Americas ■ Asia and Oceania ■ Africa and the Middle East ■ Europe (USSR until 1991)

Figure 1.2   The two IB regions are shown on this map, along with some of the states covered by this book

Key Concepts

To perform well in your IB History examinations, you will often need to consider aspects of one or more of six important Key Concepts as you write your answers. These six Key Concepts are:

- Change
- Continuity
- Causation
- Consequence
- Significance
- Perspectives

Sometimes, a question might ask you to address two Key Concepts, for instance: 'Why did the US Congress pass the Civil Rights Act in 1964? What were the immediate consequences of this legislation on the position of African Americans?'

It is immediately clear with this question that the Key Concept of Consequences must be addressed in your answer. However, it is important to note that although the word 'causes' doesn't explicitly appear in the question, words such as 'why' or 'reasons' are nonetheless asking you to address Causation as well.

To help you focus on the six Key Concepts, and gain experience of writing answers that address them, you will find a range of different questions and activities throughout these chapters.

Theory of Knowledge

In addition to the broad key themes, the chapters contain Theory of Knowledge links, to get you thinking about aspects that relate to History, which is a Group 3 subject in the IB Diploma. *Rights and Protest* has several clear links to ideas about knowledge and history. The actions of protest movements and the interaction between them have been the subject of differing interpretations by historians.

At times, the controversial nature of some of these issues has affected the historians writing about them. Thus, questions relating to the selection of sources, and to differing interpretations of these sources by historians, have clear links to the IB Theory of Knowledge course.

For example, when trying to explain the effectiveness of different protest actions or the significance of certain leaders, historians must decide which evidence to select and use to make their case – and which evidence to leave out. But to what extent do the historians' personal views influence their decisions when they select what they consider to be the most important or relevant sources, and when they make judgements about the value and limitations of specific sources or sets of sources? Is there such a thing as objective 'historical truth'? Or are there just a range of subjective historical opinions and interpretations about the past, which vary according to the political interests and leanings of individual historians?

You are therefore encouraged to read a range of books offering different interpretations of the Civil Rights Movement, considering the several different groups that comprised the movement, the protests against apartheid, the role of leaders such as Martin Luther King and Nelson Mandela, and the significance of different historical events during the period covered by this book, in order to gain a clear understanding of the relevant historiographies (see Chapter 8, Further Information).

IB History and Paper 1 questions

Paper 1 and sources

Unlike Papers 2 and 3, which require you to write essays using just your own knowledge, Paper 1 questions are source-based. Whether you are taking Standard or Higher Level, the sources, the questions – and the markschemes applied by your examiners – are the same.

To answer these questions successfully, you need to be able to combine the use of your own knowledge with the ability to assess and *use* a range of sources in a variety of ways. Each Paper 1 examination question is based on four sources – usually three written and one visual. The latter might be a photograph, a cartoon, a poster, a painting or a table of statistics.

Captions and attributions

Before looking at the types of sources you will need to assess, it is important to establish one principle from the beginning. This is the issue of captions and attributions – these are the pieces of information about each source provided by the Chief Examiner.

Captions and attributions are there for a very good reason, as they give you vital information about the source. For instance, they tell you who wrote it and when, or what it was intended to do. Chief Examiners spend a lot of time deciding what information to give you about each source, because they know it will help you give a full answer, so they expect you to make good use of it! Yet, every year, even good candidates throw away easy marks because they do not read – or do not use – this valuable information.

Essentially, you are being asked to approach the various sources in the same way that a historian would approach them. This means not just looking carefully at what they say or show, but also asking yourself questions about how reliable, useful and/or typical they might be. Many of the answers you need to provide to these questions come from the information provided in the captions and attributions.

Types of source

Most of the sources you will have to assess are written ones, which are sometimes referred to as 'textual' sources. They might be extracts from books, official documents, speeches, newspapers, diaries or letters. Whatever type of source you are reading, the general questions you need to ask about them are the same. These questions concern the content (the information the source provides), its origin (who wrote or produced the source, when and why), and its possible limitations and value, as a result of the answers to those questions.

As an example of the relative value of a source for finding out about a particular event, ask yourself this question: is a recent history book *more* valuable than a speech made at the time of that event?

Although visual (or non-textual) sources are clearly different from written sources in some respects, the same questions and considerations are relevant.

Approaching sources as a set

As well as developing the ability to analyse individual sources, it is important also to look at the four sources provided *as a set*. This means looking at them *all* to see to what extent they agree or disagree with each other.

This ability to look at the four sources together is particularly important when it comes to the last question in the exam paper - the one where you need to use the sources *and* your own knowledge to assess the validity of a statement or assertion, or to analyse the significance of a particular factor. Here, you need to build an answer – along the lines of a 'mini-essay' – that combines precise knowledge with specific comments about the sources. Try to avoid falling into the trap of dealing with all the sources first, and then giving some own knowledge (as an afterthought) that is not linked to the sources.

Exam skills

If all this sounds a bit daunting, don't worry! Throughout the main chapters of this book, there are activities and questions to help you develop the understanding and the exam skills necessary for success. Before attempting the specific exam practice questions that come at the end of each main chapter, you might find it useful to refer *first* to Chapter 8, the final-exam practice chapter. This suggestion is based on the idea that if you know where you are supposed to be going (in this instance, gaining a good grade), and how to get there, you stand a better chance of reaching your destination!

Questions and mark schemes

To ensure that you develop the necessary understanding and skills, each chapter contains questions in the margins. In addition, Chapter 8 is devoted to exam practice. It provides help and advice for all Paper 1 questions and for Paper 2 essay questions, and sets out worked examples for Paper 1 judgement questions and for Paper 2 essays. Worked examples for the remaining three Paper 1-type questions (comprehension, value and limitations, and cross-referencing) are to be found at the end of each main chapter.

In addition, simplified markschemes have been provided, to make it easier for you to understand what examiners are looking for in your answers. The actual IB History markschemes can be found on the IB website.

Finally, you will find activities, along with examiners' tips and comments, to help you focus on the important aspects of the questions. These examples will also help you avoid simple mistakes and oversights that, every year, result in even some otherwise good students failing to gain the highest marks.

Figure 1.3 A black man at a 'For Colored Only' water fountain in North Carolina, with a white man at a separate fountain in the background

Background to the period

Before the Second World War, the United States and South Africa were not the only countries in which there was segregation and discrimination based on race. In all the European colonial empires in Africa and Asia there were forms of political, economic and social segregation. Colonised people had no political rights, such as the right to vote, except in very limited circumstances. In these colonies, economic and social discrimination favoured white settlers for jobs, education and housing. For example, Aboriginal Australians had few rights: they were restricted to reserves, could be forcibly moved and were not recognised as citizens.

After the Second World War, however, attitudes around the world began to change. The idea of classifying and discriminating against people on account of their race became increasingly unacceptable. The exposure and subsequent horror of what had happened in Nazi Germany had shown the world the drastic nature of what policies based on race could lead to. As a result, there was a greater awareness of human rights issues and, in 1948, the newly formed United Nations drew up a Universal Declaration of Human Rights that recognised the equality of all people, regardless of race.

These new attitudes and a greater determination to bring about change had far-reaching consequences after the war. Colonies in Asia and Africa demanded independence and fought for freedom from colonial rule. In Brazil, where Afro-Brazilians formed 44 per cent of the population, but where positions of power were dominated by whites, the government passed the Alfonso Arinos Law in 1951, outlawing racial discrimination. In Australia, Aborigines and white liberal supporters formed groups to raise public awareness and put pressure on the government, and in the 1960s Aborigines were granted the right to vote in state and federal elections. In Britain – where immigrants from Commonwealth countries, such as India and Pakistan and those in the Caribbean, faced prejudice and discrimination for housing and jobs – a Race Relations Act was passed in the 1960s.

It was in this context of a greater determination and assertiveness in demanding human rights in the post-war period that the Civil Rights Movement in the United States and the protests against apartheid in South Africa must be seen. However, there were significant differences between these two situations. In the United States, African Americans formed 10 per cent of the population, and in the course of their struggle for equal rights, the federal government used the courts and the army to challenge segregation. In South Africa, however, where blacks formed 80 per cent of the population, the white minority government used legislation, the police and the army to enforce an even stricter system of segregation and oppression.

The Civil Rights Movement in the United States, 1956–65

To appreciate fully the growth of the US Civil Rights Movement in the 1950s and the motivation behind their protests and actions, it is necessary to have some knowledge of the historical background.

The United States of America was created in 1783, out of 13 colonies within the British Empire. The Founding Fathers of the USA were related to early colonists of predominantly English descent, along with a small number of north European origin. The 1776 American Declaration of Independence had stated: 'We hold these truths to be self-evident, that all men are created equal… with certain inalienable Rights, that among these are Life, Liberty and the pursuit of Happiness.' But in reality, Native Americans and black slaves of African origin – both of whom were a significant minority – were deprived of such equality and freedom.

Even by 1850, the majority of black African Americans remained as slaves. A few bought their freedom, some escaped and others worked in the north of the USA, where slavery was less dominant. But more than 90 per cent remained employed as southern slaves.

Meanwhile, white Americans had moved westwards and settled on new land, but tensions arose between the south and the rest of the Union (USA) about whether new states being admitted into the Union should be free or slave states. Most northerners wanted free states so that slave labour would not undercut free black men working their own land.

Many northerners were also concerned in case the south – which they deemed backward-looking – might dominate national government. Such rivalry, underpinned by the deeper political issue of free states versus slave states, triggered the American Civil War in 1861. Eleven southern states operating slavery broke away to form the Confederacy, an alliance of states who resented being patronised by what they viewed as growing interference from the federal government in Washington.

By 1865, the war had ended with the forces of the north defeating the Confederacy. President Abraham Lincoln then signed the 13th Amendment to the US Constitution, which abolished slavery, and was eventually ratified by individual states. But problems remained, such as how the defeated Confederate states were to be treated, and how four million theoretically free slaves were to be provided for. This period of Reconstruction, or the years when the government attempted to rebuild the south, necessitated bringing defeated states back into the Union and assisting former slaves to find work and achieve equality. But many white Americans – especially in the south – developed tactics designed to undermine this process and keep blacks subservient to and dependent on whites. This would preserve white supremacy – the notion that whites were superior to non-whites.

Social segregation was implemented when various states in the south enacted laws or 'Black Codes'. These determined where blacks could and could not go; it segregated them from whites in the use of public buildings and facilities, and limited the areas within towns where they could live. They were also prevented from being witnesses in court. The Codes even allowed whites to whip blacks for indiscipline and return them to previous 'owners' if necessary.

Intimidation, fear and inferiority for blacks thus continued over the next century, while their voting rights were virtually non-existent. Little wonder that after the Second World War – with the exposure of many African Americans to a wider world through military service overseas, together with greater media awareness in the 1950s – came a growing

Figure 1.4 A Civil War map showing free states and slave states in the US

indignation with respect to their continued second-class status within the postwar world's greatest superpower and biggest democracy.

Protests against apartheid in South Africa, 1948–64

To fully understand apartheid and the protests against it, it is necessary to have some knowledge of the colonial background and developments before 1948.

Discrimination based on race did not start with apartheid in 1948. It had been present right from the early days of colonialism, when parts of southern Africa were colonised, first by the Dutch in the 17th century and then by the British in the 19th century. The discovery of diamonds (in 1867) and then gold (in 1886) had a profound effect, politically and economically. Politically, it awakened British interest in the interior of southern Africa, which resulted in the subsequent annexation by Britain of the remaining independent African kingdoms and the 'Boer republics' (independent states set up by the descendants of Dutch settlers in the interior of southern Africa). Economically, it led to an industrial revolution in the region and the potential for rapid economic growth. But it also laid the foundations for a formal system of segregation by introducing strict systems of control over black mine workers. Under the system of migrant labour, black workers from rural areas did the manual labour on the mines for low wages. Their movement to the mines was strictly controlled by a system of 'passes'. These labour practices laid the foundation for segregation and apartheid in the 20th century.

South Africa as a country was established in 1910, when four British colonies united to form the Union of South Africa, as a self-governing dominion within the British Empire. Right from the start, white South Africans (who at that stage made up about 20 per cent of the population) controlled the government and the economy. Most of them were immigrants from Britain or descendants of Dutch settlers (called Afrikaners) who had colonised the Cape and set up the Boer republics.

From 1910, a succession of governments introduced segregation laws that protected the privileged position of the white minority and discriminated against anyone who was not white. The people who were most negatively affected by these segregation laws were 'Africans' who made up about two-thirds of the total population. The lives of the 'coloured' and 'Indian' minorities were also affected, but not to the same extent. The most significant of these laws, and the one that laid the basis for much of the poverty and inequality in contemporary South Africa, was the 1913 Land Act that restricted African land ownership to the 'reserves', which initially covered less than 10 per cent of the total land area of South Africa, later rising to 13 per cent.

In 1948, an Afrikaner nationalist government was voted into power, determined to introduce a more rigid system of segregation, called apartheid. This went further than previous laws had done, and was applied more harshly. So, at a time when the rest of the world was moving in the direction of a greater recognition of human rights, South Africa was moving in the opposite direction.

Terminology and definitions

Afrikaners and Boers

Afrikaners are South Africans of Dutch and French Huguenot descent who speak Afrikaans; in the 17th century their ancestors settled in the Cape, which was then under Dutch control. When Britain took over the Cape in the 19th century, some of them

Fact: South African history and 'race'

It is impossible to understand South African history without referring to race. In the sections of this book that deal with South Africa, we use the terms 'black', 'white', 'coloured' and 'Indian', which were the main racial divisions used by the apartheid system. The term 'black' had two uses: it was used to refer specifically to 'Africans', but was also used collectively for anyone who was not white. 'Coloured' was the official term used to label people of mixed descent, who formed about 9 per cent of the population. 'Indians' were the descendants of labourers brought from India in the 19th century to work on sugar plantations. In 1960, they formed about 3 per cent of the population.

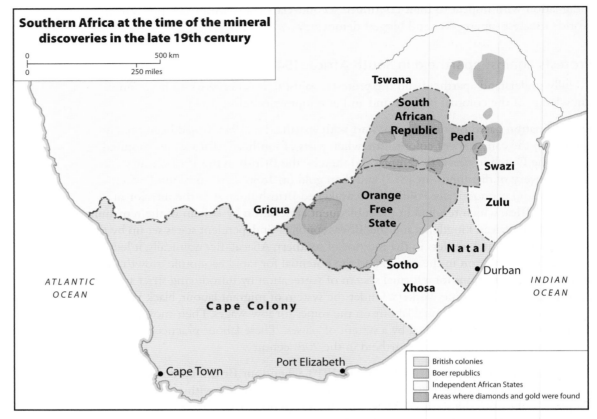

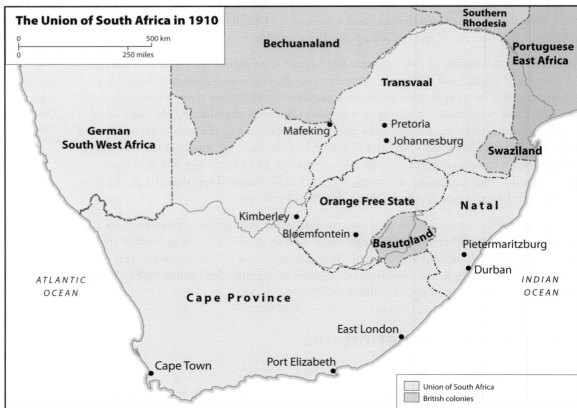

Figure 1.5 Sourthern Africa at the time of the mineral discoveries and after the formation of the Union of South Africa in 1910

moved into the interior to escape British control. There they set up two independent 'Boer' (or farmer) republics. The Boer republics joined with two British colonies in southern Africa to form the Union of South Africa in 1910. The term 'Boer' is sometimes used disparagingly to refer to Afrikaners.

Armed resistance and the armed struggle

When the apartheid government outlawed the African National Congress and the Pan Africanist Congress in 1960, this effectively meant that all forms of non-violent protest actions were banned. Both organisations decided to establish underground organisations and use violent means of resistance, including sabotage and guerrilla warfare. This is referred to as the 'armed struggle'.

Civil rights

This phrase refers to an individual's rights to freedom – both political and social – and equality by virtue of citizenship. Examples include:

- the right to equal treatment under the law
- the right to vote in elections
- the right to a fair trial
- the right to equality of opportunity
- the right to have an education
- the right to freedom of speech, expression, and religion
- the right to freedom of movement.

The Civil Rights Movement in the USA between 1954 and 1965, as examined in this book, aimed to secure these rights through protests and actions designed to change the law, or by influencing the US Supreme Court as to how the laws were interpreted. That meant that it was crucial to win the support of the US government in Washington, DC.

'Europeans' and 'non-Europeans'; 'whites' and 'non-whites'

When apartheid laws were first introduced after 1948, all facilities were segregated according to race and were initially labelled for the use of 'Europeans only' or 'non-Europeans only'. Later this terminology was changed to 'whites only' or 'non-whites only' (presumably because the use of the term 'European' implied that whites were foreign to South Africa). The term 'non-white' included Africans, 'coloureds', Indians and Chinese.

Extra-parliamentary opposition

'Extra-parliamentary' means 'outside parliament'. In apartheid South Africa, where only whites had representation in parliament, any political organisation that had support from different race groups could not use parliamentary means to bring about change. They had to use other methods, such as defiance campaigns, marches, petitions and additional forms of protest outside the parliamentary system.

'Jim Crow' laws

In the 1880s, governments in the southern states of America passed anti-African American laws, which became known as 'Jim Crow laws' after the name of a typical black minstrel show character. This term referred to discriminatory laws that prohibited African Americans from using public facilities such as restaurants, theatres, cinemas, hotels, public transport and swimming pools. Schooling was segregated according to colour, and in many states marriages between whites and African Americans were illegal. African Americans effectively had second-class citizenship, although these laws claimed to provide 'separate but equal' facilities to both whites and blacks. In reality, black facilities were poorer and in worse locations.

Minority rule and majority rule

In the context of Africa, minority rule means rule by a white minority who dominate political power and deny others the right to vote, except in insignificant numbers. Majority rule exists when a government has been voted into power in an election in which all adults, regardless of race, have the right to vote. South Africa had a minority rule government until 1994.

'Natives' and 'Bantu'

The early segregation and apartheid laws referred to Africans as 'natives', which was later replaced by the term 'Bantu'. So, for example, the Native Affairs Department became the Department of Bantu Affairs. 'Bantu' is a linguistic term referring to the more than 300 different but related languages spoken in central and southern Africa. Because of its use under apartheid, the word assumed negative connotations and Africans chose to refer to themselves as 'Africans' or 'blacks' rather than Bantu.

Reserves, homelands and Bantustans

Reserves were the areas demarcated for African land ownership in the 1913 Natives Land Act; Africans could not own land outside the reserves, which, at best, formed only 13 per cent of the land area of the country. Under the system of apartheid, the reserves were transformed into 'homelands' (also called Bantustans), in which the government tried to reinforce a tribal identity for each ethnic group. The homelands were impoverished and never viable economically, and served as pools of cheap labour for the rest of South Africa. The former homelands are the poorest and least developed regions of contemporary South Africa.

Restriction orders and bannings

The apartheid government used 'restriction orders' to silence its opponents. This meant that these opponents were confined to a specific district, had to report daily or weekly to the nearest police station, and could not attend public meetings or be quoted in newspapers. Anything they had previously written was banned. Restriction orders could be reimposed immediately after the previous term expired. People served with restriction orders were referred to as 'banned'. Sometimes whole political parties were banned, such as the Communist Party in 1950, and the African National Congress and Pan Africanist Congress in 1960.

Segregation, apartheid and separate development

Segregation was a system of laws to separate people, based on race, used in South Africa and other colonies and former colonies. Apartheid (an Afrikaans word meaning 'separateness') was the strictly enforced system of racial separation under white domination introduced by the National Party government after 1948. It was based on previous segregation policies, but was more rigid and systematic and was ruthlessly enforced. 'Separate development' was an attempt to present apartheid in a more positive light by creating theoretically 'independent' homelands where Africans had limited political rights. Sometimes separate development is referred to as 'grand apartheid' and the early apartheid laws that classified and separated people as 'petty apartheid'.

State of emergency

This extends the power of the executive and restricts the jurisdiction of the courts in order to overcome a perceived threat to the state. The usual laws are suspended and the police and army are given unrestrained powers to crush resistance, as well as indemnity from prosecution for their actions. In 1960, the apartheid government declared a state of emergency to stop countrywide protests. It lasted for five months, during which time thousands of opponents of the government were detained. During the 1980s, there were sustained and widespread protests against apartheid, with South Africa under an almost permanent state of emergency from 1985 to 1990.

The US system of government

The US Constitution aims to maintain a balance of power between the individual states and the central government in Washington, DC. When it was drafted in 1787, the founders were wary of creating an over-powerful American head of state. The solution was the creation of a federal system of government with a federal or national government in Washington, DC, then separate governments in each of the states. The head of the federal government – the president – can propose laws; but these then have to be passed by an elected parliament or law-making body – Congress, which is comprised of two houses: the Senate and the House of Representatives. The Senate consists of two elected representatives, or senators, from each state. In this way, the smaller states cannot be dominated by a few bigger states.

This format was adopted in each individual state, where there is an elected governor and legislature. The states are responsible for law and order, education and many other matters.

Unsurprisingly, disputes arise between the federal government and the states over their respective powers. So the US Supreme Court acts as the judge in such matters. As the highest court in the land, its job is to protect the US Constitution and decide, when asked, if the laws passed by federal or state governments are constitutional or not. Changes can be made to the Constitution but they have to be passed by a majority of two-thirds in both houses of Congress and be ratified by the states. These are Amendments to the Constitution. The demand for such Amendments forms a key part of the campaigns by African Americans and other minorities. Seeking changes in federal law and making appeals to the Supreme Court for interpretations of existing law, are hallmarks of the civil rights struggle.

Summary

By the time you have worked through this book, you should be able to:

- understand the background leading to the growth of the Civil Rights Movement in the USA in the 1950s;
- explain the nature and characteristics of the discrimination that led to the protests and actions carried out by the Civil Rights Movement in challenging and outlawing racial segregation;
- compare and contrast the role and significance of the different civil rights groups, in their quest for civil rights legislation;

- evaluate the role of Martin Luther King and of the federal government in achieving civil rights for African Americans;
- understand the contribution made by both the media and the Church throughout the campaign;
- understand how the policy of apartheid was implemented in South Africa after 1948 and how it affected people;
- explain how resistance to apartheid was suppressed on the pretext that it was 'communist';
- understand how the decade of non-violent protest against apartheid during the 1950s ended with the shooting of peaceful protestors at Sharpeville;
- explain how effective international protests against apartheid by the United Nations and the Anti-Apartheid Movement were;
- understand why the leaders of the resistance to apartheid switched to violent forms of protest, and were sentenced to life imprisonment as a result;
- compare the role of the National Party in implementing apartheid and suppressing opposition; and the roles played by the different organisations that opposed it.

- What were the origins and nature of racial discrimination and violence against African Americans in the USA?
- How did racial segregation operate in the 1950s in the USA?
- Why were the events at Little Rock in 1957 so significant for African Americans?

This chapter examines the origins, nature and characteristics of discrimination and violence against African Americans in the USA by the 1950s, as well as exploring the responses, and how those responses developed and changed.

Having provided a historical context to the discrimination, it examines the impact of the Second World War on the lives of all Americans. More than 14 million Americans were called up for combat, and similar numbers migrated to cities to work in war industries. Nearly one million blacks fought and a similar number were involved in the urban migration. The USA emerged from this conflict as a world superpower and an atomic power, trumpeting its leadership of the 'Free World' – but allowing racism and segregation to exist in its own states. This chapter comments too upon the early years of the Eisenhower presidency (1953–61), as the backdrop to the position of African Americans.

This chapter also considers the emergence of the Civil Rights Movement during those years, and how its actors sought to deal with the denial of social, economic and political opportunities to African Americans. Their campaign for improvement focuses on two key events that demonstrate clearly how racial segregation operated and the impact it had on lives. The first is the 1954 Supreme Court ruling on desegregation in schools, which was a significant legal breakthrough, with the potential to unlock much greater educational and social opportunity for African Americans, but aroused considerable resistance in the south. The second focus is on the significance of the stand-off between the governor of the state of Arkansas and the federal government in 1957 at Central High School in Little Rock, Arkansas, over the implementation of the 1954 desegregation ruling.

TIMELINE

1865 Apr: U.S. Civil War ends.

1870 African Americans given right to vote.

1881 Tennessee first state to pass 'Jim Crow' segregation laws,

1896 Racial segregation constitutional with Plessy *v.* Ferguson verdict ('separate but equal')

1941 Mar: A. Philip Randolph plans march on Washington. President Franklin Roosevelt bans segregation in defence industry.

1941 Dec: USA enters the Second World War.

1945 Apr: Roosevelt dies. Succeeded by Harry S. Truman.

1945 May: Second World War ends in Europe – and in August in Asia.

1948 Jul: Truman orders desegregation of the armed forces.

1953 Jan: Dwight D. Eisenhower becomes president: nominates Earl Warren as Chief Justice of US Supreme Court

1954 May: Supreme Court verdict on Brown *v.* Topeka Board of Education: segregation is unconstitutional.

1955 Dec: Rosa Parks (1913–2005) arrested in Montgomery, Alabama, for not giving up her seat on a public bus to a white man. Bus boycott for 12 months.

1957 Jan: Martin Luther King and others form Southern Christian Leadership Conference (SCLC).

1957 Sep: Eisenhower sends federal troops to Little Rock, Arkansas.

1957 and 1960 Eisenhower Civil Rights Acts.

Fact: For many years in America, civil freedom was the preserve of white Protestants of North European origin. Other ethnicities faced institutional racism and sexism. At the outbreak of the American Civil War in 1861, the majority of African Americans were slaves. Along with Native Americans, Hispanic Americans and many of the late 19th-century immigrants, they were viewed as socially, economically and politically inferior.

Progress was made during the 20th century by African Americans in their quest for civil rights, but even in 1945, they and other ethnic groups were still denied true equality. Most of the civil rights and protest movements aimed to secure these rights through legal changes and the way existing laws were interpreted. To achieve this, the support of the US government in Washington was crucial.

Figure 2.1 Segregation in education was something the Civil Rights Movement fought to eliminate

Overview

- In a number of southern states, the presence of Jim Crow laws, the Ku Klux Klan and forcible segregation in many areas of public life – including schools, restaurants and other public places – was seen as a deliberate denial of social and economic opportunity.
- To counter this, the 1950s saw black movements like the NAACP mount increasingly confident legal challenges to segregation and discrimination in voter registration, fair employment and schooling.

- The landmark Supreme Court ruling *Brown v. Topeka Board of Education* 1954 advocated the ending of racial segregation in schools. A legal precedent was set and some places outside the Deep South began to integrate. This helped to widen the potential for better education and thereby greater social and economic opportunity for blacks. But it also unleashed equally strong resistance and protest from whites in the south.

- The attempted implementation of *Brown v. Topeka Board of Education* at Central High School, Little Rock, Arkansas in 1957 resulted in federal intervention from President Eisenhower, following the bullish determination of the Arkansas governor and his troops to prevent such integration.

- Such decisions amid the tensions of the time brought further political, social and economic challenges to the government of the USA and led to the reinvigoration of the **Civil Rights** Movement.

2.1 What were the origins and nature of racial discrimination and violence against African Americans in the USA?

Historical background: the problems facing African Americans

Although slavery 'officially' ended in America in 1865 when President Abraham Lincoln signed the 13th Amendment to the Constitution, which was subsequently ratified by the states, white Americans developed new forms of discrimination over the next 100 years, such as social segregation. 'Jim Crow laws' were introduced in southern states to ensure white supremacy, while in 1883 the Supreme Court had declared that the Civil Rights Act of 1875 was unconstitutional.

In the 1880s, governments in the southern states passed anti African American laws, which became known as 'Jim Crow laws' after the name of a typical black minstrel show character. This term referred to discriminatory laws that prohibited African Americans from using public facilities such as restaurants, theatres, cinemas, hotels, transport and swimming pools. Schooling was segregated according to colour and in many states marriages between whites and African Americans were illegal. African Americans effectively had second-class citizenship, although these laws claimed to provide 'separate but equal' facilities to both whites and blacks. In reality, black facilities were poorer and in worse locations.

In 1896, the case of *Plessey v. Ferguson* had established the principle of 'separate but equal', affirming that Jim Crow laws in the south did not contravene the law and that segregation was not unconstitutional. So by 1920, interracial violence and hostility were still commonplace. The **Ku Klux Klan** and their 'crusaders' for white supremacy were a

Civil rights: are rights of individuals to social and political freedom, and to equality, by virtue of their citizenship in a free society. These entitlements include: the right to vote, to receive equal treatment under the law, the right to equality of opportunity, the right to a fair trial, the right to have education, the right to have free speech, and the right to have freedom of expression, religion and movement.

Ku Klux Klan (KKK): this was a white supremacist political organisation, which began as a club in Tennessee in 1866. Its members were youngish, middle-class men, who wore sinister white clothing with face masks and conical hats. They rode out in the night with their horses' hooves muffled. Their presence terrified blacks as they often resorted to intimidation, beatings, mutilation and lynchings. Potential informants were both afraid and reluctant to give information and testify. By the 1870s, the KKK was much diminished, but it reappeared nationwide in the mid-1920s and a third KKK became active in the 1940s and 1950s, targeting civil rights activists and their white sympathisers. But most Christian denominations condemned their tactics that instilled fear into African Americans.

Franklin Delano Roosevelt (1882–1945)

He was US President from 1933 until his death in 1945. He was a Democrat who believed he could bring the USA out of the Depression with his New Deal policies to get people back to work and restore prosperity. Roosevelt was crippled by polio in 1921, but rose to become governor of New York state in 1928, and then president.

New Deal: the name given to an extensive and unprecedented programme of government intervention to help stimulate financial recovery and give relief to the poor and unemployed. Franklin D. Roosevelt implemented this policy upon becoming US president in March 1933, when the US was in a severe economic depression.

QUESTION

Look at **Sources A** and **B**. They are both about situations facing African Americans in their everyday lives in the period up to 1941. What do they tell us about their social status? What are the points of similarity and difference between these two sources? Remember: when you make your comments, you should discuss the two sources together, pointing out similarities and differences.

menacing threat and would remain so for the next half-century – so African Americans and other ethnic minorities faced continual prejudice, discrimination and, at times, hatred.

After the economic boom and bust of the 1920s, **President Roosevelt's New Deal** of the 1930s focused on immediate relief and economic recovery and reform, while growing war clouds dictated that economic and military issues increasingly took priority by the late 1930s. There seemed to be a dearth of political will in federal government when it came to the issue of increased civil rights for the ethnic population of America.

The **Harlem Renaissance** in New York during the 1920s brought together a community of talented writers and musicians and gave them an expressive platform for challenging inequality, although ironically some of the greatest enthusiasts for the 'negro jazz music' of Harlem were the white audiences who chose to segregate them and treat them with disdain. Moreover, when black musicians entertained white audiences, fellow black people were banned. So racial prejudices remained, even in the roots of this cultural flowering.

Despite the **Great Migration of 1910–40**, when many African Americans moved to industrial cities in the north, most American blacks still lived in the **Deep South** under Jim Crow Laws. But during the Depression, black workers in the north and the south had begun to join trade unions. This provided a platform for their grievances and led to an increased awareness of their predicament. The quest for civil rights would be boosted further by African American participation in the Second World War, with almost one million being drafted to fight.

SOURCE A

Examples of Jim Crow Laws:

All railroads carrying passengers in the state (other than street railroads) shall provide equal but separate accommodations for the white and coloured races, by providing two or more passenger cars for each passenger train, or by dividing the cars by a partition, so as to secure separate accommodations.

Tennessee, 1891

It shall be unlawful for any white prisoner to be handcuffed or otherwise chained or tied to a negro prisoner.

Arkansas, 1903

Marriages are void when one party is a white person and the other is possessed of one-eighth or more negro, Japanese, or Chinese blood.

Nebraska, 1911

Any white woman who shall suffer or permit herself to be got with child by a negro or mulatto... shall be sentenced to the penitentiary for not less than eighteen months.

Maryland, 1924

Smithsonian National Museum of American History – Behring Centre (http://americanhistory.si.edu/brown/history/index.html)

SOURCE B

By the time of America's entry into the Second World War, almost three-quarters of the country's black population still lived in the south, in spite of the large-scale migrations that had taken place during the First World War and in response to the Great Depression of the 1930s. Here they were almost all excluded from voting and from serving on juries. They were refused access to white hospitals, universities, public parks and swimming pools. In urban areas, they were condemned to work in lowly, unskilled occupations. In rural areas, they struggled to survive as **sharecroppers**, tenant farmers or labourers. Their life expectancy was at least ten years less than that of white people. In the north they were subjected to racist violence and discrimination in the workplace and in housing. Unemployment rates, especially during the Depression, were significantly higher than those of white workers.

D. Paterson, D. Willoughby and S. Willoughby (2001) *Civil Rights in the USA 1863–1980*, Oxford: Heinemann, p. 246.

The impact of the Second World War on African American attitudes

The USA's entry into the Second World War in December 1941 had a significant social impact. Nearly 15 million Americans were called up to fight in Europe and the Pacific, with similar numbers migrating to cities to boost the war industries. The impact on black Americans – *equally* involved giving military service and *equally* involved in moving to the industrial north from the rural south – cannot be underestimated. They were sharing the fight against Japan and Germany 'equally' with white Americans.

Yet, although equal on the battlefield in blood and sacrifice to their white fellow soldiers, black conscripts were segregated in the army canteen, the military hospital, on the parade ground and in church. Even the outstanding black unit in the US Air Force, the Tuskegee Airmen, faced some prejudice. They were ranked among the best pilots in the US Army Air Corps, having trained with determination and, in some cases, having applied the pre-war military and mechanical experience they already possessed. Nevertheless, they still encountered racism. In due time though, their combat record gained them the respect of all colleagues, notably bomber crews who often asked for them as an escort.

But others in the military continued to harass these airmen; and the disregard or lack of respect shown at times to the famous Tuskegee unit hardened attitudes and caused African Americans in general to think about resolving this disparity in status once the war was over. Many black members of the forces now asked among themselves how the US government had the hypocrisy to ask them to fight totalitarian and racist regimes while the country upheld a racial caste system back home. They questioned how far the country could be seen as the 'arsenal of democracy' and the 'champion of freedom', as Roosevelt had described the USA.

It was no model democracy or protector of individual rights for the blacks who had inadequate protection under the law, and were not even allowed to vote in the south. Consequently, many African Americans coming home from war in 1945 had sampled a taste of racial integration, particularly if stationed in Britain and other parts of Europe.

Harlem Renaissance: the name given to the artistic, social, and cultural explosion that occurred in the New York neighbourhood of Harlem between 1920 and 1935. Harlem became a cultural centre attracting exiled African American authors, poets, musicians, artists and other scholars. Many fled the oppressive racism of the south to find a place where they could freely express their talents, championing equality and challenging racism. Writers such as Langston Hughes used black folklore in his poetry to protest against social injustice, while musicians Louis Armstrong and Duke Ellington figured prominently at places like the Harlem Cotton Club, bringing jazz to a wider, non-black audience.

Great Migration of 1910–40: more than two million blacks migrated from the rural south to the large industrial cities of the north to escape rural poverty and social oppression. New York, Chicago, Philadelphia and the car manufacturing centre of Detroit were the main areas of settlement. The African American population of New York rose from 91,000 to 328,000 during this period.

Deep South: the name given to the states of Alabama, Florida, Georgia, Louisiana, Mississippi and South Carolina. Until the mid-1960s, most people in the Deep South supported the Democratic Party (except Florida). The Republican Party was seen as a northern organisation. It was also blamed in the south for the American Civil War, which ruined the southern economy.

Sharecropping: this was when landowners divided up their land into small tenancies of 30–50 acres. Poorer white farmers and black freemen could then lease their own farms by giving half of their crops to the landowner as rent. This was beneficial to former slaves and their families, who could now work together on the land as a family.

QUESTION

How useful is this photographic source (Figure 2.2) in telling us about the involvement of African Americans in the US forces in the Second World War?

Many had forgotten how prejudiced the south was, and some suffered when they challenged the state of continuity there.

One returning uniformed black officer was badly beaten and subsequently blinded by thuggish white racists for standing his ground over segregated travelling on the bus and refusing to move to another seat. Little wonder then that many soldiers and their families were galvanised into action – more determined to lobby the government, to agitate and even to protest openly for something better. Historian Mary L. Dudziak has shown how communist critics could easily point out how hypocritical it was for the USA to portray itself as the leader of the free world at a time when many of its citizens were discriminated against. In particular, Dudziak suggests that this eventually pushed the US government into supporting civil rights legislation.

Figure 2.2   The legendary all-black Tuskegee Airmen pose in front of a P-40 fighter plane in 1943

The postwar attitudes of African Americans

Wartime experiences thus moulded and strengthened the determination of African Americans to challenge the system and its continuity of racism. In doing so, such challenges brought irrevocable change. African Americans had now gained experience in the military, the unions and in industry. They were gaining confidence at a time when improvements in communications and mass media created both a greater national awarness and the erosion of bigotry and narrow-mindedness at a local level. As Levin and Papsotiriou explain in *America since 1945* (2005), 'the South was no longer a remote and isolated region in the vast United States'. But even media modernisation did not halt the determination by many whites to resist change.

The activities of the **National Association for the Advancement of Colored People (NAACP)** increased. Founded 'to ensure the political, educational, social, and economic equality of rights of all persons and to eliminate racial hatred and racial discrimination', the association witnessed a surge of support during the war and benefited from a huge increase in membership. In the mid-1920s, the NAACP had just under 200,000 members, but by 1945 some 450,000 people had enrolled. Now there were NAACP branches and representatives in nearly every state, with workers poised to push the government for changes in the law. It gave backing to many small-scale local campaigns, while the contribution to the war by African Americans, plus the growing prominence of black lawyers and unionists, had all given the NAACP cause for optimism.

Confidence was growing politically too. It was boosted by the skill of NAACP lawyer **Thurgood Marshall**. He had argued successfully before a more liberal Supreme Court in 1944 that an all-white primary election in the south violated his black client's legal right to equal protection. African Americans in Texas had been prevented from casting a primary (first) vote to choose who would later be a party's candidate in the forthcoming general election. Now they could no longer be legally excluded, as the case, known as *Smith v. Allwright*, won an 8–1 victory.

In consequence, the NAACP worked harder than ever to get black voters on the electoral register, and in spite of threats and intimidation, the number of southern blacks registered to vote rose from just under 3 per cent in 1940, to 12 per cent by 1947. Black political power previously had been negligible, with many disenfranchised. President **Harry S. Truman** knew that this newly enfranchised constituency of black voters – likely to vote Democrat – could have a significant impact in northern cities.

Things were changing socially too for many African Americans. More than a million African Americans had served in the armed forces and, in the postwar years, their employment in armaments and other defence jobs had risen to 8 per cent of the workforce. The setting up of the **Fair Employment Practices Commission (FEPC)** by Roosevelt in 1941 had also ensured that blacks were employed in the wartime munitions industries and had gained new skills to take with them into the postwar world.

In 1946, President Truman established a Congressional Committee on Civil Rights. The Committee's findings were forthright. Homes, jobs, education and the right to vote were deemed requirements for all US citizens – regardless of ethnicity, colour or creed. But in none of these areas could black people be viewed as having the equal rights of white people. So Truman proposed a Civil Rights Bill in 1947 – but it never came to fruition. Even though Truman won the 1948 election, Congress killed off his Civil Rights Bill due to a combined effort by Republicans and reactionary southern state Democrats. Apart from looking much further at the attainment of equal rights, the Civil Rights Bill, had it passed, would also have made lynching a federal crime, established a permanent Civil Rights Division of the Federal Justice Department and outlawed segregation on all public transport.

But the scene seemed set, albeit tentatively, for a postwar era of beneficial social development. African Americans, and their white supporters, began to speak of moving forward and not returning to the old pre-war ways; and in 1948, there was some

---

The National Association for the Advancement of Colored People (NAACP): is the oldest and largest civil rights organisation in the USA. Founded in 1909. The NAACP was formed to campaign peacefully for civil and political rights through educating the public and utilising the courts. By 1914 it had 6,000 members, with W.E.B. Du Bois (1868–1963), at its helm. See also Chapter 3.

Thurgood Marshall (1908–1993)

He was a prominent black lawyer who took on cases for the NAACP concerning segregation. Challenging the Supreme Court, he won most of them, including the landmark *Brown v. Topeka Board of Education* in 1954. Such was his reputation, President Lyndon Johnson appointed him as the first black justice of the Supreme Court in 1967.

Harry S. Truman (1884–1972)

He was Democratic senator for Missouri in 1934, having previously served in the First World War and become a judge. From a mid-America farming background, Truman became prominent during the Second World War as a committee chairman in Congress. Chosen as Roosevelt's vice-president in 1944, he became president on Roosevelt's death in April 1945. He authorised the dropping of the atomic bombs on Hiroshima and Nagasaki in August of the same year. He was elected president in his own right in 1948, and retired in 1953.

The Fair Employment Practices Commission (FEPC): this was established in Congress in June 1941 by President Roosevelt after the trade unionist and civil rights activist A. Philip Randolph threatened to bring thousands of blacks to Washington, DC, albeit in a peaceful protest. The threat of such a mass demonstration had brought results and boosted the morale of the emerging Civil Rights Movement.

optimism when Truman signed legislation designed to end all forms of segregation in the US military and hopefully bring an end to all other discrimination in the forces.

Although Truman achieved little else in civil rights prior to his retirement in 1953, his identification of civil rights as a moral issue and a matter of national importance stimulated the NAACP and Thurgood Marshall. The Civil Rights Movement of the 1950s and 1960s was being conceived.

SOURCE C

The Second World War and its outcome would have a dramatic impact on the lives… of millions of black Americans as well as white. Nearly a million were called up to fight… African Americans knew that the USA's entry into the war in 1941 meant that they were fighting to defeat an avowedly racist Nazi regime. They were determined to exploit that. Black Americans were eager to play their part in the war effort, but were determined not to go unrewarded as they had done after the First World War.

M. Stacey and M. Scott-Baumann (2013), *Civil Rights and Social Movements in the Americas,* Cambridge: Cambridge University Press, pp. 63–4.

The Cold War and the social and political background in the 1950s

Figure 2.3 Ethel and Julius Rosenberg, who were executed on 19 June 1953 for conspiring to commit espionage to aid the Soviet Union

Any progress in the campaign for racial equality in the 1950s was impeded by the impact of international events. The **Cold War** rivalry between the capitalist and communist world was now at a peak. It was the era of events such as the Berlin Blockade (1948–9), the Soviet Union obtaining the atomic bomb (1949), the Chinese communists gaining power (1949), the Korean War (1950–3) and confessions of spying for the Soviet Union by officials in the USA and Canada. This deepened the acute mistrust and rivalry already present between the USA and the USSR. These events also precipitated a Red Scare, a ten-year period of strong anti-communism in the USA where suspicion of communism was almost at a level of paranoia.

In such a climate, arguing for liberal, social reform was viewed by some as tantamount to treason. Campaigning groups and individuals might be accused of communism by Senator **Joseph McCarthy** and hauled in front of the overbearing House Committee on Un-American Activities (HUAC), which he chaired. Advocating greater civil rights and racial equality became identified with communist ideas of equality for all, so few politicians were willing to question the existing social order for fear of being deemed subversive or unpatriotic. Even the NAACP itself was faced with postwar accusations of communism and was later banned in Alabama for such supposed links.

Changes in government and in race relations

In 1952, the US elected a Republican as its president, the former Supreme Allied Commander of the Second World War, Dwight D. Eisenhower. When he took office, millions of African Americans in the south still lived in conditions of poverty and faced social segregation and no voting rights; while in the north there existed unofficial segregation, with discrimination against blacks in employment, education and housing provision. But Eisenhower's previous public service had been almost entirely in

Cold War: hostile relations that do not build up into a 'hot war' (full-scale military conflict). The term was popularised in 1946–7 by the US journalist Walter Lippmann and the US politician and businessman Bernard Baruch. It is now used commonly to describe the period after 1945 until the late 1980s, when there were frequent tensions and incidents between capitalist and communist countries (e.g. the USA and USSR), but where no formal war was declared.

Joseph McCarthy (1908–57)

He was a Wisconsin senator from 1947 until his death. From 1949 to 1954 he was the most public face of the Cold War period in the USA, in which US–Soviet tensions fuelled fears of communist subversion. He claimed that the USA had been infiltrated by communists and Soviet spies. But his accusations against individuals became more and more extreme and led to him being reprimanded by the Senate in December 1954. Thereafter he lost much of his influence.

Figure 2.4 President Truman (left) and President-Elect Eisenhower meet at the White House in November 1952 to discuss the transfer of power

the military and he appeared to show no real signs of interest in the race issue. In fact, Eisenhower only met black leaders once during his entire presidency and both he and his staff felt that incidents of racial injustice were often exaggerated by black organisations, for the benefit of publicity. Sanders in *Race Relations in the USA Since 1900* (2000: p. 101) comments on Eisenhower's White House that 'one presidential aide felt that black demands were made with "ugliness and surliness"'.

Eisenhower had assumed power at a time when 1.2 million black workers had moved off the land into growing southern cities and to the industrial north since 1945. The black working class entered industry, although they were still usually given the most poorly paid, unskilled jobs. But opposition to inequality spread from the south throughout America, driven by the Civil Rights Movement, which evolved to produce real political and social challenges. At the same time, both the growth in car ownership and in television set production meant that white Americans were becoming more aware of how blacks were being treated in the south. Greater mobility combined with increased everyday exposure to news on TV opened up America like never before.

In particular, the growth in media would give civil rights organisations and white liberals invaluable visual publicity. Between 1950 and 1959, television set ownership grew from one million families to 45 million. The isolated, racist Deep South was opened up to greater national scrutiny, and pressure to change racist laws and institutions now intensified.

At the grass-roots level in the 1950s, churches, local organisations, fraternal societies and black-owned businesses all mobilised volunteers to participate in broad-based actions. The call for civil rights was adopting more direct, swifter means of bringing about change than the previously favoured strategy of launching court challenges. It was the advent of what Sanders describes as 'a combination of co-operation, coercion and confrontation when dealing with whites'.

For example, in 1952 the Regional Council of Negro Leadership (RCNL) organised a boycott of Mississippi gas stations that refused to provide bathrooms for blacks. The RCNL leader T.R.M. Howard led other campaigns too, including one to highlight brutality by the Mississippi state highway patrol, and another to urge blacks to put money into the black-owned Tri-State Bank of Nashville, an institution that offered loans to civil rights activists who were victims of a 'credit squeeze' by the White Citizens' Councils.

When change eventually came later in the 1950s, it emerged from both ends of the social spectrum: from the small towns, farms and churches of the Deep South but, significantly, also from the heart of Washington, DC, itself and from within the Supreme Court. If this proved surprising to the members of the NAACP, it also came as quite a shock to the new president. Not least because President Eisenhower's appointee as chief justice of the United States, the Republican Earl Warren, would make a momentous decision in the *Brown v. Topeka Board of Education* ruling of May 1954 (see section 2.2, Warren's verdict and its consequences). A liberal southern Republican, Warren struck a major blow against segregated schooling with his court's decision.

As black veterans returned home from the Second World War to claim their piece of the 'American Dream', they were still often restricted from moving into the newly emerging suburbs. Forced to live in cramped, urban neighbourhoods, many African American adults were unable to find suitable employment. Even candidates who were qualified for well-paying jobs faced discrimination during the hiring process, often only able to

---

Fact: The Civil Rights Movement, which was most active between 1954 and 1968, aimed to outlaw racial discrimination against African Americans and reform voting rights. By 1968, the more radical Black Power movement, which lasted into the 1970s, had enlarged these aims to include racial dignity, self-sufficiency and freedom from white oppression. Many in the Civil Rights Movement, who belonged to organisations such as CORE, NAACP, SLCL and SNCC, preferred the term Southern Freedom Movement, because the struggle was about more than legal civil rights. It also focused on wider issues of freedom, respect, dignity and equality.

Fact: Civil rights organisations

CORE – Congress of Racial Equality, a non-violent organisation founded in 1942.

NAACP – National Association for the Advancement of Colored People, founded 1909

SCLC – Southern Christian Leadership Conference, an organisation of black ministers formed in 1957 led by Dr Martin Luther King. A coordinating movement for civil rights activities.

SNCC – Student Non-violent Co-ordinating Committee. Founded in the 1960s, worked for black voter registration.

get menial jobs, and black people were still frequently subject to prejudice and outright violence.

Yet some did begin to benefit economically from the boom and felt a sense of confidence, in line with the greater postwar prosperity that was evident throughout the USA. Out of such confidence emerged a growing black middle-class, possessing an increasing number of people with the qualities of leadership. To them it became clear that there was a need for a more highly organised movement that would ensure the rights of black people in the USA and not 'take cover' when the political climate was bumpy. Indeed, there was a nationwide growth of such organisations in the 1950s, particularly in places where racism was strongly entrenched, such as those states in the south where African Americans were widely restricted from voting by illegal practices like literacy tests and imposed taxes.

But although they were shying away from direct protest, members of the NAACP continued to mount legal challenges to the system of segregation and discrimination, especially in areas concerning education, the registration of voters and fairness of employment. They worked as a pressure group, they liaised with other interest groups, they tried to raise awareness among southern blacks and, crucially, they won increasing respect from moderate whites as NAACP leaders became role models for the black community. Consequently, developments began to pave the way for the equal rights granted in the 1960s, with the *Brown v. Topeka* challenge of 1954 marking the starting point for this acceleration. But the backlash that ensued showed clearly to the outside world just how racial segregation operated in the south and the extent to which many whites were determined to protect that segregation.

End of section activities

1   Carry out further research into Senator Joseph McCarthy and the 'Red Scare'. How did it create difficulties for the burgeoning civil rights groups?

2   Look at **Source C** and then reread the text in this section. Do you feel that the postwar aspirations of African Americans had been met by 1954? If so why? If not, were there *any* grounds for optimism?

3   Draw up a chart of two halves: one highlighting the achievements and progress of African Americans in the USA and the other part showing the difficulties and oppression many faced in some parts of the country. Use your information to write a report on the social, political and economic situation of African Americans in the 1950s. Remember to have balance in your report, but you must come to a definite conclusion.

KEY CONCEPTS QUESTION

Causes and Consequences: Draw up a chart showing the main causes of growing dissatisfaction among African Americans at the end of the Second World War. What were the most important immediate consequences of this dissatisfaction and what were the main postwar social changes that affected civil rights?

2.2 How did racial segregation operate in the 1950s in the USA?

Brown v. Topeka Board of Education, 1954 – a legal breakthrough

To understand the way in which racial segregation really operated in the USA – especially in the south in the 1950s – it is necessary to examine how an existing law was challenged and to measure the response of the opposing parties. The impact of the *Brown v. Topeka Board of Education* court ruling in 1954 was one such touchstone.

2

To place this event in its context, there had been a major change in the hierarchy of the Supreme Court of the USA in 1953, and the new chief justice and its head judge was Earl Warren, a former California governor and vice-presidential candidate on the defeated Republican ticket in 1948. Warren caused immense surprise among conservatives – not least Eisenhower – by becoming one of the most reforming and liberal-minded of all the chief justices.

The 'breakthrough moment' for civil rights, a catalytic moment for the cause, came with the ruling on the case of a black girl called Linda Brown. An appeal was brought by her father, Oliver, against her having to travel to an all-black school a mile away, when there was a white school around the corner from her home in Topeka, Kansas.

The case, known as *Brown v. Topeka Board of Education*, was a landmark decision in judicial history. The US Supreme Court under Warren ruled that the existence of separate public schools for white pupils and black pupils was wholly unconstitutional. The decision meant that the Supreme Court had decided against its *Plessy v. Ferguson* ruling from 1896, which had legalised and advocated such segregation on the merits of 'separate but equal'. The legal basis for segregation was removed. This had the potential to change radically the lives of many black children and students, and it was a potential nail in the coffin of racial segregation, which all blacks faced from nursery school to the grave.

The NAACP selected Oliver Brown to headline the case by name. Brown had a solid reputation in the Topeka community and was a church pastor. A group of 13 parents was involved in the lawsuit, as these parents had failed to enrol their children in their closest neighbourhood school in September 1951. Instead they had been allocated places in segregated schools some distance from where they lived.

Interestingly, the plaintiffs did not argue that the schools in Topeka were inadequate. But the NAACP, and its chief lawyer Thurgood Marshall, used the argument that 'separate but equal' in a child's education had a detrimental effect on their intellect and health. Marshall continued by declaring that the practice of separation established a 'psychology of inferiority independent of the physical condition of the schools' and contended that even if the schools were equally good in a material sense, this could still impact greatly on future learning and upon the realisation of potential in adulthood for the child. In Kansas, the local district court had agreed with Marshall, but did not make a ruling, on the grounds that any inequality in the facilities was not deliberately state-sponsored inequality.

Warren's verdict and its consequences

The Supreme Court had first heard the petition for *Brown v. Topeka Board of Education* in December 1952, as the first of five cases brought to Washington by the NAACP. But then Chief Justice Fred M. Vinson died and delays ensued. The new chief justice, Earl Warren, finally made his ruling on the case in 1954, by which time Linda Brown was too old to take up a place at the elementary school she wanted to attend. But Warren was seeking a unanimous verdict, not a majority ruling. He wished to send the strongest signal possible from the Supreme Court that segregation in education was not only morally wrong, but a contradiction of the 14th Amendment, which required the admission of all children on equal terms to public (state) schools.

Figure 2.5 Thurgood Marshall

With his final verdict on 17 May 1954, Warren reiterated Marshall's argument in his ruling and himself endorsed the increasingly fashionable view – one supported by contemporary social science research – that black children were psychologically harmed by separate education.

The Supreme Court did not try to give immediate direction for the implementation of the ruling, because Warren and his fellow justices expected strong opposition. Instead, the court asked the attorney-generals of all states with laws allowing segregation to inform the court how they planned to proceed with desegregation. After more hearings throughout 1954–5,

SOURCE D

Although *Brown v. Topeka* neither resulted in the immediate demise of the caste system in the Deep South nor prompted a major grass-roots revolt against Jim Crow, it did crystallise the hitherto inchoate [not fully formed and developed] white opposition to the profound changes under way in southern society. Public opinion in parts of the region was polarised dramatically, forcing moderate whites to abandon thoughts of gradual reform and causing blacks to reassess their tactics and strategy. As white intransigence grew, it became increasingly obvious to African Americans living in the Deep South that neither the federal courts nor the traditional reformist strategy of negotiating with civic elite, was in itself likely to promote the kind of rapid social change that the Second World War had led them to expect. The way was left open for more militant action by blacks.

R. Cook (1998) *Sweet Land of Liberty*, Harlow: Longman, pp. 93–4.

QUESTION
According to **Source D**, what was the reaction within both the white community and the African American community, in the aftermath of the *Brown v. Topeka* ruling?

Theory of knowledge

History and emotion/
language:
Earl Warren's judgment
on the *Brown v. Topeka*
case is famous not only
for its content, but for the
language he uses and the
contemporary ideas he
conveys. How does Warren
get his message across?
What is the key reason
given by Warren in his
judgement for allowing the
desegregation of schools?
How might different groups
of people interpret this?

SOURCE E

To separate them [black students] from others of similar age and qualification solely because of their race, generates a feeling of inferiority as to their status in the community that may affect their hearts and minds in a way never likely to be undone… We conclude that in the field of education… separate educational facilities are inherently unequal.

Earl Warren delivering his judgment on *Brown v. Topeka*, 1954; quoted by D. Farber and B. Bailey (2001) *The Columbia Guide to America in the 1960s*, New York: Columbia University Press, p. 14.

the justices then ruled on a plan for how things were to proceed. On 31 May 1955, the states were commanded to commence the introduction of educational desegregation 'with all deliberate speed'. Some years would pass before full school desegregation occurred in the USA, but undoubtedly *Brown v. Topeka* and *Brown II* (as the desegregation plan became known) were responsible for getting the process underway.

Figure 2.6   The reaction to the Supreme Court decision

Eisenhower failed to take any substantial action in support of Warren, although not necessarily through racist tendencies, as he had outlawed any form of racism in Washington, DC. More likely he was keen to maintain the relative stability of Middle America in the mid-1950s, and loathe to stir up opposition with the 1956 presidential election approaching. Eisenhower also feared disorder and rioting in the south, where the social order might be upturned in too dramatic a fashion. He felt it better to backpedal for the time being.

But even Eisenhower knew that this was a milestone decision and a major legal breakthrough. The Supreme Court – the highest in the land – had ruled unequivocally that racial segregation in public schools was unconstitutional, signalling the end, in principle, of legalised racial segregation in US schools. It also overruled the 'separate but equal' doctrine set out in 1896. It was an immense morale booster for the burgeoning civil rights movements, establishing their rights in legality. Yet by the time of Eisenhower's re-election victory in November 1956, there had been little immediate desegregation. Indeed the impact of the *Brown v. Topeka* judgment with respect to growing opposition was striking.

On 24 February 1956, Senator Harry F. Byrd, Sr. of Virginia declared a policy of 'Massive Resistance'. In the state of Virginia, which geographically contains part of the suburbs of Washington, DC, Byrd ran a powerful, personal, political machine that dominated politics in the state. He stated that if Virginia could mobilise the states in the south for resistance to the Supreme Court ruling then 'in time the rest of the country will realise that racial integration is not going to be accepted in the south'.

New laws were created to punish schools within Virginia that integrated, and funding was created in order to finance white students to be able to attend private, segregated schools. Indeed, such was the resistance from Byrd and his supporters that a series of legal battles and public protests over school integration dragged on. The federal courts then had to order integrated schools to stay open. Funding was provided until 1960, in order to prevent a total breakdown of the education system in Virginia.

'Massive Resistance' was followed by the **Southern Manifesto** against school integration. Nineteen senators and 81 members of the House of Representatives consented to sign. Interestingly, they comprised all of the Congressional membership of Alabama, Arkansas, Georgia, Louisiana, Mississippi, South Carolina and Virginia. The Southern Manifesto was unveiled to the media on 12 March 1956 and it asserted that they would resist the changes called for by the *Brown v. Topeka* case and to unite the south in opposition to integration.

If further evidence of the hostility towards desegregation was needed, then the state of Mississippi provided it when it created the Mississippi State Sovereignty Commission, with the objective to 'protect the sovereignty of the state of Mississippi, and her sister states' from 'federal encroachment'. Undermining the Civil Rights Movement through covert means was the objective. The enforcement of racial segregation by stealth, blackmail and slander became one of its main ways of operating. Informants were assigned to pass on details of marches and boycotts, and police harassment of African Americans who cooperated with civil rights groups was encouraged – especially of activists who were striving for voter registration.

The extremely racist Mississippi senator James Eastland claimed that it was the communists who had 'stirred up African-Americans' into challenging segregation, and vowed to use all legal means to get the Warren ruling revoked and prevent, by use of force if necessary, the federal government from imposing the ruling.

At the federal level, FBI director J. Edgar Hoover authorised the Counter Intelligence Programme (COINTELPRO) in 1956 to monitor pro-communist groups within the United States and investigate them where necessary. By 1960, it had been extended to target so-called 'dissident' or 'subversive' groups, including civil rights activists and their leaders.

In retrospect, it now seems logical that Marshall and the NAACP should have changed course and opted for black voting rights as their first objective. Given the sympathetic and liberal nature of the Warren court, perhaps if the Supreme Court had acted in their favour – which it probably would have done – then the process of abolishing

Southern Manifesto: an agreement signed in 1956 by most southern politicians. It was a declaration of constitutional principles designed to impose the implementation of the two *Brown* verdicts. The signatories also agreed to augment the active level of southern opposition to any further integration. But two very notable southern politicians did not sign it: Senator Albert Gore of Tennessee (father of the US vice-president from 1993 to 2001, Al Gore) and Senator Lyndon Johnson from Texas. Johnson became president in 1963 after the assassination of John F. Kennedy, and it would fall to him in 1964 to bring in a Civil Rights Act with the depth so many had craved.

Historical debate:
Many historians believe that the *Brown v. Topeka* ruling was a breakthrough moment for civil rights, in that it removed the legal basis for segregation and empowered blacks by virtue of their seeing that the NAACP had got the Supreme Court to rule in their favour. But other historians consider Warren's ruling to be only of fleeting importance, with little substance, much vagueness in the requirements and ultimately, little success. What do you consider to be the real significance of *Brown v. Topeka*? Using the library and the internet, research alternative historical perspectives on this event. Then, in groups, prepare a debate examining both sides of the historical argument.

segregation might have been quicker, with many more African Americans able to register their vote.

Analysing the court ruling and its consequences, Paterson, Willoughby and Willoughby in *Civil Rights in the USA 1863–1980* (2001: p. 113) consider that the main importance was that this landmark ruling 'had created an important precedent and was expected to produce major change'. Washington, Baltimore and St. Louis now began to integrate, followed by other areas of the south 'but progress was not quick… by 1957 less than 12 per cent of the 6300 school districts in the south had been integrated… the federal government was seen as acting dictatorially in seeking to impose its values and opinions elsewhere… the Supreme Court itself had not been altogether clear about the timetable for change'.

Perhaps the lack of any follow-up plan by the Supreme Court was a means of pacifying those who were already angry by this controversial verdict. Even when in 1955 the Court's *Brown II* ruling called for desegregation 'with all deliberate speed', it failed to set a timetable and left it to lower federal courts to implement. These lower courts were often open to pressure from some of the white supremacist ruling elites in the Deep South. At the same time, Eisenhower was shocked by Warren's ruling and confessed that his appointment of the chief justice was 'the biggest damn fool decision I ever made', adding that deeply held and longstanding social traditions and racial feelings ought not to be changed simply by law. Eisenhower acknowledged: 'You cannot change people's hearts by law.' But as Traynor comments in *Modern United States History* (2001: p. 236), 'Eisenhower's record on civil rights was probably the weakest element of his entire administration'.

But possibly the main reason for a lack of response to the Warren ruling was the entrenched and widespread opposition from whites, especially in the south. *Brown II* was seen as legal justification for stalling integration, and many states devised clever means of perpetuating the existing system. They closed down school systems, apportioned state money to finance segregated 'private' schools and even supported 'token' integration. Here, selected bright black children were allowed to enter formerly white-only schools. But the majority of black children still remained in black schools, which were badly funded. States bordering the Deep South such as Oklahoma, Maryland and Missouri had complied, and even in the south moderates had urged that the rule of law ought to be obeyed. But in the staunchly racist states of Alabama, Mississippi, Louisiana, South Carolina and Georgia there was no mood for compromise, with state officials seeing Warren's ruling as an attack on the states' rights to organise education their own way.

Campaigning initially for enfranchisement would probably have been a better and more powerful tool for African Americans in their struggle for desegregation, on the premise that first unlocking the key to the ballot box might lead to better things in education and social conditions. But for the time being, this was not to be the case. Yet it must not be forgotten just how significant Warren's ruling was. It progressed the whole civil rights environment and made national and international headlines. To a largely unknowing world outside the USA, it had drawn attention to the way in which racial segregation operated from the cradle to the grave. It showed that many in the next generation of African Americans were poised to remain second-class citizens socially and economically by virtue of an inadequate education, unless more was done to remedy the situation. So the battleground was being drawn by the two sides – and it was to be tested again over segregation in the state of Arkansas in 1957.

SOURCE F

After its announcement Eisenhower refused to speak in defence of the decision. Thereafter relations between the President and his Chief Justice cooled. In the remaining six years of his tenure. Eisenhower never proposed implementing he Warren decision, nor did he defend the Court from outrageous attacks mounted by members of his own party... the Supreme Court had acted to defend the civil rights of black citizens that had remained flagrantly unenforced since the Civil War. Controversial though it was, the desegregation decision set irreversible forces into motion that eventually destroyed legal segregation in America.

J. Gilbert (1981) *Another Chance, Postwar America 1945–68*, New York: Alfred A. Knopf, p. 149.

QUESTION

How useful is **Source F** for a historian who is trying to understand Eisenhower's views on civil rights and racial equality? In what way might the source misrepresent Eisenhower? Reread the preceding section before answering.

End of section activities

1   Carry out research into the lives of both Earl Warren and Thurgood Marshall. What was it about their background and training that made them suitable for their appointments? How far might their achievements and decisions be seen as unexpected?

2   Can you think of any controversial court decisions in your country's history? If so, how influential was that decision? Did it have a long-term impact? If not, consider how influential judges are in courts. How up-to-date are they with life outside the legal system, the media and mainstream contemporary culture?

KEY CONCEPT QUESTION

Significance: 'The *Brown v. Topeka Board of Educvwation* ruling in 1954 was a significant moment in history for both the US government and for civil rights groups.' How far do you agree with this statement? Write an essay in answer to this, presenting evidence, giving explanations, making links, giving a balanced judgement, and referring to historiography.

2.3 Why were the events at Little Rock in 1957 so significant for African Americans?

The growth of the Civil Rights Movement

Following *Brown v. Topeka Board of Education*, the Civil Rights Movement was now emboldened by unfolding events. Campaigners were indignant about white attempts to stop the implementation of the law, and encouraged by evidence of a growing awareness in the US white community and abroad of the injustices many African Americans faced: a lack of decent education and unjust barriers in the pursuit of a better life, with social and economic opportunity. As we have examined, segregation in public schools had been banned – theoretically – by the US Supreme Court in 1954. Then, in 1955, a bus boycott occurred in Montgomery, Alabama when Rosa Parks, an African American seamstress, was arrested for not giving up her seat on the local bus for a white person to sit down; another manifestation of social and racial segregation. The Montgomery buses were eventually desegregated (see Chapter 3, section 3.1 for more detail), but not before a year of bus boycotting, peaceful protests and much legal wrangling.

Significantly, these actions helped to create new grass-roots organisations such as the Montgomery Improvement Association (MIA). This in turn brought a Baptist minister, Dr Martin Luther King, to prominence, and to the leadership of a new Southern Christian Leadership Conference (SCLC) in 1957 (see Section 3.1,

The consequences of a successful boycott). These would play important parts in coordinating civil rights activities.

What is apparent, however, is that in spite of both the favourable rulings of the Warren Supreme Court and the growing media awareness of the struggle for African American rights, it was mainly when these groups stood firm against their oppressors that they achieved the most decisive outcomes. Fortunately for the USA in general, they did so by non-violent means, regardless of the abuse and violence used against them. The issue of force and violence did, however, come to the fore on 4 September 1957 at Central High School in Little Rock, Arkansas.

Figure 2.7   Elizabeth Eckford walks into school at Little Rock, Arkansas, being verbally abused, spat on and taunted with cries of 'Lynch her!' and 'Two, four, six, eight, we ain't going to integrate!'

The integration crisis at Central High School

The NAACP reacted to the *Brown v. Topeka Board of Education* ruling by registering black students at previously all-white schools in southern cities. The school board in Little Rock, Arkansas opted to adhere to the ruling, and its gradual integration plan was finally approved in May 1955, with implementation required by the start of the new academic year in September 1957.

By that time, 75 black children had applied to enter Little Rock Central High. Some were rejected and others changed their minds when they became aware of the hostility of the neighbouring white community. Finally this left nine black students, registered by the NAACP and selected for their exemplary grades and attendance. They came to be nicknamed the 'Little Rock Nine'. Central High was recognised as one of the best high schools in the south and achieved great academic success. Naturally, demand for places was high.

As term began on 4 September 1957, segregationists blocked access to the school. Arkansas governor **Orval Faubus** sent in the National Guard to keep the peace, but also to support the white protestors. The governor predicted on television that 'blood would run in the streets' if the nine children attempted to enter the school – which they did on the first day back.

The event made the national news and drew attention to the general situation. Student Elizabeth Eckford was nearly lynched when she became separated from her fellow students and tried to get through a white mob that was blocking her way to a bus stop. The mob then surrounded her and threatened to lynch her. News reporter Ben Fine spotted her distress and went to protect her, as did Grace Lorch, a local white sympathiser. It was clear that the children could not enter the school. But the TV pictures of National Guardsmen resolutely blocking a school where children were trying to enter to get an education reflected very badly on both the situation and the white protestors.

On 14 September, Eisenhower met Governor Faubus in Washington and ordered him to keep control of the situation and not to challenge ruling of the Supreme Court. But things escalated to such an extent that a judge ruled that the National Guard had to be replaced by the police, who attempted to escort the students into the school on 23 September.

Orval Faubus (1910–94)

He was the Democrat governor of Arkansas from 1955 to 1967, Faubus was a staunch racist. He was due to be re-elected in 1958 and wanted to enhance his chances of winning by making a firm stand on the issue of segregated schooling. In a newspaper obituary, Faubus was deemed to be one of the best-loved politicians in Arkansas during his time, yet also one of the most feared and hated.

QUESTION

Look carefully at **Source G**. Using the information on this poster and your own knowledge, write a paragraph explaining why this poster was printed and what it was hoping to achieve. Think also what it tells us about how racial segregation operated. Write a paragraph explaining this. Remember to put your answer into a proper historical context.

SOURCE G

DO YOU WANT NEGROES IN OUR SCHOOLS?

IF YOU <u>DO NOT</u> THEN GO TO THE POLLS THIS COMING MON.

DAY AND FOR REMOVAL **VOTE** AGAINST REMOVAL

LAMB	McKINLEY
MATSON	ROWLAND
TUCKER	LASTER

THIS IS THE SIMPLE TRUTH, IF THE INTEGRATIONISTS WIN THIS SCHOOL BOARD FIGHT, THE SCHOOLS <u>WILL BE INTEGRATED THIS FALL.</u> THERE WILL BE ABSOLUTELY NOTHING YOU OR WE CAN DO TO STOP IT.

PLEASE VOTE RIGHT!!!

Join hands with us in this fight— send your contributions to

THE MOTHERS' LEAGUE

P. O. BOX 3321 * LITTLE ROCK, ARKANSAS

Ad Paid For by Margaret © Jackson, Presidents Mary Thompson,

Petition by the Mothers' League of Central High School, Little Rock

The nine black children were escorted inside by the police, as more than 1,000 whites protested in front of Central High School. Some white students, including Sammie Dean Parker, who had been part of the mob threatening Elizabeth Eckford earlier in the month, even jumped out of windows to avoid contact with the black students. But eventually, fearful of the growing anger of the mob, the police decided to evacuate the nine children from the school. Even three black journalists covering the story were physically attacked by the mob. They escaped to find sanctuary in a black area of town.

Federal intervention and white consternation

President Eisenhower called the rioting 'disgraceful' and sent the 101st Airborne Division of the United States Army to Little Rock. He used his presidential power to federalise all 10,000 members of the Arkansas National Guard. This removed power from Governor Faubus and put Eisenhower in charge. The 101st took up positions at the school: ironically the same soldiers who had barred the way now had to keep white protestors back and escort the nine students into school. They successfully entered the building the following day, 25 September. The so-called 'Little Rock Nine' had a hard time and were frequently victimised, both physically and verbally, by bullying white students. One student, Minnijean Brown, physically resisted the bullying. For this, she was repeatedly suspended and she later transferred to a school in New York City.

Some white students, including Sammie Dean Parker, were disciplined for organising the handing out of cards at school that read 'One down, eight to go'. She was suspended. In a report made by the Arkansas National Guard, both she and her mother 'viciously and physically attacked' the school's assistant principal during an after-school meeting.

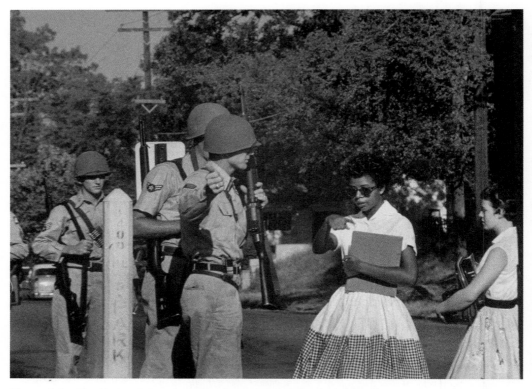

Figure 2.8   The National Guard outside Central High School, Little Rock

The family sued and Parker was readmitted a month later. But the intervention by Eisenhower simply hardened the resolve of most southern whites. They showed in many ways the extent to which they would go to retain segregation, using all legal means and, if necessary, by manipulating the law.

SOURCE H

After lunch one day, I was called to Mrs Huckabee's office. When I entered the office, I saw a girl sitting and crying. I was told that she was crying because as we came upstairs from lunch, she said, 'Thelma was in front of me, and kicked me.' It was a complete lie. I told the girl, 'If I kicked you, I apologize.' That evening on the 6:00 news, her name was called saying that I had kicked her!... I was seated across from Minnijean Brown in the cafeteria when a white male student came and dumped a bowl of soup on her head. The 101st [Airborne] had left [the school]... As I was going down a flight of steps to go home one day, someone on the landing above spat down on my poodle skirt. One day someone threw black ink on the back of my white blouse... One day it snowed... and Minnijean, Melba and I were waiting inside a hall exit door for my mother to pick us up. The Arkansas National Guard were there to 'keep peace'. Some boys found small rocks and packed them into the snow and tossed them inside the hall at us. The Guards said nothing to the boys, but ducked to keep from getting hit themselves! The guards said nothing to the boys and when my mother arrived, as we ran to the car, the same foolishness continued.

An account by Thelma Mothershed from the National Park Service – Department of the Interior: Little Rock Central High School, National Historic Site part 6 *'Every person has a story of courage: The Little Rock Nine'*.

> **QUESTION**
> How useful is **Source H** and what are the limitations for a historian trying to discover what it was like for the new African American pupils at Central High School in Little Rock in 1957?

Resistance by the governor

In 1958 Governor Faubus closed all public schools and tried to lease them privately to organisations or individuals who would teach pupils in a segregated learning environment. It was all part of a plan to maintain de facto segregation, but the plan failed partly because of the 1958 *Cooper v. Aaron* Supreme Court decision. This developed in February 1958 when members of the Arkansas school board lodged a claim with the district court in Arkansas, hoping to halt or postpone the process of desegregation. They claimed that the expression of public hostility towards desegregation was evidence enough of its unpopularity, as well as a threat to the stability of the town and the state. Unsurprisingly, Governor Faubus backed their case.

The plaintiffs asked for the African American children to be returned to segregated schools for the time being, and that Arkansas underwent a period of reflection and considered public discussion about the policy. During this time they sought postponement for the implementation of the desegregation for two and a half years. Significantly, the district court in Arkansas granted the school board's request, but the Supreme Court immediately reversed the ruling.

Again this was a landmark decision, important because it established a legal precedent stating that even if individual states in the US were opposed to a Supreme Court decision, they still had to enforce it, and that the states were bound by the decisions of the Supreme Court. The obstinacy of Faubus and the general legal wrangling resulted in Little Rock having no formal education in its schools for more than a year. This proved very costly and was grossly unfair to those high school students who were approaching exams. It subsequently became known as 'the lost year'. Integrated schools eventually reopened in September 1959, but black students had lost valuable time in seeking to assert their rights, and had become the victims of prejudiced white students and their families.

> **SOURCE I**
>
> Eisenhower's fears that *Brown* would produce a Southern backlash may seem a poor justification for his half-hearted support in implementing it [at Little Rock], but they were not unfounded. Southern violence against blacks did increase after the *Brown* decisions. New members flocked to the racist Ku Klux Klan. There were instances of blacks being killed for seeking to remain on the voting lists.
>
> P. Levine and H. Papasotiriou (2005) *America Since 1945*, Basingstoke: Palgrave Macmillan, p. 65.

The significance of Little Rock – where did it leave African Americans?

QUESTION

Look at **Source J**. Why do you think M.J. Heale suggests that by the end of the 1950s, black protest now had a 'profound moral effect on American society'? Make a list of the social changes and circumstances you consider might have had an impact or an influence on both sides of the argument about civil rights. Share your views in a class discussion.

> **SOURCE J**
>
> Inevitably there was disaffection and disappointment. Some young people were alienated by the powerlessness they felt in an increasingly bureaucratic post-industrial order… black protest also had a profound moral effect on American society.
>
> M.J. Heale (2001) *The Sixties in America: History, Politics and Protest*, Edinburgh: Edinburgh University Press, p. 111.

Undoubtedly the events at Little Rock were of real significance. The attempted integration of black students at Central High School was the only occasion when Eisenhower used his federal power to intervene, thereby enforcing the legal ruling of *Brown v. Topeka*. It is also a prime example of the lengths to which many white southerners went to in order to retain segregation – or delay the inevitability of integration. Clearly Governor Faubus in Arkansas was determined not to desegregate; but he might have also known deep down that such change was inevitable. He was reluctant to be the man who integrated, but he might have eventually complied had Eisenhower put more pressure on him. Perhaps then he could have saved face by pleading defeat to overwhelming presidential power – but not before he had offered strident, but token, resistance.

Importantly for the civil rights movements, Little Rock had revealed just how rigorously southern whites at a grass-roots level opposed Supreme Court rulings like *Brown v. Topeka*. Even when blacks showed more urgency and behaved more decisively, as at Little Rock, little was achieved. Even by 1964, fewer than 5 per cent of black children attended desegregated schools. The fact was that blacks had to do more than push for court decisions and respond to their verdicts. Significantly, Little Rock would make the Civil Rights Movement more proactive.

Nationally, events at Little Rock caused shock when TV news bulletins showed black children being spat on, sworn at and screamed at by aggressive white adults. Then there was the sight of a bullish, racist governor, surrounded by armed National Guardsmen, ranting against the rights of black children to get an equal education. All of this was now visible in the sitting rooms of millions of Americans. It could not help but polarise opinion on both sides of the racial divide. Similarly, it stimulated discussion, but also made it clear that politicians had to respond ever more quickly to events. Change had to come.

All these events had shown the USA in an unfavourable light, not least the governing Republican Party. In the 1958 mid-term elections, the Republicans lost on a huge scale. The governing party is often prone to setbacks, especially when it is in its second term, but such were the gains by the Democrats in Congress that these elections are known as the 'Mid-term Revolution'. Indeed, the Democrats made the largest Senate gain in history. The US was entering a recession, and the USSR was seen as gaining in the space race with the launch of the sputnik satellite; but there were also worries about right-to-work issues that had galvanised labour unions, as well as a general growing unease about the disparity between the lifestyle and rights of white and non-white Americans. The events at Central High School had exposed a great divide and had opened sores at the heart of the social and political system. There remained a festering problem of how school desegregation was to be achieved, in spite of a judicial ruling.

Eisenhower did respond to a limited extent. He signed the 1957 Civil Rights Act, the first civil rights legislation for 80 years. The Act called for a bipartisan Civil Rights Commission and the establishing of a division in the Justice Department to examine civil rights abuses in fields such as voting. In the south, most African Americans were

Figure 2.9 On 9 September 1957, President Dwight D. Eisenhower signed into law the Civil Rights Act of 1957

denied the vote in spite of having a right to do so. Locally invoked literacy tests, poll taxes or, in some cases, bigoted trickery meant that southern blacks were, in reality, voiceless in the electoral process. Unfortunately, the Act Eisenhower signed was much reduced from the proposal sent to Congress. Southern Democrats managed to pass an amendment in Congress that required a jury trial to determine to what extent a citizen had been denied the right to vote. But African Americans could not serve on juries in southern states, so these were unlikely to prove favourable. They would still be frozen out of the electoral process, as white juries would seldom convict for breaches of civil rights.

In 1960, Eisenhower signed the second Civil Rights Act, but there were only small improvements over the earlier law. It allowed judges to make special appointments of those who might assist blacks to get on to the voting register, and it also introduced national penalties for bombing and actions by mobs. As African Americans were often the victims of such aggression, it could be argued that at least Eisenhower had instituted the principle of federal action for such violence, removing the implementation of these laws – or the lack of it in the Deep South – from the jurisdiction of individual states. These civil rights laws were fairly weak and still gave only moderate protection, but perhaps it was a sign of things to come.

Politically, the Democrats were poised to make a strong bid for the White House in the 1960 presidential election and this fostered a sense of optimism among many in the Civil Rights Movement and their supporters.

Although not entirely typical in the history of civil rights in the 1950s, the events at Little Rock left African Americans in no doubt as to the opposition they were going to face in pushing for their legal entitlements. In this sense it provided a wake-up call of great significance, as they realised that it was no longer sufficient to trust in court or Congressional decisions regarding greater desegregation, the pursuit of voting rights and an end to the caste system in which they were at the bottom of the pile. Meanwhile, white supremacists suspected it was just the beginning of more overt action by civil rights groups, and were prepared to draw up battle lines. Consequently, the Civil Rights Movement would take off more dramatically at the start of the 1960s and arouse equally determined opposition.

QUESTION

Look at **Source K**. What insight does this source provide with respect to how Eisenhower's administration viewed the whole issue of African American civil rights? What might the general feeling be among members of civil rights groups with regard to progress for their cause, as Eisenhower's presidency came to an end in January 1961?

SOURCE K

In truth, although civil rights leaders welcomed the dramatic intervention of federal troops in Little Rock, the president had little enthusiasm for such ventures… generally wary of undermining the existing polity until pushed into a corner by some southern politician who did not, significantly, belong to his circle of political backers. While Little Rock offered the civil rights movement a model of what could happen if federal authorities were stung into action, it did not reflect the general tenor of federal policy in the 1950s… petty apartheid, racist violence and widespread disfranchisement of southern blacks continued unabated. Without a sterner test, it seemed that Jim Crow might survive the political and social changes of the post-war era – if not intact, then certainly in better health than many segregationists had feared in 1954.

R. Cook (1998) *Sweet Land of Liberty*, Harlow: Longman, p. 111.

Eisenhower's apparent apathy or lack of urgency when it comes to civil rights must be considered. William Chafe in *Civilities and Civil Rights* (1981) argues that the president was too inactive and that if he had insisted on desegregation and backed this up by enforcing it, compliance to this ruling across the south would have been much more likely. Others, like Eisenhower's biographer Stephen Ambrose, might balance this by pointing out that President Eisenhower did use his constitutional powers on occasions where he felt that they were clear. For example, Eisenhower sought to drive forward the desegregation of the US military begun under Truman, and he used them to achieve desegregation in federal facilities in the nation's capital. Most crucially, the president appointed judges to federal courts whose rulings helped to advance civil rights – although the liberalism of Chief Justice Earl Warren probably took Eisenhower by surprise. Yet even Ambrose felt that, until events unfolded at Central High School, Eisenhower provided 'almost no leadership at all' on the most fundamental social and moral problem inherent in his country. Traynor, in *Modern United States History* (2001), states that Eisenhower's upbringing in Kansas and Texas, together with his life in the military, equipped him with many qualities but 'had not instilled a clear vision for leadership in the area of civil rights'. Eisenhower was prepared to complete the process of army desegregation begun by Truman, but still retained an abiding distrust of African American militancy. Paterson, Willoughby and Willoughby, in *Civil Rights in the USA* (2001), add further to the debate by commenting that the general Cold War atmosphere in the 1950s might have prevented a great deal of progress in civil rights, with Eisenhower and the US government being preoccupied with the international situation. Also, linking to Traynor's comment about militancy, they add that some civil rights supporters who had shown communist sympathies or had criticised the actions taken against African Americans had suffered personally and professionally – but that these criticisms also unsettled the government. A. Philip Randolph said that the lack of racial equality in the USA remained a propaganda gift for the USSR and that Eisenhower ought to have been aware of this.

End of section activities

1   Carry out further research into the events at Little Rock using the internet or library. Then in pairs, write a news report from Little Rock describing the arrival of the Little Rock Nine and analysing the day's events. One report should be from the perspective of a white journalist and the other from that of a journalist writing for one of the civil rights organisations. Include eye witness descriptions and interviews with key people at the school. Then present both of your reports to your fellow students. How different is the emphasis? The perspective? The content? The bias? Where are the two accounts similar?

2   The Little Rock Nine achieved both hero status and notoriety, depending which side of the debate you were on. Can you think of an individual or group of individuals in your country who have challenged the status quo recently and made a big impact on social and political life?

3   Thelma Mothershed, Minnijean Brown, Melba Pattillo and Elizabeth Eckford are four of the Little Rock Nine. What happened to them eventually? Who were the other five? How did their future lives develop? Using the library and the internet, research the Little Rock Nine, and for each person create a short bullet-pointed mini-biography.

4   Look back at **Source I**. What is stated about the Ku Klux Klan (KKK)? Using the material mentioned in this section, plus the internet and library, carry out research into the history of the KKK, especially focusing on the years 1945–60. What significant facts have you discovered? Share your findings in class.

End of chapter activities

Summary

You should now be able to explain the characteristics and context of racial discrimination in the USA, prior to, during and after the Second World War, by being aware of the presence of the many laws and threats that enforced segregation in many areas of public life. You should understand how the 1950s saw black movements mount increasingly confident legal challenges to segregation and discrimination in voter registration, fair employment and schooling. Similarly, you should be able to explain the significance of landmark rulings and events leading to integration, but that also unleashed equally strong resistance and protest from whites in the south. You should also be able to clarify the connections between social and economic challenges to the government of the USA at the time, and how they led to the reinvigoration of the Civil Rights Movement.

Summary activity

Copy the diagrams below. Use the information in this chapter and from other sources to make brief notes under each heading.

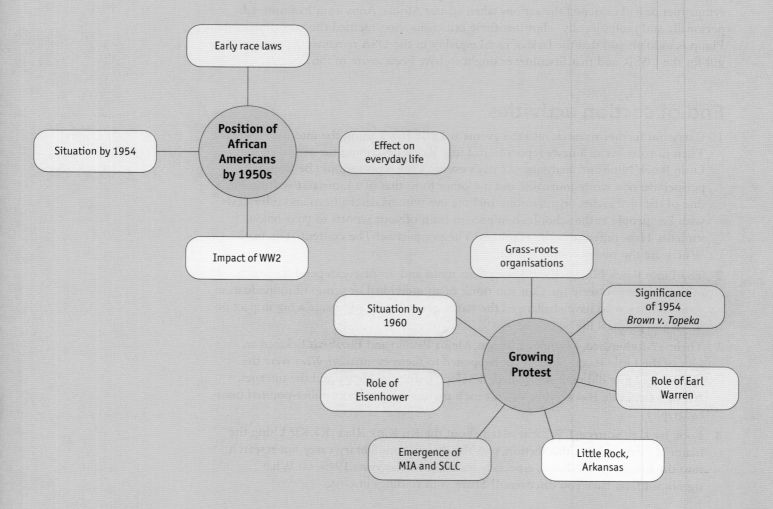

Paper 1 exam practice

Skill

Comprehension of sources.

Questions

1a According to **Source A**, what were the feelings in southern states following the *Brown v. Topeka* 1954 Supreme Court decision?   **[3 marks]**

SOURCE A

In the ground breaking case of *Brown v. Topeka Board of Education* 1954, the Supreme Court… accepted the argument put forward by the National Association for the Advancement of Coloured Peoples (NAACP) that the notion of 'separate but equal' as it was applied to education, was a contradiction in terms… and it ruled that the process of desegregating schools should begin 'with all deliberate speed'. While the decision was broadly welcomed, and seen as responsive to the changing interpretation of the Constitution in the South, it provoked turmoil… While not all newspapers in the South expressed hostility to the riling, some certainly did. The *Daily News* in Jackson, Mississippi, spoke of 'Bloodstains on the White Marble Steps' of the Supreme Court… the *Cavalier Daily* in Virginia spoke of the 'violation' of the Southern way of life, and the *Mississippian*, the newspaper of the University stated: 'though the majority of students do not want to attend school with the Negroes, we feel that the students will adapt themselves to it.

J. Traynor (2001) *Mastering Modern United States History*, Basingstoke: Palgrave Macmillan, p. 236.

1b What message is conveyed by **Source B**?   **[2 marks]**

SOURCE B

Headline from the *Topeka State Journal*, 17 May 1954

www.kshs.org/research/collections/graphics/brownvbd_headline.jpg

Student answer

1a) According to Source A, the Supreme Court decision produced turmoil in the south, where one newspaper said that the decision 'violated' the southern way of life.

1b) Source B conveys the message that this was a news item of major importance as it made the headlines of the Topeka newspaper announcing 'school segregation banned'.

Examiner's comments

In 1a) the candidate has selected ONE relevant and explicit piece of information, quoting from a newspaper of the time in a way that identifies an outcome. This would gain one mark out of three. But as no other reaction to the legislation has been identified, this candidate fails to get the other marks available.

For 1b) the candidate has identified ONE aspect of the message – that segregation was banned; but reference could have been made to the sub-heading relating to the Supreme Court and comment offered on that message. So one mark out of two obtained here.

Activity

Look again at the sources, and the student answers above. Now try to identify/make **two** other comments for **Source A** and **one** more for **Source B**. This will enable you to obtain the other marks available for the question.

Paper 2 practice questions

1   Evaluate the main problems facing the US federal government in implementing the decision made by the Supreme Court about racial segregation in schools.
2   Discuss the importance of the crisis at Little Rock, Arkansas in 1957.
3   Examine extent to which the position of African Americans changed between 1945 and 1957.
4   'Eisenhower had no interest in civil rights during his presidency, nor did he achieve anything of value in this area.' To what extent do you agree with this statement?

Protest and action

KEY QUESTIONS

- What protests and actions against racial discrimination took place before 1956?
- Why were the sit-ins and Freedom Rides launched during 1960–1 so important?
- Why was the Mississippi Freedom Summer of 1964 so important?
- What reforms were passed as a result of protests in the period 1956–65?

This chapter evaluates what is undoubtedly the most intensive period of protest and action in the campaign for African American civil rights in the USA. Beginning in 1955 with the Montgomery Bus Boycott – an action inspired by the grassroots of the Civil Rights Movement itself – it then considers the explosion of student activism in 1960–1 in the form of staged sit-ins and Freedom Rides across the Deep South and beyond. It then examines the development of other different forms of direct, popular action such as the 1964 Freedom Summer in Mississippi and a showdown at the Democratic Party National Convention. Such protests and demonstrations culminated in the Civil Rights Act of 1964 and the Voting Rights Act in 1965; but while there were militant non-violent campaigns such as the March on Washington and the campaign in Selma, Alabama, violent disturbances increasingly broke out in northern and western towns and cities, most significantly in the Watts District of Los Angeles in the summer of 1965.

Overview

- The Montgomery Bus boycott of 1955–6 influenced the future development of demands for civil rights and the methods used to challenge the authorities.
- The student sit-ins of 1960 and the formation of the Student Nonviolent Coordinating Committee (SNCC) reinvigorated the Civil Rights Movement.
- The Freedom Rides of 1961 and the violence provoked led to President Kennedy intervening and addressing the issue openly on television.

TIMELINE

1955 Dec: Montgomery Bus Boycott begins.

1956 Nov: US Supreme Court declares Montgomery bus segregation Illegal. Bus boycott ends.

1957 Jan: Martin Luther King, Jr. sets up the Southern Christian Leadership Conference (SCLC).

1960 Feb: Sit-in movement begins in Greensboro, North Carolina.

Apr: Student Nonviolent Coordinating Committee (SNCC) formed.

1961 Jan: John F. Kennedy becomes president.

May: Freedom Rides begin in the Deep South.

Nov: Attorney General Robert Kennedy enforces Supreme Court rulings on desegregated interstate travel.

1962–4 SNCC voter registration campaign in Mississippi.

1963 Mar–May: 'Project C' (Confrontation) in Birmingham, Alabama.

Aug: March on Washington; Martin Luther King's 'I Have a Dream' speech.

Sep: Killing of four African-American girls in a church in Birmingham, Alabama.

Nov: Assassination of President Kennedy in Dallas, Texas.

1964 Jun–Aug: Freedom Summer campaign in Mississippi.

Jul: Civil Rights Act passed by President Lyndon Johnson.

1965 Jan: Martin Luther King joins voter registration campaign in Selma, Alabama.

Feb: Selma– Montgomery march.

Mar: 'Bloody Sunday' and follow-up marches.

Aug: Watts Riots in Los Angeles. Voting Rights Act passed.

43

- The Freedom Summer of 1964 in Mississippi revealed the depth and strength of white supremacist feeling in southern states.

- The Mississippi Freedom Democratic Party (MFDP) went to the Democratic Convention in Atlantic City to challenge the official delegation made up of whites only. This caused problems for Lyndon Johnson and Hubert Humphrey.

- The July 1964 Civil Rights Act was passed by President Johnson in the aftermath of Kennedy's assassination. It outlawed work and social discrimination on the basis of colour, ethnicity, national origin, religion or gender.

- The 1965 campaign for voter registration in Selma, Alabama accelerated the passing of the 1965 Voting Rights Act.

- Serious rioting in the Watts District of Los Angeles and in other industrial cities now focused the campaign for civil rights away from the south. Urban areas in the north and west became significant.

3.1 What protests and actions against racial discrimination took place before 1956?

The Montgomery Bus Boycott of 1955–6

In the last chapter, we considered the significance of the *Brown v. Topeka* Supreme Court ruling, its consequences – as shown by events at Little Rock, Arkansas in 1957 – and the impact that this had on the direction of the Civil Rights Movement. Equally significant was the Bus Boycott of 1955–6 in Montgomery, Alabama. In contrast to the *Brown v. Topeka* ruling and its aftermath, events at Montgomery were determined not by the actions of a court ruling but were driven by the grass-roots of the movement.

Even in 1955 across the US, African Americans were still required to sit at the rear of city buses and even had to vacate their seats in favour of white passengers if seating at the front of the bus reserved for whites was full. On 1 December 1955, a 42-year-old black seamstress and staunch Methodist, **Rosa Parks**, was returning home from her job at a local department store and had seated herself at the front of the area marked 'coloured section'. When all of the white seats became occupied, the driver ordered four black passengers, including Parks, to vacate their seats. The others complied, but Parks refused. Subsequently, she was arrested.

Her defence was taken up by the black community in Montgomery, which quickly moved into action. Edgar D. Nixon, a past president of the National Association for the Advancement of Colored People (NAACP) in Alabama, had previously spoken to Rosa Parks – herself in the NAACP – and discussed a 'test-case' and a boycott, if a suitable incident could be found.

The Rosa Parks incident was not an isolated one-off event, as imagined by many people for years. Some years earlier, Parks had encountered the same driver, to whom

**Rosa Parks
(1913–2005)**

She joined the Montgomery branch of the NAACP in 1943, later becoming branch secretary and running its youth council. During the Bus Boycott, she was supported by both the president of the Alabama NAACP, Edgar D. Nixon, and the liberal white lawyer Clifford Durr. She was harassed and lost her job, and received death threats. The Parks family moved to Detroit in 1957 and set up the Rosa and Desmond Parks Institute for Self-development, giving job training to black youth. In 1996, US President Bill Clinton awarded her the Presidential Medal of Freedom, and in 1999 she received the Congressional Gold Award.

she had paid her fare at the front of the bus before getting off to re-enter through the back door as required. But the driver had then pulled away smirking before she could reboard. Earlier in 1955, a 15-year-old black girl, Claudette Colvin, was arrested in Montgomery following a similar incident. Montgomery's black leaders were all prepared to protest, until they found out that Colvin was pregnant. They reconsidered their intentions, believing that she was not the ideal symbol for their cause. But Parks was respected in the black community in Montgomery, and it seemed that this was now the moment to act.

On 5 December, she appeared in court and was duly fined $10, plus $4 in court fees. But, on the same day, blacks boycotted the buses. In Montgomery, 30,000 black people usually travelled by bus, providing most of the bus company's income, but on this day they walked to work or shared lifts, if they knew someone with a car.

Following the imposition of the fine on Parks, plus the success of the one-day boycott, black leaders in Montgomery decided to prolong the protest. So they established the Montgomery Improvement Association (MIA) to coordinate the boycott. Among the black leadership were many church ministers and they invited one of them, a young Baptist minister named **Martin Luther King**, to lead the boycott. His local Baptist church thus acted as the base for the campaign.

Martin Luther King Jr (1929–68)

He was born in Atlanta, Georgia. Martin Luther King's grandfather and father were both Baptist ministers, and King became one himself, having completed a PhD at theological college. In 1953 he married Coretta Scott, a fellow activist from the south. By this time, he was also a civil rights campaigner for African Americans and a member of the NAACP. He came to public attention because of his role in coordinating the Montgomery Bus Boycott in 1955–6. In 1957 he was elected president of the Southern Christian Leadership Conference (SCLC). A brilliant orator, he spoke more than 2,500 times about injustice, racial prejudice, protest and action. His ideas were founded on the Christian belief of reconciliation through love, as well as being influenced by the non-violent, mass actions of Mahatma Gandhi in India. In 1964 he won the Nobel Peace Prize and is considered the key figure in the 1960s civil rights struggle and an iconic hero to millions. He was murdered by a white gunman in Memphis on 4 April 1968.

Figure 3.1 Rosa Parks being finger printed after her arrest in December 1956, prior to the Bus Boycott that followed

What was the significance of the Montgomery Bus Boycott?

The boycott began with high spirits among the black population of Montgomery, as they believed firmly that they held the moral high ground and that their requests were moderate. Although their demands did not include the total desegregation of Montgomery buses, the campaigners pressed for more polite treatment of black passengers from white bus drivers; seating to be first-come, first-served; and an end to black passengers having to stand when the bus was not full in the white seats. It was felt that there was also a need to employ some black drivers, given that African Americans comprised more than 75 per cent of the Montgomery bus passengers. The bus company was adamant it would not give way and refused any compromise, but the black protest was a success from the start. Most of the bus company managers and many of the city politicians believed that the boycott would not last long. They assumed wrongly that the blacks lacked the ability to sustain their campaign. Many also reasoned that they would start reusing public transport when the weather was bad. But it was a huge miscalculation. Significantly, the boycott had resulted in the first mass, non-violent mobilisation of black people. They walked, cycled, shared lifts and hitch-hiked. They improvised in many different ways.

To further enhance the chances of success, black leaders in Montgomery organised carpools, with black taxi drivers charging the same fee as the bus company – 10 cents – for African American passengers. They organised regular mass meetings to keep African American residents mobilised around the boycott. The authorities reacted by harassing the drivers and customers, by damaging the cars and by threatening to arrest

Figure 3.2 Carpooling in Montgomery

those taxi drivers who charged below the standard fare. But morale was high and many just decided to tough it out and walk.

Rosa Parks was sacked from her job by her white bosses, and bombs were thrown into black churches. Cars were also targeted, as was the house of Martin Luther King in January 1956. His wife and daughters were inside when their home was bombed, though they weren't injured. Yet the boycott persisted as the spring of 1956 moved into the summer.

In June 1956, the NAACP took the case to a federal district court, which ruled that segregated transport was unconstitutional in the light of the recent *Brown v. Topeka* decision. It violated the 14th Amendment to the US Constitution, which had guaranteed all citizens, equal rights and equal protection under the law.

Montgomery's civic leaders appealed to the Supreme Court, but their ruling declared that Montgomery's buses had to be integrated. This happened on 21 December 1956 after a boycott of 381 days. The day after the order became effective, Martin Luther King and other local leaders took their first ride on a desegregated bus.

SOURCE A

The Montgomery Bus Boycott was a remarkable event. Even though a good case can be made for arguing that the 381-day protest did not result directly in the desegregation of local buses, the boycott constituted the first real indication that southern blacks could organise effectively on a community-wide basis to defeat Jim Crow.

R. Cook (1998) *Sweet Land of Liberty*, Harlow: Longman, p. 98.

QUESTION

Look at **Source A**. What is meant by the phrase 'organise effectively on a community-wide basis to defeat Jim Crow'? Why has the Montgomery Bus Boycott been seen as a significant moment for the Civil Rights Movement?

The consequences of a successful boycott

The Supreme Court ruling and the victory at Montgomery had showed that the black community could protest and take an active part in remedying their previous sense of hopelessness. Although the Deep South still remained in the grip of segregation, and in spite of the persistence of beatings, the occasional lynching and a general sense of intimidation and discrimination, it proved that with coordination and persistence, the Civil Rights Movements could achieve great things through their solidarity, their grass-roots activism and the determination of their leaders in standing up for their rights.

The Montgomery boycotters did not back down at all, since the authorities would not give ground either. This set a tone and made the Montgomery Bus Boycott the template for future challenges. In this respect, it is significant as the starting engine for the growing activity undertaken by the Civil Rights Movement over the next decade. It also made a significant impact on northerners who were supportive of civil rights, many of whom felt that the momentum provided by the success at Montgomery could be built upon and encourage more direct action in the south.

The success at Montgomery saw Martin Luther King emerge as a key figure in the Civil Rights Movement on the national stage, through his leadership role in the MIA. He advocated non-violent resistance. This approach helped to forge the movement's mission statement, which continued throughout the 1960s. Moreover, after the boycott ended,

King helped found the Southern Christian Leadership Conference (SCLC), which became one of the most influential civil rights organisations in operation, as they fought segregation throughout the south (see Chapter 4, section 4.1, The Southern Christian Leadership Conference (SCLC).

Finally, the boycott drew international attention to the treatment of African Americans in the south. More than one hundred reporters from around the world visited Montgomery to investigate the effort and interview its leaders. Significantly, the horizon of the black protestors was now raised from wanting 'reasonable status' for their race to an ultimate goal of integration.

Interpretations of the Montgomery Bus Boycott

The Montgomery Bus Boycott has stimulated debate about why the tactics succeeded, and has led to examination of certain aspects of this event. The 'heroism' of Rosa Parks, and the perceived triumph of the boycotters over the segregationist authorities have allowed events in Montgomery to be cast as a David versus Goliath struggle, where spontaneous response and communal determination slayed the giant of the city authorities. But it is not as simple as this. Montgomery was not a standalone achievement. While M. Marable, in *Race, Reform and Religion* (1991), believes that the 'challenge to racism blossomed into an international event', Sanders (2006, p. 107) reminds us that bus boycotts were not new and that the Montgomery blacks were using tactics first employed at Baton Rouge, Louisiana in 1953, noting: 'the boycott did not just come out of the blue: it was the result of black organisations (the church and NAACP) that had been developing for years', while Paterson, Willoughby and Willoughby (2001, p. 287) add a cautionary note, warning 'once the initial euphoria of the magnificent success at Montgomery had died away, it was clear that much more of this campaigning was going to be required if black people were to gain their full civil rights'. Stacey and Scott–Baumann argue in *Civil Rights and Social Movements in the Americas* (2013) that Rosa Parks was no ordinary black woman as depicted, but that she and her husband, Raymond, were active in the local NAACP. They also show that that there was a real network of burgeoning support at hand. Upon Parks' arrest, she called Edgar D. Nixon, who bailed her out of jail and determined that she would be a good role model to call as a plaintiff in the legal challenge over segregation. They also draw attention to a strong female organisation, the Women's Political Council (WPC). This was a group of 300 educated black women who had been campaigning for voter registration and the desegregation of the buses for several years. What Farber and Bailey (2001) call 'a remarkable group of veteran African American activists', the WPC began circulating flyers calling for a bus boycott on 5 December, the day of Parks' court trial. They were led by Jo Ann Robinson, a professor of English at the all–black Alabama State College. This adds weight to the notion that the boycott was not necessarily as spontaneous and as emotionally fuelled by outrage as time has led us to believe: as Stacey and Scott-Baumann comment, 'Nixon and Robinson took responsibility for mobilising the blacks of Montgomery. They had just four days to organise the boycott if it was to take place on the day of Parks' trial … the bus boycott was not completely spontaneous. It was the result of years of grass–roots activism and was sustained by a strong, well–organised black community in Montgomery. The community's leaders were no longer afraid to stand up for their rights, despite ongoing intimidation.' Clearly, Rosa Parks did not just happen to be in the right place at the right time. Nonetheless, whatever slant the debate might take, it was evident that African American confidence in removing segregation was growing.

End of section activities

1   Carry out further research on the Montgomery Bus Boycott and its organisers. What do your findings reveal about the nature of the opposition to segregation in Montgomery and in Alabama generally?

2   Write two press releases about the Bus Boycott: one to be released by the civil rights groups at their supporters, the other by the Montgomery Bus Company and/or the city leaders. In your statements, make sure you analyse the boycott with respect to how it affects the interest of that particular group. Don't just narrate the events.

3   Using the library or the internet, undertake some more research into Rosa Parks. Think about her own words and reasons. What do you think motivated her to stay seated and why? Write your own interpretation of the events that led up to and took place during the Montgomery Bus Boycott. Cite the reasons and sources you have found to support your view.

KEY CONCEPTS QUESTION

Causes and Consequences: Draw a chart with two columns, one showing the main reasons for the Montgomery Bus Boycott and the other showing the consequences of the twelve-month boycott. Take care to include the position and responses of both sides in the dispute. What was the most important consequence of this event?

3.2 Why were the sit-ins and Freedom Rides launched during 1960–1 so important?

How did sit-ins develop?

On 1 February 1960, a sit-in protest movement began at the lunch counter of the Woolworth store in Greensboro, North Carolina, when four black students refused to leave a whites-only area. This and similar protests highlighted the fact that meal segregation was a symptom of a much deeper sickness. Support groups sprang up in northern colleges and among white students. It was a seminal moment, and the SCLC helped different civil rights groups and organisations

On the first day at Greensboro, four smartly dressed, polite black students – Franklin McCain, Joseph McNeil, Ezell Blair, Jr and David Richmond – bought items to eat and then sat down in the store all day, refusing to move from a segregated area for whites. They chatted, wrote or read the Bible, and only left at closing time.

The next day more than twenty people joined them. By day three, journalists were reporting this story on the national news, and the sit-in students were joined by sixty more. They remained passive in response to the tone set by the speeches of Martin Luther King, yet were heckled and verbally abused. Whites hit them and threw ketchup and soda drinks over them; some even stubbed cigarettes out on their bodies. But they failed to retaliate. The Woolworth company stated officially that it would maintain its segregated policy, where it coincided with local custom, but the store was forced to close temporarily on 6 February when more than 300 people became involved. It was a critical moment in the Civil Rights Movement and within six weeks, people in more than 30 cities and towns across seven states were engaged in various sit-in campaigns.

SOURCE B

Ezell Blair Jr, Franklin McCain, Joseph McNeil and David Richmond leaving the Woolworth store after the first sit-in on 1 February 1960.

americanhistory.si.edu

The development and spread of sit-ins

The Civil Rights Movement knew that in order to make lasting progress, meticulous planning was necessary. Seeing the efforts of the Greensboro students, the movement instigated a general boycott on the Woolworth chain of stores. Memories of Montgomery and Rosa Parks were reignited, and the success was of similar proportions.

Nationwide sales at Woolworth stores dropped by more than one-third. Seeing the financial effects of this boycott, the Woolworth management realised they would have to end their segregation policy. On 25 July 1960, the desegregation process began when black employees at Greensboro's Woolworth were served first at the store's lunch counter as a gesture of intent. The following day, every Woolworth store in the US was desegregated.

The Greensboro Four had inspired other protests, with students in Kentucky, Tennessee and Virginia being motivated. In Nashville, Tennessee, Vanderbilt University student James Lawson organised campaigns and led workshops on non-violence. 'Rules of Conduct' for the protests and sit-ins were produced, emphasising courtesy, no sarcasm, no violence and no retaliation. Students also followed a policy of 'jail, no bail' – refusing to pay bail so that the police would have to keep them in prison. As jails filled up, Nashville police reduced bail to $5 – but they still refused to settle. Consequently, many had to be released as the jails would soon be overflowing.

By mid-1960, Nashville was serving blacks at its bus station lunch counter, as were a number of department stores. Cinemas, hotels and leisure facilities would prove to be more resistant, but it was an important first set of achievements for the movement. The organisation was also impressive. Lawson's seminars had drawn many notable thinkers and activists. Future leaders of the Civil Rights Movement were trained here and notable workers such as Diane Nash, John Lewis and Marion Barry were able to gain valuable experience for the future. The student sit-in movement was aided by sympathetic media coverage. Newspapers printed positive articles in praise of the sit-in participants' courage, and reported on the movement's growth.

In Philadelphia, retail stores that relied on black customers in overwhelmingly black areas but were refusing to employ blacks were targeted. Leon Sullivan, the pastor at the Mount Zion Baptist Church, gathered a church group around him whose motto was 'Don't buy where you can't work!' By mid-1960, more than 250,000 black Americans had joined Sullivan's campaigners.

During 1960–1, students and activists across the US began other forms of sit-ins in their local communities. This fed the growing national movement, and by the end of 1961 more than 800 towns and cities had desegregated public areas. The original sit-ins at 'whites only' lunch counters inspired swim-ins at segregated public pools, kneel-ins at segregated churches, sleep-ins at segregated motel lobbies, read-ins at segregated libraries and many more attention-drawing tactics. More than 70,000 people had participated and over 3,000 arrests had been made.

The significance of the sit-ins

It is significant that the origins of this protest had taken place in North Carolina, as this state was marginally less racist than Alabama, Mississippi, South Carolina or Georgia. As a result, prominent white liberal politicians were able to express sympathy for the students' cause. Terry Sanford, later elected governor of North Carolina, was particularly supportive. He knew, as did the authorities, that the instigators of the sit-ins were articulate, idealistic and intelligent college students. They were fired by a determination that was in itself fuelled by the knowledge that they had no jobs to be dismissed from. This also brought a new dimension to the protest.

The student-led demonstrations were typically non-violent, in spite of their being routinely heckled and assaulted by segregationists and police. But they remained resolute and determined, believing that peaceful protest could still yield results. However, many areas in the Deep South remained largely untouched by this level of protest and many people were still highly outspoken against such attempts at discrimination.

The student movement had pointedly pursued tactics of direct action, but still upheld the idea of non-violence. This had instilled in the movement what Martin Luther King described as 'the extraordinary power and discipline which every thinking person observes'. Segregation was now being seen as a moral as well as a legal issue, and the dignity of the black sit-in students in the face of white supremacist rage went a long way to win both black and white support for their cause, at both the national and international level. The next stage of the campaign to outlaw segregation was now about to hit the roads of the US highways.

What were the Freedom Rides of 1961?

A month after the election of **John F. Kennedy** as president in November 1960, the Supreme Court made a significant ruling. In *Boynton v. Virginia*, the court pronounced that racial segregation was illegal in all waiting-rooms and restaurants used in terminals serving buses that crossed state lines, would violate the Interstate Commerce Act. In combination with the 1946 *Morgan v. Virginia* and the 1955 *Keys v. Carolina Coach* Supreme Court rulings, segregation was outlawed on all interstate bus travel. But, as with the continued segregation of hotels and other public facilities in many of the southern states, many of these rulings were conveniently ignored.

In 1961, Freedom Rides were initiated by young activists, both black and white. They boarded buses heading south toward segregated terminals. They aimed to test the *Boynton* decision, hoping that where confrontations arose, media attention would be captured, at the same time nudging Kennedy's new government into action. But these were dangerous journeys.

The purpose of the Freedom Rides and the challenges faced

The first 'Freedom Ride' left Washington, DC, on 4 May 1961, scheduled to arrive in New Orleans, Louisiana on 17 May. Thirteen Riders left Washington, DC, on Greyhound and Trailways buses, intent on riding through Virginia, North and South Carolina, then on to Georgia, through Alabama, into Mississippi, and ending with a rally in New Orleans, Louisiana. The Riders were from the Congress of Racial Equality (CORE) and the **Student Nonviolent Coordinating Committee** (SNCC) and were led by CORE director James Farmer. Most were over 40 years old.

This Freedom Ride (and others that subsequently took place) was designed to publicise the fact that in spite of the different Supreme Court rulings of recent years, segregation was still legally enforced in the southern United States. Riders were arrested for disregarding these racist laws and for trespassing, as well as for allegedly violating state laws and contravening local Jim Crow laws (see Chapter 2, section 2.1, Historical background).

The Riders' tactics were designed to provoke a reaction. For example, they would have at least one interracial pair sitting in adjoining seats. Then they would position a black Rider at the front of the bus, occupying a seat traditionally reserved for white passengers. Several others would then sit throughout the bus. Cleverly, one of the Riders would avoid arrest by deliberately following the segregation rules for travel. He or she could then contact CORE to inform them of the situation and arrange bail for those who were arrested. Virginia proved relatively trouble-free, but some Riders were arrested in Charlotte, North Carolina and parts of South Carolina.

In Alabama, violence was actively organised by Birmingham Police Commissioner 'Bull' Connor to end the Freedom Ride. In May 1961, a mob was given 15 minutes to attack Freedom Riders in Anniston without any arrests being made. The Greyhound bus was hit and its tyres slashed. It then had to stop several miles out of town, whereupon the mob, chasing it in cars, hurled firebombs. They then attempted to hold the doors of the burning bus shut, aiming to kill the Riders trapped inside. The Riders managed to escape both the mob and the flames, but many were beaten viciously. When two white Riders attempted to intervene, they were assaulted. A retired college professor was permanently invalided because of the severity of his injuries and spent the rest of his life in a wheelchair.

Figure 3.3   Freedom Riders in shock outside their firebombed bus in Anniston, Alabama, May 1961

The Freedom Riders were prevented from being lynched due to warning shots being fired into the air by highway patrolmen. A Trailways bus then set off to continue the onward journey and was attacked by a police-aided mob when it arrived at Birmingham, Alabama. The police themselves had tipped off the local leader of the Ku Klux Klan, and allegedly said that they would gave the Klan 15 minutes to do what they wanted before they intervened. On trying to leave this second bus, the Riders were beaten with baseball bats and piping, with white Riders being singled out for particular punishment.

On 21 May 1961, the remaining Riders en route to Montgomery were abandoned by the Alabama State Highway Patrol as they approached the city. The local police ignored the brutal beatings the Riders got at the main bus terminal in Montgomery. The police did not intervene, nor did they protect white Freedom Riders, who were singled out for vicious assaults. A Justice Department official sent by the Kennedy administration to accompany the Riders and observe the situation was beaten unconscious. Local ambulances refused to take the injured to hospital for treatment, so it was left to a few brave blacks to assist the victims.

The same night, more than 1,500 people, including Martin Luther King, filled the Reverend Ralph Abernathy's First Baptist Church in Montgomery. The church was surrounded by a crowd of shouting whites, many of whom attacked blacks in the street. Only a few US Marshals protected the church from assault and firebombs. The black leaders in Montgomery feared a bloodbath and asked President Kennedy for assistance. Kennedy told State Governor Patterson to send in the National Guard to protect the blacks, or he would dispatch federal troops. Patterson finally ordered the Alabama National Guard to disperse the mob.

The Kennedy administration now hoped for a cooling-off period, but many hundreds of activists continued to defy segregation on the Freedom Rides and in bus stations. Jails were filling up, not only in the Deep South, but also in Chicago, Illinois. Here 2,500 blacks rode nearly fifty buses to City Hall with banners demanding better jobs, better pay and decent housing. Throughout the summer of 1961, other Freedom Riders continued protesting and campaigned by sitting together in segregated places.

SOURCE C

White protestors, considered 'race traitors' by other white people, were the focus of particular hatred. Jim Zwerg, a white student from Fiske University, Nashville, was kicked and punched until his teeth were knocked out. Then he was punched to the ground time and time again. His back was severely injured and he was temporarily disfigured. But in a television interview from his hospital bed he showed remarkable courage and bravery. 'We are dedicated to this…we are willing to accept beatings… we are willing to accept death… segregation must be broken down!'

D. Paterson, D. Willoughby and S. Willoughby (2001) *Civil Rights in the USA 1863–1980*, Oxford: Heinemann, p. 133.

QUESTION

Compare **Sources C** and **D**. What do they tell us about the relationship and the empathy between the US government and civil rights activists in 1961? What are the points of similarity and difference between the two sources?

SOURCE D

Racist mobs attacked the freedom riders viciously, raising the spectre of large-scale racial violence in the south… Kennedy initially reacted to this racist violence by telling a civil rights aide: 'Can't you get your goddamned friends off these buses?' At this point, he seemed worried primarily about the damage the violence was doing to the international image of the United States. Kennedy was not unmoved by the plight of the blacks; if necessary, he decided that he would protect civil rights. But he sought to delay movement on this contentious issue, hoping, much like Eisenhower, that in time the South would come to accept reform.

P. Levine and H. Papasotiriou (2005) *America Since 1945*, Basingstoke: Palgrave Macmillan, p. 98.

The consequences of the Freedom Rides

Media coverage of the Freedom Rides achieved the desired results. Millions of people in America and across the world were shocked. Alabama Governor Patterson was unsympathetic when interviewed by the press, saying: 'When you go somewhere looking for trouble, you usually get it.' But to many, this served to reinforce the perception of America's south as being racist and living in a social time warp. Also, somewhat ironically, the SNCC and CORE had virtually forced the whites into violent retaliation although they themselves professed non-violence. Overall, it finally kick-started Kennedy's

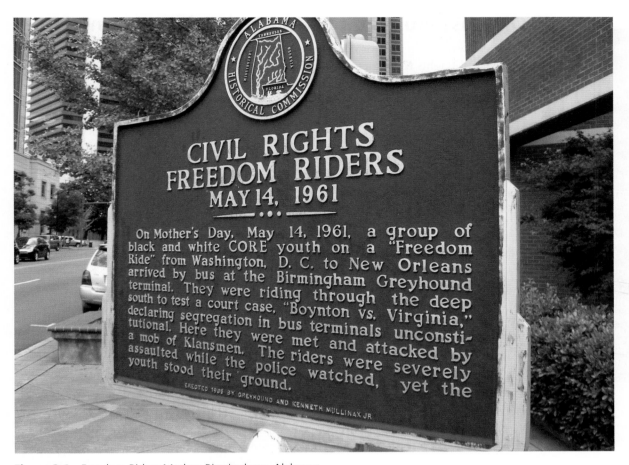

Figure 3.4 Freedom Riders Marker, Birmingham, Alabama

government in the field of civil rights legislation as the violence and arrests continued to attract national and international attention.

Under pressure from Kennedy, regulations prohibiting segregation in interstate transit terminals were issued. Bus signs, as well as those in waiting rooms, toilets and eating areas, all had to be changed. The giveaway signs of segregation such as 'black waiting room' and 'whites only here' were finally removed. But it had taken 15 years to enforce the original Supreme Court decision from 1946, which ruled that interstate transport segregation was illegal.

But Kennedy had to proceed with caution; he needed southern votes in Congress. As Traynor (2001) observes: 'Kennedy was slow to take a strong stand on the issue… Executive action, he believed, could do more for blacks than legislation.' Although Schlesinger felt that black leaders 'never doubted that Kennedy was on their side', Kennedy also felt that an all-out drive to support civil rights would have alienated support in the south for social and educational legislation he wanted to enact as part of government policy. Boyer, Clark and Kett (2008) believe that he viewed civil rights as a thorny thicket to avoid, not a moral issue, 'and only after scores more freedom rides and the arrests of hundreds of protestors did Kennedy act'.

3

James Meredith (1933–)

He was the first African American student admitted to the segregated University of Mississippi. He believed he had a God-given mission to integrate a university where few black people had ever applied and none had been previously accepted. Meredith sought to pressure the Kennedy administration on Civil Rights for African Americans, becoming a leading writer, campaigner and thinker in the movement, especially after the Freedom Rides of 1961 led to the desegregation of interstate bus terminals.

Ole Miss, Bull Connor and action from Kennedy

But there was another major consequence of the Freedom Rides: the buoyancy it gave to the Civil Rights Movement as its various actors gathered increasing white support and world media attention. Their sense of determination inspired other 'tests' against white supremacist rulings and attitudes, and events in 1962–3 would further force Kennedy's hand.

James Meredith was a black US Air Force veteran denied admission to the all-white University of Mississippi, known as 'Ole Miss' for the start of the academic year beginning in September 1962. When Meredith had applied the previous year, he had written at the bottom of his application: 'I sincerely hope that your attitude toward me as a potential member of your student body… will not change upon learning that I am not a white applicant.'

Other African American students had also tried unsuccessfully to gain admission to other all-white universities in the state. For example, in 1959 Clyde Kennard, a former paratrooper in Korea, returned home to Mississippi and was denied admission to Mississippi Southern College. Following a perfunctory 15-minute interview, Kennard left the college only to be arrested for speeding and possessing alcohol that in all likelihood was planted in his car. He was subsequently imprisoned for seven years, charged with stealing chicken feed. He died shortly after being released.

Meredith's rejection was challenged by Medgar Evers of the Mississippi NAACP, and the case went to the Supreme Court. In June 1962, Justice Hugo Black ruled that Meredith was entitled to attend the university and ordered Ole Miss to admit him. This was indicative of how much legal progress had now been made with respect to educational integration. But the segregationist Mississippi Governor Ross Barnett vowed to keep Meredith out and his refusal led to a showdown between state and federal authorities.

Meredith arrived on campus, where angry mobs had assembled. A segregationist mob tried to storm Ole Miss. They had virtually laid siege to the campus, attacking some of the 170 federal marshals who were anxiously trying to keep order. Meredith emerged unscathed, but the clash left two onlookers dead and dozens injured. A TV reporter was even attacked inside his own car. But ultimately Ole Miss, the state of Mississippi and the entire nation were forever changed. The SNCC and CORE also reaped much of the publicity for these legal successes.

The Meredith episode proved to be one of the most violent conflicts in Mississippi for many years, fuelled by the power wielded by the racist Citizens' Council. But change would eventually come, although not before more travesties of justice occurred. Sadly, Meredith had to endure the humiliation of being segregated on campus and eating alone. Nonetheless he was an inspiration to others

Theophilus Eugene 'Bull' Connor (1897–1973)

He was commissioner of public safety in Birmingham, Alabama and was renowned for his opposition to desegregation and his actions during SCLC's Birmingham Campaign of 1963.

Then, in spring 1963, police arrested Martin Luther King and other ministers demonstrating in Birmingham, Alabama, turning fire hoses and police dogs on their marching supporters. As with the earlier Freedom Rides, Police Chief **'Bull' Connor** not only failed to organise protection but actually encouraged the violent protests, and so became a symbol of bigotry. His use of fire hoses, police attack dogs, and even a small tank against protesters provoked national disgust when it later appeared on TV.

SOURCE E

An Associated Press photographer captured the image of a large German shepherd dog mauling a fifteen-year-old bystander. Kennedy privately remarked that he 'felt sick'. Within a month Kennedy gave a national television address from the Oval Office on the issue of civil rights: 'we are confronted primarily with a moral issue. It is as old as the Scriptures and is as clear as the American Constitution. If an American, because his skin is dark, cannot eat lunch in a restaurant open to the public, if he cannot send his children to the best public schools available, if he cannot vote for the public officials who represent him...then who among us would be content... It is time to act in Congress...'

J. Traynor (2001) *Modern United States History*, Basingstoke: Palgrave, p. 272.

QUESTION

Look at **Source E** and the preceding text. Why do you think Kennedy finally proposed legislation at this point in 1963 to bring about changes in race relations? If he did not, what might the reaction of moderate blacks be?

Figure 3.5 Martin Luther King acknowledges supporters at the Lincoln Memorial on 28 August 1963, where he delivered his famous 'I Have a Dream' speech, which is credited with mobilising supporters of desegregation. King was assassinated five years later

Fact: African Americans were largely debarred from voting in the south, even in the mid-1960s. White election officials and local officials sought to prevent them from exercising their right by imposing literacy tests and comprehension requirements. Not only could highly educated blacks not pass these requirements, but the majority had low levels of literacy, if any at all.

To pressure Congress, the 'March on Washington for Jobs and Freedom' took place on 28 August 1963. It gained lasting prominence with the historic 'I Have a Dream' speech delivered at the Lincoln Memorial by King and shown live on TV. Organised by civil rights, labour and religious organisations, the number marching reached around 250,000; 80 per cent were African American and the rest were white or from other ethnic groups. This march was part of the rapidly expanding Civil Rights Movement, although some objected, saying it was 'watered down' by having whites participating in the march, as opposed to a rally showing the influence of blacks alone. Others differed over the purpose of the march. Yet the march did help to push through Johnson's Civil Rights Act (1964) and National Voting Rights Act (1965). It was also the high point of Martin Luther King's influence. This will be examined further in the next chapter, when consideration is given to the role and significance of key groups and leaders, and attention is focused on civil rights protests in Albany, Georgia and in Mississippi – perhaps the most racist of all the southern states.

How important were the sit-ins and Freedom Rides?

The indignation created by the Greensboro sit-in and its successors, together with widespread violence provoked by the Freedom Rides, sent shockwaves through much of the US. On one side of the argument – predominantly from white communities – came accusations and press editorials accusing the Riders of provoking social unrest and accusing CORE of playing dangerous games with their direct action approach. Conversely, the Freedom Rides were viewed in more liberal quarters as having a heroic quality and being inspirational, as well as morally right. Above all the Freedom Riders from the north, who had acted fearlessly on behalf of southern blacks, gained enduring respect in the south. It inspired others to join the Civil Rights Movement and promote campaigns such as voter registration throughout the south.

The Freedom Rides enabled CORE, the SCLC and the SNCC to rise to prominence. The 'big three' movements that shaped the latter years of the civil rights struggle, these organisations were firmly in the tradition of pursuing more direct action. They also had a tendency to organise members in their own communities. They were a contrast to the NAACP, an organisation much more grounded in fighting legal battles and promoting changes in legislation.

CORE and its leader James Farmer were now in the public spotlight and, being active in many major northern cities, soon became the principal civil rights organisation outside the south to advocate direct action. In a similar vein, the SNCC as an organisation was previously little known outside Civil Rights Movement circles. But after the Freedom Rides, the public and the press were more aware of the SNCC as an organisation. Therefore, the sit-ins and the Freedom Rides had brought a small ray of early light into the darkness of segregation in the south.

End of section activities

1 'The African American sit-ins of the early 1960s were totally spontaneous and owed little to the past work of existing civil rights organisations.' How far do you agree with this statement? Using this section, together with your own research, write an answer to this interpretation. Consider whether or not existing

activism may have played a part. You might also need to consider the role of the government.

2   How big an impact did the sit-ins and the Freedom Rides have on the system of racial segregation in the south? Divide into two groups and prepare a debate on this. You will need to plan carefully and do extra research. Consider not only events, but movements, individuals and the importance of outside agencies like the media.

3   Like *Brown v. Topeka* and Little Rock, Arkansas, the story of James Meredith's bid for admission to 'Ole Miss' is a case study of school and university integration in the Deep South. Find out what you can about other attempts to break down the racial barriers in education in the 1960s. Researching George Wallace and the University of Alabama, plus looking on the website of the US Federal Judicial Centre (www.fjc.gov), would all be good starting points.

4   Imagine that you are *either* James Farmer *or* James Meredith, *and* that you are *either* Bull Connor *or* the governor of a southern state where major events are being played out. How do you view all the events that have taken place between 1960 and 1963? Write two diary entries for your chosen pair, backed up by factual events as well as your opinion. It must show what you hope, and fear, and how you view the role of the federal government. The two entries will obviously be very contrasting and highly personal to who you are.

3.3 Why was the Mississippi Freedom Summer of 1964 so important?

What did the Freedom Summer aim to do?

In 1964, a voter registration drive known as the Mississippi Summer Project, or Freedom Summer, was organised. It sought to increase black voter registration in Mississippi and throughout the south prior to the presidential election in November of that year. The SNCC and CORE worked on the project, which was run by the local Council of Federated Organizations (COFO) – an association of civil rights groups of which the SNCC was the most active member.

An initial voter registration in November 1963 was undertaken by the SNCC. The hundred white college students on this project were then joined in the summer of 1964 by hundreds of other students, predominantly white volunteers from the north, often from privileged backgrounds.

The Freedom Summer workers were frequently impeded and bullied by members of the white population in Mississippi. But false arrests, arson and beatings all led to more serious happenings. Eventually, all of America took notice of the Mississippi Freedom Summer when three activists – two of whom were white – were murdered by segregationists who were probably also members of the Ku Klux Klan. These events provided the backdrop for the highly successful Alan Parker film *Mississippi Burning* (1988).

3

How the summer of 1964 unfolded

Mississippi was targeted because of its social and political demographics. It was virtually the poorest of all US states and it also had the highest percentage of black people – 45 per cent. But Mississippi also had one of the most hard-line white supremacist state governments, with blacks experiencing more beatings, lynchings and racial crime there than in any other state. Significantly, it had historically low levels of African American voter registration, with only 5 per cent of voting-age blacks in the state being registered to vote in 1962, 16 per cent below the national average. Moreover, no black had been elected to any office within the state since the end of the American Civil War in 1865.

The workers clearly operated under the most difficult and dangerous circumstances. The police force of Mississippi's capital city of Jackson was fully equipped to meet any disturbances, being heavily reinforced with extra shotguns and tear gas. There was even a tank on standby. Jackson's authorities were prepared to deal with the Freedom Summer workers in the same way as the authorities in Birmingham. Segregationists were appalled at the thought of white northern liberals encroaching on the Mississippi way of life, and local newspapers spoke of an invading army from the north. Governor Johnson denounced the invaders and their scheme, stating: 'We are going to see that law and order is maintained – and maintained Mississippi-style!'

The first 300 helpers arrived in mid-June, and shortly afterwards two white students – Michael Schwerner and Andrew Goodman from New York – both disappeared, together with a local black SNCC worker, James Chaney, after they had investigated a church bombing.

The trio were detained for a traffic violation, whereupon the police informed the Ku Klux Klan that they would be freed that night. Upon release, they were followed by three vehicles and subsequently disappeared. There was huge media attention and President **Lyndon Baines Johnson** ordered a major investigation. FBI agents questioned hundreds of people in an operation codenamed 'Mississippi Burning'. Six weeks later, their bodies were found. It was apparent that, following an abduction, they had been severely beaten and killed.

The state of Mississippi refused to prosecute anybody, although 18 people were implicated. Neshoba County Deputy Sheriff Cecil Price had coordinated the kidnapping and murder of the three. In 1967, Price and six others were convicted on a lesser charge of conspiracy to violate the civil rights of the victims; yet this was a key moment in Mississippi legal history. A jury had convicted white men, and some of them members of the Klan, in connection with the death of a black man. But it was the killing of two white men that made the Mississippi murders so notorious.

SOURCE F

The murders… rocked me to the core of my very being. Lynchings were not unusual. And they were legal, as far as we could see… but I was not used to white men killing white men because of black men… So those murders in 1964 were shocking. And I felt for the mothers of the white boys. You see, the mother of a black boy knows that when he leaves home, she may never see him again, no matter where. But the white mother didn't know that. Those three young men… had the courage to go to the lion's den and try to scrub the lion's teeth… [they] are unmitigated heroes, so we have to lift them up and show them to the world.

Maya Angelou (2013) foreword to C. Goodman with B. Herzog, *My Mantelpiece: A Memoir of Survival and Social Justice*, New York: Why Not Books.

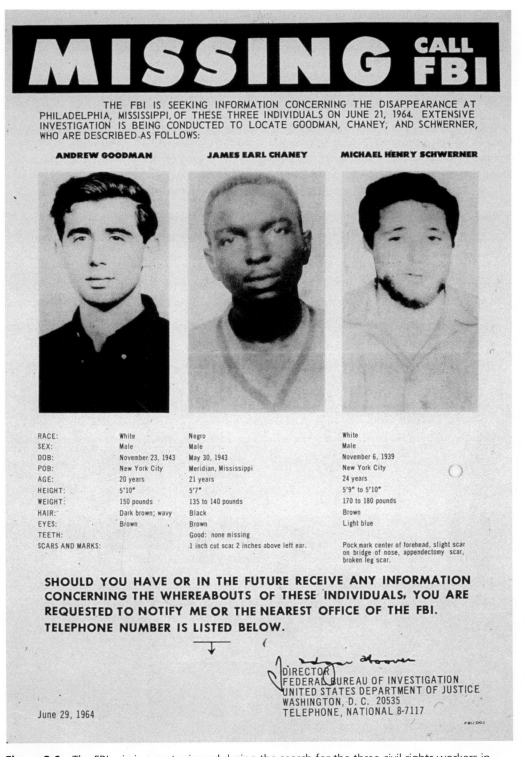

Figure 3.6 The FBI missing poster issued during the search for the three civil rights workers in Mississippi who were murdered

Theory of knowledge

History and film: Watch the film *Mississippi Burning*. How useful is a film like this when studying the history of the Civil Rights Movement? Does the film manage to convey the view held by many historians that events in Mississippi became a turning point for the entire Civil Rights Movement, in terms of to how to respond to racism in the future? Does the portrayal of events in the film help to support a widely held view that the Mississippi Freedom Summer was the most heavily deployed and intensive project of all for the civil rights campaigners?

During the search for the missing victims, a sense of outrage grew across the US. Freedom Summer workers were dismayed by the lack of protection they were offered, and civil rights supporters were critical of the speed of the Mississippi Burning investigation. In such a climate of disgust, the passage of a long-pending Civil Rights Bill in Congress was undoubtedly speeded along and any thoughts that the disappearance of the three workers might intimidate or discourage other volunteers backfired. Support for the campaign grew.

Also, although securing voting rights was the main focus of this campaign, it became apparent that restricted access to the polls was only one of the social problems facing Mississippi blacks. The state had spent $82 per head on white students, but only $22 on blacks. It also became evident that the educational curriculum was

Figure 3.7 Students and teachers at a Freedom School at the Friendship Baptist Church in Cleveland Ohio, April 1964. These were run under the auspices of Staughton Lynd, director of the Freedom Schools in the Freedom Summer Project

controlled, with state textbooks praising the 'southern way of life' and ignoring black achievements.

CORE, the SNCC and the NAACP were able to establish fifty Freedom Schools to carry on community organising in Mississippi towns. People volunteered as teachers, and the curriculum now included black history and the Civil Rights Movement philosophy. They sought to correct the educational imbalance in Mississippi, allowing political debate and artistic expression, and offering key subjects such as mathematics, science and remedial reading.

The schools promoted courses in acting, public speaking and journalism, and more than 3,000 students attended – three times greater than the anticipated number. Directed by **Staughton Lynd**, the experiment proved very popular and it provided a model for future educational programmes.

The formation of the Mississippi Freedom Democratic Party

Other workers died that summer, and the attacks continued, but the campaign carried on with determination. Ultimately only 1,600 were able to register to vote, although 17,000 blacks had attempted to do so. But even though a mixture of fear and state conniving had precluded many from exercising their right, the subject of black disenfranchisement was now high on the political agenda. The events of the Freedom Summer would hasten the passing of the 1965 Voting Rights Act.

The SNCC also maximised the opportunities for publicity during the Freedom Summer, as inequality and racial segregation in the Deep South got frequent national and international media exposure during 1964.

The formation of the Mississippi Freedom Democratic Party (MFDP) was a real achievement, catapulting the racial issue into the midst of the 1964 US presidential election campaign – an immense arena for international publicity. Around 80,000 black Mississippians joined the party and elected 68 delegates to go to the national Democratic Party Convention in Atlantic City, New Jersey. Here, President Lyndon Johnson was seeking the Democrat nomination for the 1964 election, along with Senator **Hubert Humphrey** as his vice-presidential candidate. The emergence of the MFDP and its challenge to the official (segregated) Mississippi delegation demonstrated the dangers of the situation to Johnson and Humphrey.

The MFDP was a mechanism whereby black Mississippians might get proper political representation, in contrast to the '**lily-whites**' of the mainstream Democratic Party. They sought official recognition at the Convention, presenting the assembly with two delegations claiming the same seats.

MFDP's Fannie Lou Hamer made an impassioned speech and claimed equal representation, arguing that it had widespread support in the state. Eighty thousand blacks voted for MFDP in unofficial elections, yet a majority of these were not allowed to register.

Television viewers across the US sent messages to their delegates urging support for the MFDP, and there was even a protest on the Atlantic City boardwalk urging delegates to accept the MFDP as opposed to the segregationist whites. The official Democrats were very alarmed by these developments and President Johnson himself didn't want to jeopardise his re-election by losing southern Democrats to the Republicans.

Staughton Lynd (1929–)

He is an American Quaker, sociologist and historian who became a civil rights militant. His socialist leanings had seen him blacklisted during the McCarthy era. Lynd became the director of the Freedom Schools of Mississippi and he was a peace activist during US involvement in Vietnam, urging Americans to withhold their taxes in protest. Lynd was especially critical of the treatment of blacks by the military.

Hubert Horatio Humphrey Jr (1911–78)

He was a Democrat senator from Minnesota; assistant majority leader or whip of the US Senate from 1961 to 1965, and vice-president under Lyndon Johnson from 1965 to 1969. He lost narrowly to Richard Nixon in the 1968 presidential election. Humphrey was the chief negotiator in the Senate at the time of the passage of the Civil Rights Act. As floor leader, he had to ensure the legislation had enough support. Ultimately, he obtained four more votes than the minimum requirement.

---

lily-whites: a nickname for the majority of southern Democrats who opposed civil rights.

Figure 3.8 Fannie Hamer of the Mississippi Freedom Democratic Party, approaches the Democratic Party convention hall entrance in Atlantic City in August 1964. She and other members of her group were eventually admitted

A compromise was offered to the MFDP. Their representatives could speak, but not vote; and they could have two token seats in the Mississippi delegation. They were also given a promise that the Democratic Party would ban any group guilty of discrimination from future conventions.

Johnson's offer was viewed as being paltry by Martin Luther King and it caused dissatisfaction all round. All but four of the white Mississippi Democratic Party members walked out in protest, while the MFDP turned down the compromise, protesting that Johnson 'can't just issue two seats at large for a moral issue'. The MFDP did occupy the seats vacated by the white Mississippi Democratic Party members as they left the Convention in protest, but did not officially take the place of the white Democratic Party.

One consequence of these events was that many civil rights campaigners became increasingly unhappy with white liberal reformers like Johnson and Humphrey, although the events at Atlantic City did lead to racially segregated delegations being prohibited at future conventions. The MFDP's stand-off with the national Democratic Party thus brought the Freedom Summer of 1964 to an unseemly close.

What does **Source G** tell us about:

- the feelings of the MFDP?
- the 'politician' in Lyndon Johnson?
- the potential consequences for the Civil Rights Movement, arising out of what happened?

SOURCE G

Johnson, however would have none of it. Afraid not only that the white Mississippi delegates would bolt the convention but that other Southern delegations would join them, the president ordered Hubert Humphrey – if Humphrey wanted the vice-presidency – to convince the MFDP delegates to accept two at-large seats, with a promise that their grievances would be addressed before the 1968 convention… Humphrey did Johnson's bidding. Led by Fannie Lou Hamer, the MFDP delegates refused to budge… in the end Johnson preserved outward peace, but the MFDP delegates left Atlantic City disenchanted with the Democratic Party and convinced that the system really did not mean to accommodate them. Liberalism had failed in their eyes, and younger activists turned to more radical solutions for systemic change.

J.A. Andrew (1998) *Lyndon Johnson and the Great Society*, Chicago: Ivan R. Dee, p. 33.

Consequences of the Freedom Summer

The Freedom Summer had undermined the solidarity that had existed in the Civil Rights Movement during previous years. There was a growing disparity between those who pursued King's tenets of integration and non-violence, and those who felt that peaceful protest was not necessarily the best means of getting full racial equality, with many now feeling that a more radical approach was required. These people considered that white liberals, when pressured, lacked the mettle or conviction necessary in the pursuit of racial justice. The Democratic Convention had revealed this and had caused disappointment.

The registration of around only 1,600 African Americans on the electoral roll was also viewed as a dismal failure by some; yet others saw this as a small but vital step towards the democratisation of voting in Mississippi. Moreover, the MFDP actions at Atlantic City had ensured that there would never be a completely white delegation again at a Democratic Convention, and had proved by its very existence that a new way forward was possible.

So the Freedom Summer had managed to secure enfranchisement for some blacks in Mississippi and had highlighted their struggle before the media of the world, while giving a voice to the newly formed MFDP. But, more significantly, many in the Civil Rights Movement now began to look for different remedies in solving the persistent problem of African American subordination.

End of section activities

1 Explain the significance of each of these in contributing to a sense of growing protest and action by the Civil Rights Movement:

a) the abduction and killing of Goodman, Chaney and Schwerner:

b) the growth of Freedom Schools;

c) the MFDP and the 1964 Democratic National Convention.

2 Draw a mind-map to illustrate the factors contributing to the increased sense of activism by civil rights campaigners after the summer of 1964. You might wish to include events of 1961–3 from the previous section.

3 Research activity; find out more about **three** of the following: Robert F. Kennedy, Fanny Lou Hamer, James Meredith, Governor Terry Sanford, Staughton Lynd, Sheriff Cecil Price and Vice-President Hubert Humphrey. Share your findings with the class.

4 Draw up a list of reasons why the summer of 1964 can be seen as a time of great significance for the Civil Rights Movement, then place them in order of importance. Share your list with your neighbour and explain to them the reasons for your ordering.

3.4 What reforms were passed as a result of protests in the period 1956–65?

As a result of the protests and demonstrations over the previous decade, the US government passed the Civil Rights Act in 1964, followed by the signing of the Voting Rights Act in 1965. They had enormous legal implications for African Americans and changed the United States. Between them, the two pieces of legislation wiped out Jim Crow laws, banned segregation in public places and racial discrimination in schools, jobs and public accommodations, and then ensured that blacks were not prevented from registering to vote. African Americans now seemed to have full access to all social amenities and were no longer party to exclusion from the democratic political system. Both Acts were implemented with greater efficiency and scrutiny than previous civil rights legislation, and it seemed that the main goals of the Civil Rights Movement had been achieved. In this sense, the legislation was beneficial and highly significant. Many in the USA now envisaged much greater social harmony, hoping that the measures introduced were sufficient to remove the ugly carbuncle of racism. But many in the Civil Rights Movement remained unconvinced that the struggle was over and thought that greater benefits were still to be had. The consequences of this legislation were therefore not always what President Johnson had wished for.

The Civil Rights Act 1964

The Civil Rights Act of 1964 enabled the federal government to end *de jure* (in law) segregation in the south, both in public places and in places of employment. The passing of this legislation is viewed as a crowning moment for the Civil Rights Movement. Having been proposed initially by President John F. Kennedy, the Act was made law by his successor, President Lyndon Johnson, who signed it on 2 July 1964. Thereafter, the US Congress added to the legislation and also passed the Voting Rights Act of 1965.

Figure 3.9   President Lyndon Johnson signs the Civil Rights Act of 1964, watched by Martin Luther King

The Civil Rights Act specifically stated the following:

- There was a ban on exclusion from restaurants, stores and other public facilities such as theatres, hotels and sporting venues; blacks and other minorities could not be denied service based on the colour of their skin, nor could they be segregated.
- Racial, religious, ethnic and sexual discrimination by employers and labour unions was banned.
- The attorney general could now file lawsuits directly to 'fast-track' or speed up desegregation, mixed education and voting rights.
- The Office of Education had to assist with school desegregation.
- An Equal Employment Opportunity Commission was created with the authority to commence legal proceedings on behalf of workers with a grievance.
- There was to be no discrimination on any federally aided programmes.
- The Commission on Civil Rights had greater powers.
- The inequality in voting requirements was outlawed.

Martin Luther King called it a 'second emancipation', while historian Irving Bernstein described it as 'a rare and glittering moment in the history of American democracy'. It was a moment of unprecedented significance.

The Civil Rights Act was later expanded to accommodate the disabled within the legal system; it also made provision for the protection of the elderly and for women in athletics. The Voting Rights Act of 1965 (see section 3.4, The Voting Rights Act 1965) and the Fair Housing Act of 1968, which outlawed discrimination any aspects of the property market, were logical consequences of the Civil Rights Act of 1964.

The passage of the Civil Rights Bill

filibuster: originally a lawless adventurer, it has evolved into a political term. It is used to describe an attempt in the US Senate to prevent a bill from passing by talking continuously against it for hours on end, until no time remains for voting on it. The Civil Rights Act of 1964 holds the record of 736 hours of debate over eighty-three days.

It had not been easy to get this legislation through Congress. There had been southern attempts to block the bill by a **filibuster**, but it eventually passed through both houses of Congress. In the House of Representatives, 152 Democrats voted in favour and 96 voted against. The opponents were representatives mainly from the south. Lyndon Johnson had persuaded 138 of the 202 Republicans to support the bill, thus when it went to the Senate, it passed by seventy-three votes to twenty-seven.

It had passed for a variety of reasons, including: the joint lobbying of Congress by the NAACP, trade unionists and the churches; the hard work of key congressional leaders like Hubert Humphrey; Johnson himself devoting a huge amount of time and energy to win members over and break the Senate filibuster; by Johnson and Humphrey appealing to southern self-interest in that the bill would get blacks and Hispanics working and help the economy in the south; emotive appeals by people to honour the recently assassinated Kennedy and to pass this bill as a tribute to his groundwork; and the work of black activists in highlighting the injustices in US society to the whole nation, especially after Birmingham, Alabama.

After much persuasion, Congress noted the shifting public mood. It was a career triumph for Johnson, and it propelled Humphrey towards the vice-presidency; but even more significantly, it had justified the approach of Martin Luther King and his non-violent followers. They had achieved success by working with the existing political system – whatever their misgivings – as opposed to rebelling against it.

The consequences of the Act

The Supreme Court moved quickly to uphold the Act, so segregation and discrimination were now prohibited by law. African Americans would no longer have to go to court to contest acts of discrimination; rather it was the responsibility of the federal government to ensure that such acts did not occur. Legal action would be more speedy and effective, while the government had the power to penalise or withhold funding from any school, business or institution that failed to comply with the law. In the Deep South, almost 90 per cent of schools had integrated by the start of the new academic year in September 1965.

It opened up the prospects of more equal employment and educational opportunities, and changes in black mobility certainly occurred during the 1960s. According to US government statistics, whereas around 15 per cent of black males were employed in middle-class occupations in 1950, more than 35 per cent held such jobs in 1970. Whereas 62 per cent of all black employed males were in what would be described as basically lower-class jobs in 1950, only 36.4 per cent were deemed to hold such posts in 1970. Although unemployment remained higher among blacks than among whites, a more prosperous black middle-class was emerging. Undoubtedly, government enforcement of the Civil Rights Act, plus new opportunities, must have had a beneficial knock-on effect. Although racism would continue, African Americans were arguably at the dawn of a real opportunity with the legal destruction of segregation.

But Johnson knew that, in reality, de facto segregation still remained, notably in the urban areas of Los Angeles, Detroit, Cleveland, Chicago, Philadelphia and New York. African Americans had been free to vote here for many years, but in these northern and western city ghettoes, the black communities remained stuck in a rut. They had poor housing, menial jobs and inadequate schooling. In some respects, life after the Civil Rights Act for these people was little different. But the impact of this legislation on the southern states, and the wider moral impact, was significant.

It also provoked a white reaction, with Alabama Governor **George Wallace** – who barely hid his racism – becoming popular in the early Democratic primary elections of 1964 in states outside the south. In fact, race relations were not improved significantly by the Act, and there were signs of growing discontent among working-class whites in the north. So both blacks and whites in the north and south were disgruntled for varying reasons.

Even in 1965, parts of the south resisted the law, if state authorities could avoid applying the law properly. Segregation and discrimination were now wholly illegal, but a loophole existed with respect to voting rights, and the Civil Rights Movement became aware that some states were not registering black voters. Alabama was particularly lax, given its entrenched racism, and Martin Luther King decided to pressure the federal government into action.

The Selma to Montgomery March

The Southern Christian Leadership Conference (SCLC), led by Martin Luther King, decided to test the provisions of the 1964 Civil Rights Act in the Alabama town of Selma. The voting rights of black voters became the particular focus. Evidence showed that Dallas County, Alabama, was especially bad. Here 57 per cent of the population was black yet only 300 of the 15,000 black residents were registered to vote – 2 per cent – compared to 9,500 whites – 64 per cent. Alabama Governor George Wallace opposed desegregation, as did Jim Clark, the county sheriff in Selma, Dallas County. Martin Luther King knew that this was an irresistible yet dangerous challenge. It might provoke a reaction as in Birmingham and so create massive publicity for the disfranchised blacks; equally it could lead to a tragic loss of life.

King was arrested in Selma on 1 February 1965 with more than 700 others for taking part in what Governor Wallace deemed an illegal parade. He was released later that week. Then on 7 February 1965, 165 students who were demonstrating about voting rights were arrested then sent on a forced 4km run by Clark. They were poked by live electric cattle prods much of the way. On 18 February, white segregationists attacked a group of peaceful demonstrators in the nearby town of Marion. Jimmie Lee Jackson, a young African American demonstrator, was fatally shot by police while trying to protect his mother and aged grandfather from police beatings.

It was after this that the SCLC and King planned a civil rights march from Selma to the state capital, Montgomery, 85 km away. On Sunday, 7 March, a group of 600 set off, but they had only got as far as a bridge on the outskirts of Selma when police violently forced the marchers back, using whips, sticks and tear gas. The events were captured on TV for everyone to see, and it succeeded in making religious leaders of all faiths come to Selma to support the civil rights marchers.

King attempted again to march to Montgomery, this time on 9 March. Governor Wallace tried to ban it legally, but a district court judge overruled him. So police again blocked the route and asked King to turn back. The walkers duly stopped on the same bridge as before, and began to pray. King then abandoned the march. The same night, segregationists beat to death a young white northern protestor, the minister James

**George Wallace
(1919–98)**

He was initially a Democrat and served as Governor of Alabama four times. Wallace strongly supported racial segregation and blocked the enrolment of African American students at the University of Alabama in 1963. He emerged as one of the leading opponents of the Civil Rights Movement. In 1968, he stood as an independent in the presidential election and won more than 13 per cent of the vote. In May 1972, he was shot and wounded during a presidential campaign rally in Maryland, which partially paralysed him and led to his withdrawal from politics.

Figure 3.10 On 25 March 1965, Martin Luther King and wife Coretta led non-violent campaigners to the completion of an 85 km march from Selma to Montgomery

Reeb. The outcome of the second and abortive Selma to Montgomery march was that President Johnson backed the marchers on national television and pledged that he would introduce legislation in Congress to give new voting rights.

QUESTION

Look at **Source H**. What does it reveal about President Johnson's opinion of the behaviour of officials in Alabama? Consider Johnson's language and his choice of words. Write down the key principles he advocates. What does it also tell us about his mood?

SOURCE H

At times history and fate meet at a single time in a single place to shape a turning point in man's unending search for freedom. So it was at Lexington and Concord. So it was a century ago at Appomattox. So it was last week in Selma, Alabama. There is no Negro problem. There is no southern problem. There is no northern problem. There is only an American problem. Many of the issues of civil rights are very complex and most difficult. But about this there can and should be no argument. Every American citizen must have the right to vote… Yet the harsh fact is that in many places in this country men and women are kept from voting simply because they are Negroes… No law that we now have on the books… can ensure the right to vote when local officials are determined to deny it… There is no Constitutional issue here. The command of the Constitution is plain. There is no moral issue. It is wrong – deadly wrong – to deny any of your fellow Americans the right to vote in this country. There is no issue of States' rights or National rights. There is only the struggle for human rights.

President Lyndon Johnson introducing the 'Voting Rights Act' to a joint session of Congress, 15 March 1965.

On 21 March a third and ultimately successful march began when 2,000 walkers set out from Selma under the protection of US Army troops and the Alabama National Guard, which Johnson had placed under his direct federal control. As the world's media watched, the protesters walked twelve hours a day, for three days, sleeping in fields en route. They finally reached Montgomery on 25 March and in doing so powerfully raised awareness of the position of black voters in the South,

The Voting Rights Act 1965

The 1965 Voting Rights Act was carved out of the 1964 Civil Rights Act, the passage of which had unsettled whites in the south and encouraged white supremacists to try and hold back the inevitable. In particular, methods were employed to keep

Figure 3.11   Vice-President Humphrey and civil rights leader Martin Luther King before the signing of the Voting Rights Act, August 1965

African-Americas from voting. Using literacy tests, constitutional-interpretation tests and other measures – all administered by white voter-registration officials in a patronising and discriminatory manner – it became virtually impossible for black southerners to register to vote, even after 1964. The SCLC campaign in 1963 in Birmingham (see Chapter 4, section 4.2, Good King or bad King?) had attracted world attention; now in 1965, the Selma to Montgomery march had done likewise.

The actions of Jim Clark, the meanness of George Wallace and the general brutality of many police and ordinary southern people now meant that public opinion virtually guaranteed the passing of Johnson's legislation, introduced to Congress in March 1965. Parallel to this came the networking in Congress from Vice-President Hubert Humphrey. Both the Senate and the House of Representatives knew that the government would simply persist if they hindered or failed to back it. Americans would then view the failure as that of Congress alone.

The Voting Rights Act was passed and duly became law in August 1965. It specifically stated the following:

- Insisting on literacy tests and the ability to read or interpret material became illegal.
- Demonstration of academic achievement as a requirement to vote was now illegal.
- The ability to pay poll taxes or furnish proof of moral character as ways of assessing whether anyone was fit or unfit to vote were outlawed.
- American citizenship and an individual's name on an official electoral list were the only voting requirements.

The law courts would not tolerate any attempts to undermine the law.

Selma, Alabama had duly registered over 60 per cent of its black population within a month of the act becoming law and, by 1967, nine of the thirteen southern states had more than 50 per cent of African Americans registered to vote. The hard-line state of Mississippi had registered almost 60 per cent by 1968 and, overall, between 1964 and 1970, the average percentage of black registration in the Deep South rose from 35 per cent to 65 per cent. It was nothing short of a revolution in voting rights and Stacy and Scott-Baumann (2013, p. 120) state that the Voting Rights Act changed the entire tone of southern politics: 'There were no more open declarations of race hatred and white supremacy. Men such as Sheriff Clark were voted out, and most white politicians became more conciliatory.'

SOURCE I

Election to public office of black candidates

YEAR	IN THE SOUTH	IN THE USA
1965	less than 100	300
1970	500	1400

H. Sitkoff (2005) *The Struggle for Black Equality*, New York: Hill and Wang, p. 229.

SOURCE J

The number of blacks holding office in the South swelled from fewer than two dozen in 1964 to nearly twelve hundred in 1972, including half the seats on Selma's city council and the first two African Americans elected to Congress from the former Confederacy since the nineteenth century. Electoral success brought jobs for African Americans, contracts for black businesses, and improvements in facilities and services in black neighbourhoods.

P. Boyer, C. Clark, J. Kett, N. Salisbury, H. Sitkoff and N. Woloch N. (2008) *The Enduring Vision*, New York: Houghton Mifflin, p. 868.

QUESTION
Look at **Sources I and J**. What are the differences between them in how they present the statistics relating to African American progress? What do the sources reveal about the progress made? How far are they a comment on the success of the 1965 Voting Rights Act?

In the long term, more African Americans were elected into public office, which demonstrated the ability of blacks to have responsibility, so eventually there was an increase in African Americans being voted into to public office by whites, as if to reinforce the perceived shift in public opinion.

The Voting Rights Act was clearly the boost that the civil rights cause needed and the US president deserved great credit for using his power wisely. Johnson and Humphrey were also fortunate in gaining a landslide election victory in November 1964, so they worked with a Congress containing a majority of Democrats over Republicans serving in it. But five days after the signing of the Voting Rights Act, a drink-driving arrest and an ensuing scuffle between a black woman and white police in the Watts District of Los Angeles, California ignited the most destructive race riot for years. It is therefore necessary to consider why this occurred after the introduction of two key pieces of legislation.

The Watts Riots

Watts District was a deeply impoverished neighbourhood in South Central Los Angeles, with the city's highest proportion of African Americans. On 11 August 1965, Marquette Frye, a young African American motorist, was driving his brother home when he was pulled over and arrested by a white California highway patrolman, Lee Minikus, for suspicion of driving while intoxicated. As Marquette was being held, his brother went home for their mother. Mrs Frye retuned to the scene of the arrest and grappled with the police officer, tearing his shirt. Another officer struck Marquette's head, and ultimately all three of the Frye family were arrested. By this time, hundreds of onlookers had been drawn to the scene. Anger and rumours spread quickly and residents stoned cars and beat white people who entered the area. This triggered looting, arson and further assaults.

Eventually a curfew was set, with 15,000 police and National Guard patrolling an 80km area. For five days, the neighbourhood seethed, by which time thirty-four people were dead, more than 1,000 injured and 4,000 arrested. Damage in excess of $40 million had destroyed the local community. The social and economic situation in Watts, together with an existing, tense relationship between police and community and the heat of the Los Angeles summer, had ignited the situation.

Martin Luther King was swift to disapprove of the rioting, but he hastened to state that the violence-related problems were more to do with the environment than racism. He reasoned that poor housing and jobs, social isolation and growing despair were sowing the seeds of unrest not only in Watts, but in many other urban ghettoes across the USA, and he was concerned that this might unleash a wider series of violent events. King visited Los Angeles to support those living there, and in the hope of strengthening the alliance between the black community and those whites who supported civil rights.

He also offered to act as an intermediary between local people and government officials, who were insistent that rioting was part of a left-wing plot by agitators from outside the area, although a woman in Watts had told him that rioting was the only way to get the authorities to take proper notice of her community and its problems. A few months later, the official investigation into Watts found that the unrest was a result of longstanding community grievances, and King told President Johnson that it was about personal dignity and working and living conditions in the north and west, not simply racism and civil rights as in the Deep South. After the Watts Riots, Johnson introduced a federal anti-poverty programme in Los Angeles on the suggestion of King, and the Firestone Rubber Company then moved into the area to create around one hundred jobs. Finally, the Martin Luther King Hospital was built. But these improvements only made a moderate impact.

In 1966, black unemployment in Los Angeles exceeded 1930s levels during the Depression, while statistically the population density of Watts was almost the worst in the USA. There was inadequate schooling for blacks, plus poor public transport to carry them to city suburbs where new industries were developing. Having migrated from the south, many were poorly educated and therefore only found menial work. Furthermore Los Angeles had not provided sufficiently for the spin-off from mass migration, when more than four million blacks had moved from the Deep South to the north and west urban areas between 1940 and 1965.

For such people the Civil Rights Act and the Voting Act, while fundamental and relevant, were not necessarily the main priority. Thus far the Civil Rights Movement had focused primarily on the political rights of black southerners, but Watts had demonstrated that race was not just a problem confined to the south. The riots also had the potential to cause backlash from white Americans. Their timing also dismayed Johnson, Humphrey and King, coming just days after the Voting Rights Act.

ACTIVITY

Look at **Source K** and in particular, some of the language used. What is meant by 'Lotusland' and 'the American dream' in the context of the extract? Explain the difference between *de jure* and de facto in respect to how it applies to African Americans. What is the author trying to say?

SOURCE K

The Watts riot in August 1965 made clear that no region, not even 'Lotusland' would escape the violence and destruction exploding from pockets of deprivation secluded amid suburban affluence. African Americans in northern and western cities fully expected racial equality, economic opportunity and all the rights of American citizenship denied them by legal segregation in the south. Although they escaped the dehumanising conditions of *de jure* segregation – enforced by law, they endured de facto segregation – enforced by custom or practice – in employment, housing and education… proximity to the American dream with little chance of obtaining it led to relative deprivation and resentment.

D. Farber and B. Bailey (2001) *The Columbia Guide to America in the 1960s*, New York: Columbia University Press, p. 267.

Figure 3.12　An aerial view of the aftermath of the Watts Riots in Los Angeles, August 1965

The significance and the legacy of Johnson's reforms

In evaluating both the significance of the civil rights legislation and its consequences, historians must never forget the standalone importance of these landmark acts introduced after that momentous decade of protest and action.

The Civil Rights Act and the Voting Rights Act are seminal events in US history, touchstones for addressing wrongs. The scope of the legislation at that moment in time, and its effects on African Americans and other ethnicities and minorities, cannot be understated. Their very existence on the statute book is significance enough. Their enactment was also the culmination of years of work by civil rights groups and open-minded, liberal politicians. But they were not the legal, social and cultural cure many African Americans – and quite a number of Democrat politicians – thought they might prove to be.

The Civil Rights Act of 1964 fundamentally changed things by eradicating discrimination and segregation laws and, most significantly of all, giving the government the legal tools to ensure enforcement. It also targeted the long-standing tradition of second-class citizenship for women by outlawing job discrimination based on gender as well as race. But it did not go far enough with respect to the **franchise** – hence the Voting Rights Act – nor did it address deeper social problems away from the south.

The Voting Rights Act of 1965 was a comprehensive and logical follow-up to the shortcomings of the Civil Rights Act, specifically those highlighted in the events at Selma and Montgomery. It aimed to remove any legal barriers that prevented African Americans from voting, as had been their right since 1870, under the 15th Amendment to the US Constitution. The franchise was widened considerably and so this piece of civil rights legislation is viewed as one of the most successful and far-reaching in legal history. It also helped increase black congressional representation from the 1970s onwards – a real victory in the civil rights struggle.

But it also coincided with the expanding era of television, linking the nation as never before. Just as the nightly news reports from the Vietnam War would penetrate into sitting-rooms, and eventually impact fatally on President Johnson, so governmental shortcomings and social failures were now equally exposed. The sight of poverty in the midst of plenty and the ironies of urban unrest, social squalor and racial discrimination were difficult to reconcile when the USA was claiming to be the leader of the free world. It was inevitable that the excluded would want 'more' from their government and demand better from their society.

Such frustration and expectation meant that Watts was the first of three long hot summers of rioting. Newark and other predominantly northern cities experienced similar, and in Detroit 43 people were killed in 1966. In 1967, serious racial upheaval had occurred in over 150 cities, while the assassination of Martin Luther King in 1968 (see Chapter 4, section 4.2) finally unleashed a wave of violence in 125 urban centres.

While a black middle-class was developing in the aftermath of the Civil Rights Act and the Voting Rights Act, a social imbalance was going unnoticed by the federal government. White northerners were deserting their cities for the suburbs, and a black inner-city ghetto was developing. Poor education and housing plus limited opportunities still persisted, and the income of most white households was almost double that of any black family.

In 1967, Johnson created a commission to examine civil disorder and report back on the urban violence of the previous three summers. As John Morton Blum (1991) related, the commission praised the legislation of 1964–5 and commended the positives visible three years on, but added: 'What white Americans have never fully understood... is that white

---

franchise: is a right to vote, officially granted by a government to an individual or a group of people. In a political sense, to be able to elect people to represent you in an Assembly, Parliament or Congress.

society is deeply implicated in the ghetto. White institutions created it, white institutions maintain it and white society condones it.'

It struck a chord with the many northern African Americans who felt that civil rights legislation had still not brought the desired consequences – even after a decade of protest. It did not address what affected them and trapped them socially in lives of underachievement. Many turned in another direction, where whites were seen clearly as the enemy. This ongoing rupture in American politics, society and culture would distinguish the late 1960s.

End of section activities

1   How did the terms of the Civil Rights Act and the Voting Rights Act benefit African Americans? Reread this section then draw up a table with two columns. On one side, make a list of the benefits for both Acts, and then in the other column note down where there were failings. Exchange your ideas with a fellow student. Then prepare a short speech ready to give to your class on your findings.

2   Carry out some research on the Watts riots and other urban disturbances. What do your findings tell us about the impact of the Civil Rights Act and the Voting Rights Act on the northern and western states of the USA?

3   Using the library or the internet, find out what you can about the passing of the Civil Rights Bill of 1964. Why do you think Johnson and Humphrey had such difficulty in getting the bill through Congress? What do you notice about the tactics used by opponents of the bill?

KEY CONCEPT QUESTION

Significance: To what extent did the Civil Rights Act of 1964 meet the demands of all those who had protested for civil rights over the previous decade? Did it have any shortcomings? Were there any perspectives from which it might be said to be insufficient? Draw a mind-map and fill it in with information from this chapter and any other resources you may have. Now write bullet-point answers to the three questions below. Present these in class and debate your findings.

End of chapter activities

Summary

You should now understand the origins, development and growth of protests and actions by civil rights movements in the USA from 1956 to 1965. You have studied the Montgomery Bus Boycott, the sit-ins and Freedom Rides, the Freedom Summer in Mississippi and the often turbulent events surrounding the passing of the Civil Rights Act of 1964 and the Voting Rights Act of 1965. You should be able to analyse and appreciate how each event built on the previous one. You also should be aware of how signs of tension were present in the Civil Rights Movement, in spite of the passage of major legislation, and that only limited progress had been made in improving the lives of African Americans in the north and west of the USA.

Summary activity

Copy the diagram below, then using the information in this chapter, and from any other available sources, make brief notes under the headings shown. Remember to include information on historical debate/interpretations – including names of historians – where appropriate.

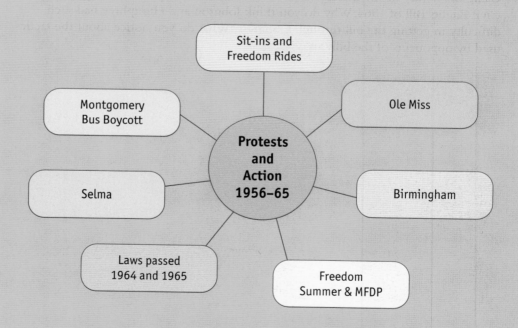

Paper 1 exam practice

The terms 'origin', 'purpose', 'content', 'value' and 'limitations' are explained in Chapter 8.

Question

With reference to its origin, purpose and content, analyse the value and limitations of **Source A** for a historian studying the achievements of Civil Rights Movement in the United States. **[4 marks]**

Skill

Value/limitations (utility/reliability) of a source.

SOURCE A

Rosa Parks seated at the front of newly desegregated bus on December 1, 1956; the day the public transportation system was legally integrated in Montgomery, Alabama

From M. Stacey and M. Scott-Baumann (2013) *Civil Rights and Social Movements in the Americas*, Cambridge: Cambridge University Press.

Student answer

Source A was produced from the time that buses were desegregated in Montgomery, Alabama (December 1956), and it shows that at this early stage, there was some success and some optimism for the Civil Rights Movement. Rosa Parks had defied the Jim Crow laws and been arrested. Now she could sit at the front of a bus and this was just the beginning. So it is quite useful, even though it is a photograph and we cannot always see everything that may be going on around.

Examiner's comments

The question requires the student to look at this source in order to make explicit or developed consideration of *both* its origins, purpose and content *and* its value and limitations. The value of the source could be addressed in a much more concise and clear fashion. In fact it is rather vague and quite poor, although the candidate does realise that there is a potential sense of limitation about this type of source. But there is nothing developed and little comment about the achievements of the Civil Rights Movement following the growth of direct action and protest between 1956 and 1965. So with limited comments all round, it is only awarded two in Band 2 marks at the most.

Activity

Look again at **Source A**, the simplified mark scheme in Chapter 8 and the student answer above. Now try to write another paragraph to push the answer up to Band 1, and obtain four marks. As well as assessing origin and purpose, try to develop more explicit comment on the content, value and limitations for this source. Think about your historical knowledge to provide examples. You should also try to make a linking comment between your paragraphs.

Paper 2 practice questions

1 Examine the changing style of protest and action by the Civil Rights Movement contribute to the federal government's decision to implement legislation in 1964–5.

2 'The use of non-violent protest had only limited success in improving the position of African Americans in US society between 1956 and 1965.' To what extent do you agree with this statement?

3 Compare and contrast the impact of the Montgomery Bus Boycott and the Freedom Rides as protests against segregation.

4 Evaluate the reasons for, and the results of, Lyndon Johnson's decision to introduce the Civil Rights Act of 1964 and the Voting Rights Act of 1965.

The role and significance of key actors/groups

KEY QUESTIONS

- How important were the new civil rights organisations and the churches to the success of the civil rights cause?
- What was the significance of the role played by Martin Luther King?
- What influence did the mass media have on developments in the struggle for civil rights?

This chapter examines the role and significance of key groups and people in the struggle for civil rights from 1956 to 1965. The postwar modern Civil Rights Movement was characterised by large masses of African Americans directly confronting and effectively disrupting the functioning of many of those institutions and organisations held responsible for their oppression.

The innovative quality of these protests was that they were widespread and sustained over a decade or more. They involved the participation of several movements such as the National Association for the Advancement of Colored People (NAACP), the Congress of Racial Equality (CORE), the Southern Christian Leadership Conference (SCLC) and the Student Nonviolent Coordinating Committee (SNCC). Attention will be focused on these often very different but sometimes complementary groups, and reference will be made to the role of the Church, as a crucial connection between the indigenous black Church and the Civil Rights Movement existed.

The role and significance of Martin Luther King is examined too, and reference will be made to key historiography in order to evaluate his leadership.

Finally, the role of the media will also be discussed. Journalists and the media empowered the Civil Rights Movement by virtue of more advanced news reporting and analysis, which also educated and influenced the public. Hence, change was demanded at a time when television was now accessible to most of America.

Overview

- The Montgomery Bus Boycott of 1955–6 and the actions of the NAACP influenced the future development of demands for civil rights and the methods used to challenge the authorities.

TIMELINE

1955 **Dec:** Montgomery Bus Boycott organised by NAACP activists

1956 **Nov:** Bus segregation in Montgomery, Alabama, is declared illegal.

1957 **Jan:** Martin Luther King, Jr. helps establish the SCLC.

Sep: NAACP spearheads campaign to integrate public schools in Little Rock, Arkansas.

1960 **Feb:** Students begin the sit-in movement at Greensboro, North Carolina

Apr: SNCC formed out at Shaw University.

1961 **Jan:** John F. Kennedy inaugurated

May: Freedom Rides organised by CORE begin in the Deep South

Nov: SNCC and King organise protests in Albany, Georgia.

1962–4 SNCC voter registration campaign in Mississippi.

1963 **Mar–May:** SCLC spearhead 'Project C' (Confrontation) in Birmingham, Alabama

Jun: Council for United Civil Rights Leadership established

Aug: March on Washington – Martin Luther King's 'I Have a Dream' speech.

Sep: Killing of four African-American girls in Birmingham, Alabama.

Nov: Assassination of Kennedy.

1964 **Jun-Aug:** Freedom Summer campaign in Mississippi.

Jul: Civil Rights Act passed.

Aug: Mississippi Freedom Democratic Party (MFDP) at Democratic Convention.

1965 **Jan:** Martin Luther King joins a voter registration campaign in Selma, Alabama.

Feb: Selma–Montgomery March.

Mar: 'Bloody Sunday' and the follow-up marches.

Aug: Voting Rights Act passed.

- The founding of the SCLC was seen as broadening the role of Martin Luther King and as a key moment in widening participation in the Civil Rights Movement, with its tie to both the churches and the NAACP.

- The SCLC campaign in 1963 in Birmingham, Alabama was seen to have attracted world attention and given the civil rights campaign a whole new dimension.

- The formation of the SNCC added a further strand to the movement, notably when it launched a sustained campaign for the right to vote in Mississippi from 1961 to 1963 and assisted CORE in the Freedom Summer of 1964 in the same state.

- The 1964 Civil Rights Act and the 1965 Voting Rights Act were finally passed in the full glare of the world's media. The influence of the press and especially that of television throughout this decade of campaigns and protests was highly significant.

- The civil rights story became the first major domestic news story to be reported on television in the US, with events unfurling almost daily in the sitting-rooms of America. Also, the strategy of the movement was based on getting media coverage and wide publicity.

- The main strength of the Civil Rights Movement during the period of 1956–65 was its orientation toward struggle and its phases of mass action. Because African Americans took their demands to the streets, they achieved many concrete gains. The input and actions of several different key groups within the Civil Rights Movement, such as the NAACP, CORE, the SCLC and the SNCC, all helped to infuse the campaign in many different ways.

- At all levels of government, equality of treatment regardless of race now became a key tenet as laws and policies reflecting this began to be implemented.

4.1 How important were the new civil rights organisations and the churches to the success of the civil rights cause?

The nature of the Civil Rights Movement

Strategy and tactics

strategy: is the means by which a principal long-term objective being fought for by a group or organisation, such as the Civil Rights Movement, should be undertaken.

tactics: are the everyday activities undertaken by the movement – either in response to the day-to-day ups and downs of the struggle or more proactively to promote the cause and attract publicity.

The US in the period between 1945 and 1965 witnessed a social and economic contradiction that undoubtedly helped fuel the Civil Rights Movement. Most African Americans were divided between the rural agricultural lifestyle and being part of the urban industrial experience. As discussed previously, the urban industrial north had some civil rights freedom in principle, while in the rural south the white minority used legal and illegal means to dominate the black population. What differentiated the two conditions politically was the degree of oppression faced.

So the postwar Civil Rights Movement confronted contradictions in the system and fought for consistent democracy: no second-class citizenship and no denial to African Americans and other minority groups of the political and civil rights guaranteed to whites. In assessing any organisation, it is necessary to define and evaluate its **strategy** and **tactics**.

For the Civil Rights Movement, the tactics of the struggle would change periodically (for example, legal challenges, petitions, sit-ins, mass demonstrations), but the overall strategy of the movement – how it aimed and expected to achieve freedom of rights – would remain unchanged.

Reform or revolution?

The strategy of the Civil Rights Movement was **reformist** and not **revolutionary** in seeking solutions under the existing system. The movement saw the US federal government in Washington, DC, as largely positive, although they would argue that the government had acted against the interests of black people because its leaders had been neither sensitive enough to the moral implications of the system's discrimination, nor daring enough to try to change the system for fear of electoral backlash for their respective party.

The existing system was not condemned in its entirety; the criticism was more that racist policies resulted from both a lack of good politicians and over-dependency on the white-dominated economic system in the USA. So the mainstream Civil Rights Movement ruled out revolution and total restructuring of society in order to solve these problems.

Yet by 1963 the nature of the movement was changing. African Americans – previously united in their support of activities such as the Montgomery Bus Boycott and the Greensboro sit-in – began to disagree over what political action should be taken to improve their situation. The rise of charismatic figures such as **Malcolm X** and the influence of an organisation called the Nation of Islam led to more open expressions of dissatisfaction and doubts about both the doctrine of non-violence, as well as the wider aims of the movement.

So the tactics of the Civil Rights Movement must be viewed within the context of its strategy, and its tactics *are* reformist as they operated within the confines of accepting the existing political and economic system. Yet sometimes the Civil Rights Movement worked within the system (such as placing lawyers in courts to spearhead challenges), but also outside it (organising boycotts, sit-ins and protest marches without permits) in order to mobilise people. It engaged both in spontaneous short-run actions and prolonged bureaucratic slog.

A pattern to the tactics

Campaigners used all tactics at all times, but to many historians a three-stage pattern is discernible.

- **Legal action** – ensuring recognition and support for the rights of black people by the legal system was the main tactic during the first phase of the modern civil rights struggle through to the 1950s. *Brown v. Topeka Board of Education* in 1954 is a prime example. Then the strategy of courtroom litigation began to shift towards 'direct action'.
- **Mass action** – by 1945, African Americans were now rooted into urban life in the north and into its industrial workforce. This paved the way for the next stage of development in the movement: mass or direct action. These were bus boycotts, sit-ins, Freedom Rides, pickets and demonstrations – all of which relied on mass mobilisation, non-violent resistance, and civil disobedience. The first new organisation to emerge during this stage of mass struggle was CORE.

reformist: a person who wishes to bring definite change and improvement to the social, economic and political system; although would work for this within the existing system and its structure.

revolutionary: a person who wants to overthrow both the existing government and the political system in which it operates, and usually wants to change the economic and social structure around it.

Malcolm X (Malcolm Little, 1925–65)

Growing up in Michigan, Malcolm Little distrusted white Americans. The Ku Klux Klan had burned his house and murdered his father. He converted to Islam after being jailed. Believing his lineage lost when his ancestors were forced into slavery, he took the last name of a variable: X. Malcolm X joined the Nation of Islam, which declared that Christianity was forced on blacks during slavery, with Islam being closer to African identity. Nation of Islam members became known as Black Muslims. They wanted blacks to set up their own schools, churches and support networks. Malcolm X called for a separate state for African-Americans, and inspired urban audiences with his style of delivery. He left the Nation of Islam in 1963, and was assassinated in February 1965 by rival Black Muslims.

From its inception in the 1940s, CORE was led by group of black and white integrationists who adhered to the principle of non-violent direct action. But in the early 1960s, when CORE led the Freedom Rides in the south against transport segregation (see Chapter 3, section 3.2), it got nationwide attention. Then, following the passing of the Civil Rights Act in 1964, CORE concentrated more on confronting segregation in the urban areas of the north. Now CORE membership became predominantly black and advocated greater militancy and more direct action.

- Electoral politics – this emerged as a dominant tactic with both the campaign for voter registration in Mississippi (see Chapter 3, section 3.3, the formation of the Mississippi Freedom Democratic Party) and the 1965 Voting Rights Act. It was also linked to the mass actions such as the Freedom Summer, the March on Washington and the Selma to Montgomery March. Focusing on electoral politics was an inevitable tactical development, given the reformist tendency to seek change within the existing system. Voting and voter registration became a main feature. In 1960, for example, Kennedy's election was helped greatly by the support of black and other minority group votes. Voter registration of blacks in the south doubled over the next four years, and the black vote was firmly established. Black people sought political office, especially in urban areas where their vote was concentrated, and this subsequently became the main tactic by the 1970s for middle-class activists.

But central to this struggle is the input and actions of different key groups within the Civil Rights Movement: some of them longstanding, such as the NAACP and CORE, others more recent in their formation such as the SCLC and the SNCC. An overview of these different groups is therefore required, together with analysis of the inter-organisational relationship that developed between them.

The key groups

The National Association for the Advancement of Colored People (NAACP)

The NAACP was the pre-eminent black protest organisation prior to the development of the modern Civil Rights Movement. Founded in 1910 in New York by black and white intellectuals appalled by racism, it sought equal rights for African Americans: hence it was both interracial and northern-based, desirous of organising the black masses to demand their rights. NAACP members believed that white man's ignorance of blacks was at the root of racism. Early leaders such as Booker T. Washington and W.E.B. Du Bois were literate scholars who sought to use educational persuasion and legal action to change the perception of many whites. NAACP branches developed in the southern states in the 1920s and 1930s, where they wanted to move faster than in the north due to the severity of the racism. Many legal cases regarding segregation, political disfranchisement and lynchings originated in the south, where the NAACP was closely tied to the churches. They were often the only safe place to meet, by virtue of its independence from the white power structure. Equally, many southern NAACP members were church ministers and the organisation was largely funded through the black churches.

But the NAACP was not only significant for its ties with the churches: over the decades it also brought other influential community people together such as local lawyers, teachers, doctors, union organisers and political activists. Although NAACP membership was seldom more than 2 per cent of the adult African American population, the ordinary black masses respected the organisation as one fighting for their rights. Hence it was important in providing the opportunity for local leaders to acquire skills in organisation, in speaking and in developing networks through which resources could be pooled. It also provided links between north and south. Thus the NAACP was the training ground from which the leadership of the modern Civil Rights Movement would eventually emerge, and by 1950 it had spread widely across the south, in spite of efforts to sabotage the organisation.

Figure 4.1   Representing the NAACP at a picket

The Legal Defence and Educational Fund (LDF) was the non-profit-making legal arm of the NAACP, established in 1940. In the 1950s, under the guidance of Thurgood Marshall (see Chapter 2, section 2.1, The postwar attitudes of Africa-Americans) the LDF lawyers filed several lawsuits questioning the legality of school segregation. They won the significant *Brown v. Topeka Board of Education* case in 1954, which ruled that segregated education was unconstitutional (see Chapter 2, section 2.1).

When NAACP member Rosa Parks refused to give up her seat on a Montgomery bus in December 1955, her action became the catalyst for the Montgomery Bus Boycott (see Chapter 3, section 3.1). The boycott was supported throughout its duration in 1956 by the NAACP, which provided lawyers and helped to meet legal costs incurred. NAACP executive secretary **Roy Wilkins** personally encouraged branches everywhere to raise funds and support the boycotters, thus marking the birth of a powerful grass-roots movement in the civil rights campaign: the first occasion an entire community had rallied against segregation, with the NAACP at its centre. Martin Luther King's involvement pushed him into national prominence too, and he encouraged Montgomery churches to become lifetime members of the NAACP. In 1956, King addressed the NAACP national convention, and it subsequently gave him its highest

Fact: The Montgomery Improvement Association (MIA) was the first predominately black civil rights organisation to operate independently of the NAACP. It originated in December 1955 at the time of the Montgomery Bus Boycott. Led by Martin Luther King, it helped coordinate the boycott and was significant in that the MIA became the first organisation to promote the tactic of direct action.

Roy Wilkins (1901–81)

He was a journalist and activist who succeeded W.E.B. Du Bois as editor of NAACP's *Crisis* magazine. He ran this for almost twenty years before being voted in as NAACP's executive secretary in 1955. He was one of the key figures in getting the *Brown v. Topeka Board of Education* case to the Supreme Court, and was one of the main coordinators of the March on Washington in 1963. He oversaw a rise in NAACP membership from 25,000 before the war to more than 400,000 by the 1970s.

award, the Spingarn Medal. In his appreciation letter, King said the organisation had his moral and financial support at all times.

King's new organisation, the SCLC (see section 4.1, The key groups), now began collaborating with the NAACP, to the extent that in 1958 King and Wilkins met jointly with President Eisenhower to push for further legislation. Both men refuted the idea that there might be any disagreement between their two organisations, although inevitably tensions did surface.

The NAACP itself faced coordinated and highly effective attacks from the southern white power structure, which fought to prevent the implementation of desegregation. This so-called 'massive resistance' was an outright defiance of federal law and set up the conflict at Little Rock, Arkansas in 1957 (see Chapter 2, section 2.3, Interactions and comparisons of key civil rights groups, 1954–65). So in 1962 NAACP joined forces with SCLC, the SNCC, the National Urban League, and CORE to launch a grass-roots campaign to develop black voter registration and mobilisation: the Voter Education Project. The organisations joined with the Brotherhood of Sleeping Car Porters – the first labour union led by African Americans to receive its formal charter status – in 1963 to organise the March on Washington for Jobs and Freedom.

By the mid-1960s, the NAACP had distanced itself from the more radical, action-oriented organisations, while King continued to work with the youthful activists of CORE and the SNCC. However, by 1966 the NAACP and SCLC were at variance with CORE and the SNCC when these groups began to exclude white sympathisers from membership and spoke of becoming more militant. The NAACP, under Roy Wilkins' leadership, was accused by these organisations of being too moderate, and by the early 1970s had lost some of its membership during a more radical period within the Civil Rights Movement.

QUESTION

What does **Source A** tell us about Martin Luther King's opinion of the NAACP? Research more about King's Prayer Pilgrimage of 1957.

SOURCE A

We have won marvellous victories through the work of the NAACP. We have been able to do some of the most amazing things of this generation, and I come this afternoon with nothing but praise for this great organisation. Although they outlawed the NAACP in Alabama and other states, the fact still remains that this organisation has done more to achieve Civil Rights for Negroes than any other organisation we can point to.

Martin Luther King speaking at a Prayer Pilgrimage in Washington, DC, 17 May 1957. Quoted in A.D. Morris (1984) *The Origins of the Civil Rights Movements,* New York: The Free Press, p. 128.

The Congress of Racial Equality (CORE)

CORE advocated non-violent direct action, and its members came to prominence when they provided advice and support to Martin Luther King during the Montgomery Bus Boycott of 1955. Prior to this, CORE had become moribund at times, with no deeply rooted base in the south. It was after the end of the Montgomery Bus Boycott that CORE began to revive, primarily due to its association with King, until the mid-1960s, when the organisation abandoned non-violence as it turned towards black separatist policies.

A number of CORE activists had been affiliated with the Fellowship of Reconciliation (FOR), an international peace and justice organisation. FOR had organised the Journey of Reconciliation in 1947, a multi-state bus ride through parts of the south (and a forerunner to the 1961 Freedom Rides), to protest against interstate segregation in travel. This meant that **James Farmer**, Bayard Rustin, Homer Jack and George Houser had all gained valuable experience – which would prove crucial to CORE a decade later.

Martin Luther King became much more involved with CORE in the months after the Montgomery Bus Boycott, and by October 1957 had agreed to serve on CORE's Advisory Committee. Thereafter, King's organisation, the SCLC, did liaise with CORE on various projects, such as the Prayer Pilgrimage for Public Schools in Virginia, which protested against attempts to block public school integration.

But CORE was also proactive in its own right; the organisation supported southern blacks during the sit-ins of 1960, and its field secretaries travelled through the south, advising student activists on non-violent techniques. Much attention has been focused on the role of King during this period, yet there can be little doubt that CORE, under James Farmer, played a crucial role during the campaigns of the early 1960s.

> **James Farmer (1920–99)**
>
> He was a director of CORE and one of its founders in 1942. As a boy, Farmer had seen his father, a college professor, being humiliated by whites. He was one of the advocates of the sit-in technique during the Second World War. He also organised the Freedom Rides, and was one of the speakers at the March on Washington in 1963.

SOURCE B

CORE under Farmer often served as the razor's edge of the [civil rights] movement. It was to CORE that the four Greensboro, NC, students turned after staging the first in the series of sit-ins that swept the South in 1960. It was CORE that forced the issue of desegregation in interstate transportation with the Freedom Rides of 1961. It was CORE's James Chaney, Andrew Goodman and Michael Schwerner who became the first fatalities of the Mississippi Freedom Summer of 1964.

Claude Sitton, journalist for *The New York Times,* quoted in R. Severo (1999) 'James Farmer, civil rights giant in the 50's and 60's, is dead at 79', Obituary, *The New York Times*, 10 July.

> **QUESTION**
>
> Look at **Source B** What is meant by the phrase 'razor's edge of the movement'? What does the tone of this source suggest in general about the significance of CORE?

CORE organised the Freedom Rides in the spring of 1961 (see Chapter 3, sections 3.2.4–6), which aroused immense hostility among white southerners. They were nearly suspended, until a Freedom Ride Coordinating Committee was formed by representatives of CORE, SNCC and SCLC to continue the momentum.

Then CORE focused on voter registration and subscribed to the Council of Federated Organisations (COFO), an umbrella for all the other civil rights groups. COFO worked predominantly in Mississippi and provided liaison for activists and organisers alike. These efforts culminated in the 1964 Freedom Summer (see Chapter 3, section 3.3) and the activities of Mississippi Freedom Democratic Party (MFDP), which challenged Mississippi's segregated, all-white delegation at the 1964 Democratic Party National Convention in Atlantic City. However, there was growing frustration with the precepts of non-violence in general following the murder of three CORE workers in Mississippi in the summer of 1964 (see Chapter 3, section 3.3.2).

CORE also ran a voter registration campaign in Louisiana, which was subjected to intimidation by white supremacists and was directly attacked by the Ku Klux Klan (KKK), who burnt crosses on the lawns of black voters and set fire to a Masonic hall, a Baptist centre and several other churches.

In November 1964, African Americans in Jonesboro, Louisiana founded a group called Deacons for Defence and Justice. Its aim was to protect civil rights workers, their communities and their families from the KKK, and most of the Deacons had army combat experience from the Second World War and Korea. The Jonesboro Deacons later ran a regional organising campaign, forming twenty-one 'chapters' in Louisiana, Mississippi and Alabama. The federal government was forced to intervene following a confrontation between the Deacons and the KKK. But the safeguarding of CORE meetings and demonstrations by the Deacons was indicative of changes taking place in CORE.

The changes displeased CORE's James Farmer. He eventually resigned as the movement's director in 1965, believing that CORE was moving away from its initial goal – a non-violent end to discrimination. Farmer felt vindicated after CORE officials made a foreign policy statement and called for the US to withdraw troops from Vietnam. Floyd McKissick took over and CORE then advocated black nationalism and greater self-determination for the black community.

The Southern Christian Leadership Conference (SCLC)

After the success of the Montgomery Bus Boycott, the SCLC was formed in 1957 to widen participation in the Civil Rights Movement by attempting to coordinate the actions and policies of local protest groups throughout the south. Churches in general – and black clergymen in particular – was particularly prominent in the movement, and Martin Luther King became the organisation's president. Based in Atlanta, the SCLC utilised the influence and independence of black churches to widen its field of activity.

Activist **Bayard Rustin** wrote about the need to build on the success of the boycott in Montgomery, taking the grass-roots activism to other cities throughout the south. He suggested that an organisation was needed to coordinate such activities. King invited southern black ministers to a meeting at Ebenezer Baptist Church in Atlanta, from which came a manifesto. It asked white southerners to consider that the treatment of blacks was a basic spiritual problem, while black Americans were encouraged to seek justice and dedicate themselves to the principle of non-violence 'no matter how great the provocation'. The SCLC was born.

The SCLC certainly played its part, helping to coordinate mass protests and voter registration drives all over the south. It augmented small, local, grass-roots movements, notably Albany, Birmingham and Selma. It later played a major role in the March on Washington in August 1963 and brought real visibility to the struggle. This assisted the passage of the Civil Rights Act of 1964 and the Voting Rights Act of 1965.

The SCLC now considered wider issues such as poverty, lack of opportunity and economic inequality. King viewed poverty as the cause of social inequality, and in 1962 the SCLC began Operation Breadbasket in Atlanta in an attempt to create new jobs in the black community. The reasoning was that blacks did not need to support businesses that denied them jobs, career advancement or plain courtesy. The SCLC also aimed to encourage black entrepreneurial independence, and by 1966 the programme had spread to Chicago. By this time, however, the SCLC was viewed by some black organisations as being too moderate, too much of a do-gooder movement and ultimately too dependent on white liberal Democrats. The increased militancy of the SNCC and CORE led to tensions between them and King.

The SCLC was certainly a key player during that turbulent decade following 1954, but its early years are delineated by teething troubles and competition from other organisations. The SCLC was significant in that it did not take individual members, so as not to undermine the NAACP. Its aim was to widen participation in the Civil Rights Movement and, in this respect, black clergymen were especially prominent.

Figure 4.2   Bayard Rustin (1912–87)

A Quaker who briefly recruited for the Young Communist League in the 1930s, Rustin was imprisoned during the Second World War for being a conscientious objector. He became an influential advisor to the NAACP and to Martin Luther King, and was instrumental in establishing the SCLC. He helped to organise the March on Washington in 1963. But his political past, and his being gay, ensured that he remained more of a background figure than a prominent leader.

Even though its first few years have been seen as fallow, it had a dynamic centre, with what Aldon D. Morris called 'institutionalised charisma'. This charisma, not least that of Martin Luther King, would eventually lead the SCLC to play a major role in the Civil Rights Movement.

Role of the Church

The SCLC's mission statement argued that movements could be generated, coordinated and nurtured by activist clergy, supportive congregations and organised black masses working in harmony: mass protest, mobilised through the churches. So the SCLC was firmly anchored in the black churches and had the capability and the captive audience to mobilise a mass base, which the NAACP did not by virtue of its more civilian contingent. The SCLC was thus linked to the two existing and enduring sections of the black community – the churches and the NAACP – and was rooted in the tradition of black protest.

The SCLC was building a viable network of church-related protest groups, a fiscal base, and harnessing it all to the cultural content of black churches. It was launched in the south, just when NAACP was losing some of its potency due to attacks and persistent undermining by the opposing white power structure. Indeed, so central were the churches to the SCLC that various clergy believed that the organisation was actually the black churches coming alive across denominational and geographical lines. Their tactics also demanded mass mobilisation; a slow and sometimes indeterminate mode of protest, without exact parameters – hence the accusations of 'fallow years'. King and his acolytes would have to wait for events to drive people to such activism. But as the organisational power and status of Martin Luther King grew, so did the efficiency and the voice of SCLC.

SOURCE C

SCLC differed from organisations such as... the National Association for the Advancement of Coloured People, in that it operated as an umbrella organization of affiliates. Rather than seek individual members, it coordinated with the activities of local organisations like the Montgomery Improvement Association and the Nashville Christian Leadership Council. 'The life-blood of SCLC movements,' as described in one of its pamphlets, 'is in the masses of people who are involved – members of SCLC and its local affiliates and chapters.' To that end, SCLC staff... trained local communities in the philosophy of Christian non-violence by conducting leadership training programmes and opening citizenship schools. Through its affiliation with churches and its advocacy of non-violence, SCLC sought to frame the struggle for civil rights in moral terms.

A. Fairclough (1987) *To Redeem the Soul of America: The Southern Christian Leadership Conference and Martin Luther King Jr.*, Athens, GA: University of Georgia Press, p. 40.

QUESTION
What does **Source C** reveal about the nature of the SCLC? How does the organisation differ from the NAACP and CORE?

SOURCE D

In addition to charismatic authority, King had organisational power. As president, King had ultimate power in the SCLC. King's former officers and colleagues unequivocally state that the power of the SCLC resided in the man they affectionately refer to as 'Martin'... that the power in the SCLC was supposed to reside in the board, but it resided in the person who had the greatest contact with the outside world and Martin became the great person out there.

A.D. Morris (1984) *The Origins of the Civil Rights Movements*, New York: The Free Press, p. 93.

QUESTION
Read **Source D**. What does it reveal about the organisational running of the SCLC?

Figure 4.3   Ella Baker (1903–86)

She was a civil rights organiser for more than fifty years and mentored many emerging activists such as Stokely Carmichael and Rosa Parks. She was a promoter of grass-roots organising and became the first female president of the NAACP in New York. She later helped to arrange the founding meeting of the SCLC and helped to set up the MFDP in Mississippi, but by 1967 had drifted away from the SNCC as it became more radical. She has been called the most influential woman in the Civil Rights Movement.

The Student Nonviolent Coordinating Committee (SNCC)

Founded in April 1960, the SNCC evolved out of the Greensboro sit-in (see Chapter 3, section 3.2, How did sit-ins develop?), when students occupied the local Woolworth store. The students who had protested were articulate, independent men; keen activists who wanted to remain independent of Martin Luther King, who had ideas about these student leaders becoming a youth section of the SCLC, and had made the appropriate overtures to them. The two organisations did cooperate frequently during the early years of the Civil Rights Movement, although ideological differences eventually caused the SNCC and SCLC to be at variance.

SCLC official **Ella Baker** invited black students who had participated in the sit-ins to Shaw University in Raleigh, North Carolina later that April. She tried to persuade the 200 students in attendance to remain independent as a student civil rights group, rather than to merge or affiliate with any of the other existing organisations. Even King issued a press statement and urged the students to form some type of organisation to continue their work and to delve deeper into the philosophy of non-violence.

At the conference, the students initially voted to establish only a temporary organisation to help coordinate future sit-ins and other protests, although by May 1960 the group had become a permanent organisation. This was in no small measure due to James Lawson, a black theology student from Vanderbilt University. Lawson's workshops on non-violent direct action would prove beneficial for future civil rights leaders and student protesters, but at the conference he drafted a statement that characterised the SNCC's early years. It affirmed the ideal of non-violence as the foundation of their purpose and their faith, and the manner of their actions.

The 1961 Freedom Rides (see Chapter 3, section 3.2) really saw the SNCC emerge as a force in the Civil Rights Movement. CORE initially sponsored the rides, but when segregationists viciously attacked riders travelling through Alabama, SNCC students from Nashville, Tennessee resolved to complete them. Other students then joined the movement and by the time the Interstate Commerce Commission had finally enforced the ruling for equal treatment in interstate travel in November 1961, the SNCC had directed its attention to the issue of black voter registration in Mississippi. It was also at the forefront of campaign for desegregation in Albany, Georgia, known as the Albany Movement.

Albany Movement

The Albany Movement promoted a campaign to challenge all forms of discrimination and segregation. It was formed by the Freedom Riders of the SNCC, but was augmented with members of other organisations including the NAACP, the Ministerial Alliance, the Federation of Women's Clubs, and the Negro Voters League. Members of the SNCC targeted the Albany bus station, which had ignored the orders to desegregate. Students from the (black) Albany State College took part in sit-ins, and when hundreds were arrested, blacks boycotted white businesses. Yet there was no reaction from the Albany town authorities.

Then, older members of the Albany Movement invited King and the SCLC to join them. SNCC leaders in Albany were annoyed and argued that the Albany Movement was for local people, local blacks. When King and other campaigners then staged a demonstration and refused to disperse, they were arrested and fined. This attracted national publicity. But the fear of fostering more adverse publicity did not go unnoticed by the city government. Local police chief **Laurie Pritchett** knew that he must avoid violence, and instructed his officers to treat demonstrators gently during arrest and prevent white demonstrators from becoming violent.

King initially refused to pay his fine and was jailed, but city officials and Albany Movement leaders soon agreed that if King paid his fine and left Albany, the city would desegregate facilities and release jailed protestors on bail. King paid the fine instead of remaining in jail over Christmas 1961, as he had originally vowed; but his payment was strongly criticised by some blacks and he was accused of hypocrisy. Indeed, the campaign had involved large numbers of black adults from varied backgrounds and, unsurprisingly, tensions had arisen. After King left Albany, the city failed to uphold the agreement in full. The interstate terminal facilities were desegregated and more black voters were allowed to register; but as Sanders (2006) comments, 'the city closed the parks, sold the swimming pool, integrated the library only after removing all the seats, and refused to desegregate the schools.....the local police chief had carefully avoided violence, so the federal government had not had to intervene'.

Laurie Pritchett (1926–2000)

He was a police chief of Albany, Georgia and an ardent segregationist. Pritchett gained national attention when he stifled the efforts of the Albany Movement in 1961–2. He adopted a non-violent approach to the protests and ordered his deputies not to use violent tactics to make arrests. It is possible that he arranged for anonymous 'benefactors' to bail out King and other SCLC leaders. King believed Pritchett was inherently a good person who had been trapped by the system.

Figure 4.4 Martin Luther King and Sheriff Laurie Pritchett confront each other in Albany, 1962

Clearly, the Albany Movement had mobilised people into big protests during December 1961; these also continued on-and-off during 1962. Although it had secured few concrete gains, it was an important learning curve for the SNCC. Albany had mobilised the entire black community, it had gained national attention, and SNCC's 'jail not bail' strategy could fill the jails with protestors and bring the courts and jails to a standstill. King had also realised that the SCLC could not be effective without a strong operational presence in the area, or where another organisation dominated. This realisation would guide King when he came to Birmingham, Alabama in 1963 (see below).

SNCC members now felt the need for greater grass-roots radicalism, believing the SCLC measured success more by national, political power, with King – in the eyes of both

NAACP and SNCC members – developing a leadership cult. Problems with funding reinforced this disenchantment, and tensions arose between the SNCC and the SCLC. SNCC members felt that it was their direct action that had brought in money from sympathisers, but that it was being diverted to promote SCLC, while even the NAACP saw King in Albany as meddling on their patch. But at this stage, the SNCC was still playing a key role in campaigning, one that was beneficial to all movements.

Post-Albany SNCC

The SNCC now became actively involved in the Mississippi voter registration campaign, bringing together three key groups: influential civil rights leaders from Mississippi, SNCC field secretaries and white student volunteers who participated in the Freedom Vote mock election of October 1963 and the Freedom Summer of 1964.

Then the SNCC supported the formation of the Mississippi Freedom Democratic Party (MFDP) in an effort to challenge the all-white Democratic Party at the National Convention meeting to choose the presidential candidate (see Chapter 3, section 3.3, The formation of the Missisipi Freedom Democratic Party). The so-called Black Freedom Movement in Mississippi was an outstanding moment for the SNCC, and this experience, plus the MFDP, politicised many poor black Mississippians – especially women – and helped develop new grass-roots leaders.

But the Mississippi Freedom Summer campaign of voter registration caused division among civil rights workers. SNCC fieldworkers often resented the involvement of northern, white student volunteers. The students were seen as trendy, liberal, middle-class 'do-gooders' and 'fly-by-night freedom fighters' – privileged whites who were only there for the summer. Yet for the black population of Mississippi, the bombings and lynchings would continue. Many felt that white students had taken over many of the key jobs that local blacks had done, undermining them and perpetuating the stereotype of black inferiority. Some SNCC workers criticised the integrationist approach and questioned the need for blacks and whites to work together.

Finally, the voting rights demonstrations that began in 1965 in Selma, Alabama (Chapter 3, section 3.4, The Selma to Montgomery March) ignited bitter ideological

QUESTION

Look at **Source E**. What does it tell us about the ethos of the SNCC? What did SNCC members think of Martin Luther King? Explain your reasons carefully.

SOURCE E

Dedicated at the outset to non-violence, SNCC was an example of King's desire to see others develop their own institutions, and he welcomed the students to the centre of the historical stage. 'What is fresh, what is new in your fight,' he told them, 'is the fact that it was initiated, led and sustained by students. You now take your honoured places in the world-wide struggle for freedom.' King christened the most energetic but also the most controversial organisation within the movement… SNCC mostly thrived on shared ideals and eventually, on an intimacy bred of danger and crisis. SNCC students also insisted on their independence from the mainstream group. As much as they owed King, the students increasingly saw him as the sort of 'hero' who undermined true democracy. The students stepped to the working motto: 'Go where the spirit say go. Do what the spirit say do.'

D. Steigerwald (1995) *The Sixties and the End of Modern America,* New York: St Martin's Press, p. 46.

debates within SNCC. The Selma to Montgomery March organised by the SNCC and the SCLC was something of a turning point. King refused President Johnson's request to call off the second march, believing that it would be a betrayal of his followers; but unknown to the SNCC, he had ordered the marchers to approach the state troopers, then come to a stop, pray and, finally, retreat. King then abandoned the march. The SNCC felt let down by King and accused him of cowardice.

Yet even during the August 1963 March on Washington, there were signs that change was looming. The SNCC chairman John Lewis was scheduled to speak alongside King at the rally after the march. He told organisers of the march that he intended to criticise President Kennedy's proposed civil rights bill for being too little, too late, and that he would refer to the SNCC movement as 'a serious revolution'. He later softened the tone of the delivered speech to appease march organisers, but it was the first sign that the SNCC was gathering militancy – especially with talk of 'revolution'. Then, distracted by division after 1965, where the SNCC had once attracted considerable black support, its influence waned in many southern communities.

But the overall significance of the SNCC was that the members were real activists in a time of official 'non-violence'. They knew that their job was to move into a community, evaluate its local leadership and then teach the community to stand up for itself. SNCC members made efforts to identify with those they wished to influence, so they adopted the traditional habits and dress of wherever they were, be it among youth, shopkeepers or sharecroppers. They aimed to leave behind self-reliant and self-governing organisations of fellow activists who could both 'spread the word' and work for their own interests in their own way.

After the Selma to Montgomery March, **Stokely Carmichael** and other more militant SNCC organisers entered rural Alabama and helped launch the all-black Lowndes County Freedom Organisation, later known as the Black Panther Party. They were disillusioned with the lack of federal protection and increasingly irritated by the apparent omniscience of King. This more militant stance helped to fracture the coalition of co-operation among the different Civil Rights Movements.

Interactions and comparisons of key civil rights groups, 1954–65

Even at the height of its success between 1963 and 1965, the Civil Rights Movement was showing signs of strain and a lack of unity. This became increasingly evident during the Mississippi Freedom Summer of 1964. The Selma to Montgomery March in March 1965 would prove to be almost the last occasion when whites outside of the south offered full and widespread support to a protest campaign in the south.

This support would diminish in part due to white resentment of growing black militancy, an increase in urban racial violence in the north and west, together with the realisation that non-violent protest was losing some of its impact. There was also a growing determination to construct separate spheres: black cultural identity and black-controlled institutions. Not only did it make many white supporters of civil rights nervous, but it also had an effect on the movements themselves – and, inevitably, stresses and strains over ideas, principles and tactics were ever-present. There were disagreements over the non-violence principle, over whether or not integration of

Figure 4.5   Stokely Carmichael (1941–98)

Born in Trinidad, Carmichael lived in the USA from 1952 to 1969. He worked with SNCC on the Mississippi Freedom Summer project and the Mississippi Freedom Democratic Party. He saw non-violence as a tactic, not a guiding principle. He replaced John Lewis as chairman of the SNCC, and emphasised black militancy rather than non-violence and integration. Carmichael was opposed to the SNCC decision to expel whites, but later joined black nationalists in advocating racial unity rather than class unity as a basis for struggles. He left the SNCC in 1967 to join the Black Panthers.

black and white was the proper aim – or even a desirable one – and also to what extent different concerns or aspects of improvement should take precedence: legal, political, social, economic. Then in middle of the 1960s, more radical viewpoints became dominant and the question of 'black supremacy' moved to the fore. For these reasons, increasing numbers of historians have analysed the interaction and cooperation between different civil rights groups.

A united movement?

Given that no one individual civil rights group existed without variation at different levels within its own organisation, how far can students of civil rights make comparisons regarding the interaction and cooperation between them?

In his study of the Civil Rights Movements of Georgia, Louisiana and Mississippi, Lawson sees the Civil Rights Movement as intertwined in a complex mix of local, regional and national groups and events. For example, local and state NAACP organisations did not necessarily fall with the cautious leadership of the NAACP nationally, and that there was what Mark Newman calls, 'a degree of… disagreement, between the NAACP's local, state and national bodies… and their approaches to the black struggle for equality ranged from timidity and caution, to voter-registration and litigation efforts and even direct-action campaigns'. This prompts the question, just how united was the Civil Rights Movement up to 1965?

By 1965 there was a shift in emphasis from the Deep South to the industrial north and west, and concern was focusing on social and economic problems as well as legal and political issues. The principle of non-violence and the Christian-based tenets of the movement were both being challenged by more radical groups, while much of the sympathy that the movement had won from the federal government was diminishing in the aftermath of the passing of legislation in 1964 and 1965.

The NAACP had led the way by bringing many legal cases to the Supreme Court. CORE was present 'on the launchpad' of modern civil rights during and after the Second World War, so it too is crucial. But CORE depended on a small group of disciplined activists to conduct their campaigns to desegregate public accommodations, workplaces and housing; it had no mass base in the north or the south before 1957, and had only attracted sporadic attention, for example at Montgomery. But there was no constant dynamism about the organisation. The arrival of the SCLC in 1957 changed things, given the momentum of the moment. And with King at its head, it became a leading civil rights organisation from the outset.

The Voter Education Project (VEP): ran from 1962 to 1968, raising and distributing funds to civil rights organisations, to assist in their work in the south on political awareness and ballot registration. The US government formally supported the VEP and hoped that it would enable the Civil Rights Movement to switch its focus from segregation.

In trying to compare the different organisations, many historians see commonality at the root of these groups, however divergent or ill-tempered they later became.

The NAACP was a national organisation and was persistent in mounting legal challenges both before and after *Brown v. Topeka Board of Education* in 1954 – the high watermark of its achievement – and it must not be forgotten that in 1962 NAACP partnered with the SCLC, the SNCC, CORE and others, to launch the **Voter Education Project (VEP)**. So cooperation was possible between these varied groups, although inter-organisational tensions would lurk beneath the surface – often because of their natural differences. For example, CORE had a presence in both the north and the south, but no real mass black base and remained predominantly secular, while the SCLC was rooted in the black churches of the south. King joining CORE's Advisory Committee enabled the SCLC to play a key financial role in

CORE's revival and expansion between 1957 and 1960. His presence meant that his name could be added to the letterhead on CORE's correspondence. This gave CORE prestige and also led to other influential civil rights workers joining. It also enabled SCLC to work with CORE on several projects described previously in this chapter.

The student sit-ins at Greensboro then brought the SNCC into being. These protests brought the Civil Rights Movement to life, so in this sense the SNCC acted as a unifying factor for the NAACP, CORE and the SCLC. The sit-ins provided more funds, because blacks as well as sympathetic whites sent donations; they also gave CORE the chance to become a much larger organisation, reflected in the fact that during 1960 it added three full-time staff members. But the SCLC perhaps takes the most credit for the success of the movement. The organisation provided a platform for the greatest black orator, Martin Luther King, and his eloquence inspired many important figures in the Civil Rights Movement to join the ranks of the SCLC. But as Paterson, Willoughby and Willoughby (2001) note, 'it was not run democratically and King had to take some flak for imposing his wishes on it and deciding where the next campaign would be and exactly what tactics would be followed. Its detailed organisation left much to be desired... but its lack of organisation enabled the SCLC to adapt with the minimum of bureaucratic delay to a new situation.'

Later the NAACP and the SCLC were both at odds with CORE and the SNCC as the latter began to take a more militant political stand over Vietnam, and then called for the exclusion of white sympathisers from membership. While the NAACP and the SCLC felt that the federal government was finally delivering on its legislative promises, with respect to the 1964 Civil Rights Act and 1965 Voting Rights Act, the SNCC felt that King and other SCLC leaders had betrayed the cause by agreeing to 'that compromise' with Johnson and Humphrey over the MFDP delegates at the Atlantic City Democratic Party Convention of 1964 (see Chapter 3, section 3.3, The formation of the Mississippi Freedom Democratic Party). They had been so confident that working with – not against – the Democratic government in Washington would bring more reform. To many SNCC activists, this was a total betrayal. Yet King was probably the only leader who could maintain some unity between different organisations.

But the non-violent protest championed by King became increasingly unrealistic. In the north, bitterness and disillusionment were widespread, as echoed by a Harlem student who supported the ideas of Malcolm X. The student told some visitors from Mississippi to New York: 'Turning the other cheek is a load of trash. Up here we understand what snake is biting us.' Non-violence was no longer the preferred option.

SOURCE F

[O]ne SNCC worker expressed what many felt: 'The days of singing freedom songs and the days of combating bullets and billy clubs with love are over.' Furthermore, increasing opposition to US involvement in the Vietnam War was causing more divisions in the Civil Rights Movement. In July 1965, the SNCC declared that blacks should not 'fight in Vietnam for the white man's freedom until all the Negro people are free in Mississippi'.

M. Stacey and M. Scott-Baumann (2013) *Civil Rights and Social Movements in the Americas*, Cambridge: Cambridge University Press, p. 143.

QUESTION

From **Source F**, what can we learn about the changing nature of the Civil Rights Movement by the end of 1965?

By 1965, the Civil Rights Movement had lost the relative unity it had achieved in the early 1960s. Impatience with the lack of federal action in economic and social affairs, combined with a sudden escalation of US involvement in Vietnam after August 1964, meant that Stokely Carmichael and his 'Black Power' advocates began providing an alternative agenda, increasingly heard. It became a radical alternative to the SCLC's chant of 'Freedom Now!', and it also meant that King's dominant sway with the SCLC had lessened. Nevertheless, where the different organisations were able to work together, the impact for the Civil Rights Movement – through Montgomery, Greensboro, Mississippi and Selma – was significant.

How important was the role of the churches?

Many of the key figures engaged in civil rights derived much inspiration from their religious faith, and an unshaken fundamental belief that justice and equality was afforded to all men, women and children – regardless of cultural background, race or religious faith. These clergymen so prominent in civil rights felt morally bound to do their best when serving these 'children of God'.

The sociologist Johnathan Rieder, writing about King and the religious roots of the Civil Rights Movement, has argued that religion was not just an opportunistic accessory but 'it was his driving force and utter motivation… and it was the source of their vision of justice......The Civil Rights Movement fused the political promise of equal votes with the spiritual doctrine of equal souls' (Rieder, 2013, p. 7).

It is easy to see how religion and the community of the black churches served as a motivator; and nowhere was this association between religion and civil rights made more manifest than in the March on Washington for Jobs and Freedom on 28 August 1963, where a real alliance of different religious groups pushed the civil rights agenda further forward.

Different denominations converged on Washington, DC, then some ministers travelled to Mississippi to help register voters. Quakers helped to rebuild black Christian churches destroyed by segregationists, and white activists took part in protests and voter registration drives in the south in their thousands. According to Rieder, they were also disproportionately Jewish.

On the day of the rally, a Catholic archbishop, a Jewish rabbi and a Baptist minister offered prayers. This preaching of Christian and Jewish leaders on the steps of the Lincoln Memorial was to an interracial crowd of about 250,000 – a quarter of whom were white – with millions watching on television. Among the nine speakers were four religious leaders who exhorted the crowd to join the cause that would make them and their brothers and sisters free. This was followed by perhaps the most enduring memory of that significant gathering: the famous 'I Have a Dream' speech given by the Martin Luther King.

Based on the March on Washington, the role of the black churches seemed both central and crucial. But their impact cannot be underestimated, because of their relative independence and by being a natural venue for African Americans. In the racist south, a church was a place in the community that remained beyond white control. It was somewhere that people could express themselves or feel empowered without reprisal. It was also the community bulletin board. So the social, political, economic, educational and spiritual power of the movement was there.

Figure 4.6 The March on Washington, August 1963

These experienced ministers who fought injustice in the 1950s and 1960s and were at the forefront of the civil rights struggle came from a world where taking the initiative and working with organisations like the NAACP was one of the only ways to affect change. By virtue of their clerical role, some were able to represent an independent voice in the community and become proactive. The church was the place where different social and economic groups came together. These communities could also help enlist others outside of the black Church to support them.

The Montgomery Bus Boycott was spearheaded by the local church, who viewed the shabby treatment of black passengers on the Montgomery buses as immoral and running contrary to their understanding of biblical scriptures. The sit-in movement that began in 1960, at Greensboro, was led by students, some of whom were seminary students and several were college chaplains. In Nashville, the local affiliate of the SCLC sponsored the workshops that trained the leadership of the Nashville sit-in movement. The students planned their action strategies at a Methodist church and staged their sit-ins from a Baptist church, while student leaders from several campuses were trained by a divinity student from Vanderbilt.

People of different faiths joined the Freedom Rides and helped eradicate segregation in interstate travel by the end of 1961, and gradually churches started to rethink their racial constituency. There is evidence that seminaries made increased efforts to recruit non-whites and provide scholarships to attract them, while events in Birmingham and Washington, DC, in 1963 reinforced this enlightened thinking.

The local Birmingham Movement (see section 4.2, Good King or bad King?) was sponsored by the Alabama Christian Movement for Human Rights and was led by people of faith, including the Rev. Fred Shuttlesworth, a local leader at the Sixteenth

Figure 4.7 A meeting of support held in a Montgomery Baptist Church, 1956, during the Bus Boycott

Street Baptist Church. Here, a bomb killed four young girls in September 1963 when Shuttlesworth was targeted by dynamite-wielding white supremacists. People from other places and other faiths added spiritual force to the Birmingham Movement. For example, the Jewish Council in St Louis, Missouri gave support to the Birmingham march by sending a large group of rabbis to join the protest. So activists, motivated by a sense of justice and sustained by their church and their scriptures, contributed significantly in the struggle for racial justice in American life.

The southern black churches were not the only indigenous black institutions to provide aid for the Civil Rights Movement. Secular organisations and grass-roots community institutions such as labour unions, women's civic clubs and teachers' associations all played their part. Even fraternal societies like the African American Freemasons from the Prince Hall Lodge of Ohio played key roles in the movement.

It has been suggested that many of the major southern campaigns were initiated by individuals without formal ties to the black churches, and that the role of the churches has been exaggerated due to a narrow focus on Martin Luther King. But it would be unkind to accuse the southern black churches of dereliction of duty; their belief in non-violence worked admirably in the early years of the struggle, as it resonated with the spirituality of so many ordinary black people.

The significance of the churches and other religious communities in the Civil Rights Movement remains debatable in terms of the importance of the role of the black churches as opposed to the work of small groups of individuals, often secular in nature. Clayborne Carson believes that churches were fundamentally conservative and often held back activists. Yet black churches played a key role in the Civil Rights Movement – although this began before the ascendancy of Martin Luther King, with black ministers being the voice and conscience of the community. With high illiteracy among former slaves and plantation workers, combined with poor comprehension of their rights as free citizens, it fell to the churches to protect, inform and educate. This progressed logically into lobbying and protesting. So the role of Churches in the Civil Rights Movement was a natural extension of an already pivotal role in black culture and community.

SOURCE G

It would be wrong to suggest that the institution (and still less the evangelical world-view of so many southern blacks) played a minor part in the events of the mid-twentieth century. The black church was an immensely diverse institution. The dominant Baptist and Methodist churches embraced a wide variety of opinion on the wisdom and necessity of civil rights involvement… the majority of socially aware southern black clergymen, cognisant of the church's historic role in spreading the gospel of deliverance, but wary of stirring up white opposition and internal dissent, advocated a composite form of social action which combined self-help with moderate protest in varying proportions… the important point is not that King and others like him were initially secondary actors in the movement, but that their involvement in the struggle was deemed critical by secular leaders.

R. Cook (1998) *Sweet Land of Liberty,* Harlow: Longman, pp. 237–8.

QUESTION

Read **Source G** and the previous text. How does this source add to the debate about the role of religion in the struggle for civil rights? Explain your answer carefully.

Figure 4.8   African American Freemasons from the Prince Hall Lodge of Ohio, 1958

Perspectives: '*The
cooperation of
various groups in
the Civil Rights
Movement had a
major impact on the
campaign against
racial segregation
and voting exclusion.*'
Consider this
perspective. How far
do you agree with
it? Using this section,
together with your
own research, write
an answer to this
statement. Consider
whether or not
existing conditions
may have had an
influence. You
might also need to
consider the opposing
perspective and give
greater importance to
role of the churches,
the government or to
key individuals at a
local or state level.

End of section activities

1   Draw a table like this one below and make notes for each of the groups you have
    studied in this chapter. Use this book together with your own research in the library
    or on the internet.

	Background	**Aims**	**Methods**	**Achievements**	**Failures**
NAACP					
CORE					
SCLC					
SNCC					
Black churches					
Secular groups					

2   Research further into one of the significant individuals referred in this chapter – with
    the exception of Martin Luther King. Activists such as Roy Wilkins, Ella Baker or
    Stokely Carmichael would be good examples.

4.2 What was the significance of the role played by Martin Luther King Jr.?

PROFILE OF MARTIN LUTHER KING

1929 Jan: Born in Atlanta, Georgia.

1944–8 Studied at Morehouse College, Atlanta; ordained as a Baptist minister.

1953 June: Marries Coretta Scott.

1954 Becomes Pastor of Dexter Avenue Baptist Church, Montgomery.

1955 Receives his PhD from Boston University.

    Dec: Headed Montgomery Improvement Association (MIA) during Bus Boycott.

1957 Jan: Founded SCLC and spoke at Prayer Pilgrimage for Freedom in Washington,
       DC.

1958 Jan: Nearly killed when stabbed by an assailant in Harlem.

1959 Resigns from pastoring and moves to Atlanta to direct the SCLC.

1960 Apr: Sent SCLC's Ella Baker to organise students at sit-ins in Greensboro. Arrested
       for participating in Atlanta sit-in, then released following intervention from
       Senator John F. Kennedy.

1962 Arrested and jailed during the unsuccessful Albany campaign.

1963 Apr: Arrested by Police Commissioner Eugene 'Bull' Connor for demonstrating
       without a permit. One day later the Birmingham campaign was launched. King
       remained in jail for eleven days, during which time he wrote his 'Letter from
       Birmingham Jail'.

Jun: Leads 125,000 people on a Freedom Walk in Detroit.

Aug: Makes his famous 'I Have a Dream' speech at the March on Washington, attended by nearly 250,000 people. Named as *Time* magazine's Man of the Year.

1964 Dec: Presented with the Nobel Peace Prize in Oslo.

1965 Mar: Leading figure in the Selma to Montgomery Campaign.

1967 Publishes *Where Do We Go From Here?* rejecting Black Power and criticising US conduct in the Vietnam War. Initiates the Poor People's Campaign, which strives for employment and freedom for the poor of all races.

1968 Apr: Assassinated in Memphis, Tennessee.

Historians and King

Martin Luther King's role and place in the history of the Civil Rights Movement is immensely significant, and he remains to this day a revered international figure, often spoken of with the same tones of respect as the likes of Gandhi, Mother Teresa of Calcutta and Nelson Mandela. Yet he is still the subject of great debate among students and historians alike. Historian Harvard Sitkoff wrote: 'despite good intentions, he had little success in desegregating the North, alleviating the misery of the impoverished or promoting world peace'. Another historian, Clayborne Carson, believed that even if King had never lived, the black struggle would still have mapped out in a way similar to how it did. William T. Martin Riches stated that, with his assassination in 1968, 'America lost the greatest black spokesperson of the century… who also could speak with the emotional passion of an Old Testament prophet that would galvanise black congregations to follow the non-violent road to justice'. Anthony Badger concluded that King was important in providing a revolution in southern race relations. Ella Baker was critical of the adulation he received at the expense of the grass-roots efforts of thousands of civil rights workers all over America, but even she conceded that his contribution to the movement was massive. As Stacey and Scott-Baumann (2013) note, 'King led by example, showing great courage and stamina in the face of opposition, assaults and threats of assassination… With his appeal to American values, such as the belief in liberty, justice and democracy, he inspired millions, both black and white. Above all, he could influence the federal government and Congress. With his preaching background, his intellectual training and his experience of life in the North, he was a brilliant communicator with white America.' There is little doubt then that King's association with civil rights is of immense importance. But as historians and political scientists now assess the Civil Rights Movement in earnest, with much lively debate in historiography, King's administrative ability, his leadership role and his personal character have all been subject to close scrutiny and no little criticism.

Good King or bad King?

Undoubtedly King brought publicity to civil rights activities and he was always keen to emphasise the importance of non-violent protest and resistance. He provided leadership, support and guidance during the Montgomery Bus Boycott and he was instrumental in establishing the SCLC – an organisation following the philosophy of non-violence. Because of his commitment to peace, non-violence and equality, King was able to make genuine progress as a black man dealing with the highest authority figures in the land.

This became a major factor in the growing respect and acknowledgment given to the Civil Rights Movement.

Albany, Birmingham and Washington

King's reputation was forged greatly between 1961 and 1964 with the campaigns in Albany and Birmingham, his speech at the March on Washington, and then his being awarded the Nobel Peace Prize in the year President Johnson passed the Civil Rights Act.

Albany

As discussed previously (see section 4.1, The key groups), King left Albany with little change having been effected. The campaign had failed to create a situation where federal authorities felt compelled to act – unlike at Little Rock, Arkansas. Sanders (2006) feels that King followed rather than led and that he recognised Albany as a defeat, while Steigerwald (1995) says that King had put his own prestige on the line and criticism came from all sides. But Albany proved to be a learning experience for King. He now needed to apply different tactics that would give him a victory elsewhere.

Birmingham

Birmingham, Alabama was home to the most violent Klan group. Nicknamed 'Bombingham' as it was the site of 50 bombings since 1945, it was also the centre of probably the harshest fight against segregation in the south. It was a large town with a population of around 350,000, of which 140,000 were black. It became King's next target.

In 1963 there was a significant direct action campaign against the segregation system in Birmingham, Alabama, through applying pressure to the city's merchants during the Easter shopping season. Martin Luther King and the SCLC worked alongside a local group, the Alabama Christian Movement for Human Rights (ACMHR), in this effort. ACMHR founder **Fred Shuttlesworth** believed that the campaign was needed in order to give the black community the chance to survive.

On Good Friday (12 April), King was detained by the police for violating an injunction designed to prevent protests. He was jailed and placed in solitary confinement. During this time, King penned his celebrated 'Letter from Birmingham Jail' in reply to a newspaper letter statement from eight Birmingham clergymen condemning the protests. King hoped to shame these clergymen into supporting what he said was his cause and God's cause.

King was also denied a call to his wife, Coretta Scott King. She then relayed the situation to the Kennedy administration, whereupon officials in Birmingham allowed King to use the telephone. Eventually bail money was raised and King was released after eight days.

But with a shortage of volunteers to continue the protest, SCLC organiser James Bevel proposed the recruitment of teenagers and younger children. King endorsed this and soon more than 1,000 black students gathered to march into Birmingham. Many were arrested, and when hundreds more gathered the following day, Commissioner Theophilus Eugene 'Bull' Connor (see Chapter 3, section 3.2, Ole Miss, Bull Connor and action from Kennedy) ordered both the fire and police departments to halt the protests, by force if necessary. Unsavoury images appeared on television and in newspapers: children as young as eight or nine coming out of

---

Fred Shuttlesworth (1922–2011)

He was the founder of the Alabama Christian Rights Movement for Human rights in 1956. Shuttlesworth invited King and members of the SCLC to Birmingham in 1963 to lead a major campaign to desegregate it through mass demonstrations. He was an advocate of non-violent direct action and constantly sought to challenge the white authorities, such as when he tried to enrol his children in a previously all-white Birmingham public school in 1957 (resulting in an attack on Shuttlesworth and his wife by a mob of Klansmen). He was abrasive and often unpopular with his own side, but in 2007 Alabama state authorities changed the name of Birmingham's airport in his honour to Birmingham-Shuttlesworth International.

Fact: While in jail in Birmingham, Alabama in 1963, King wrote a very important document on scraps of paper. His 'Letter from Birmingham Jail' became the classic justification of civil disobedience (non-violent actions that break the law in order to draw attention to an even greater injustice).

church to join a demonstration and being clubbed by uniformed officers, attacked by police dogs and drenched by high-power fire hoses.

It triggered outrage at home and abroad, but also provided important worldwide publicity for the Civil Rights Movement. Whether children should have been allowed to join in is a major ethical point; but it gave the media a big story and brought King great support from outside the south, from whites and blacks alike. Many Birmingham residents now felt disgust and were appalled by the brutal reaction. They also felt the effects of the economic disruption caused by the demonstrations.

Attorney General Robert Kennedy sent a civil rights assistant to mediate between prominent black citizens and members of Birmingham's Senior Citizens Council. Campaign leaders were asked to cease protesting and to accept a temporary compromise while negotiations continued.

Some black negotiators were in favour, although Shuttlesworth was in hospital and not consulted. King told the mediator that he would accept the compromise and call off the demonstrations. Shuttlesworth was angered by the decision to take pressure off the white business owners and the fact that had not been consulted as the local leader. Shuttlesworth rebuked King for interfering and stated that he could not speak for the black population of Birmingham on his own. He even threatened to lead them back into the street and bring King into disrepute if he made a public announcement. King made the announcement anyway, and by 10 May negotiators had reached an agreement. Shuttlesworth and King seemed to patch up their differences, and they stood together as King read the prepared statement that detailed the compromise:

• Public restrooms and fountains were to have discriminatory signs such as 'whites only' and 'blacks only' removed.

Figure 4.9 Seventeen-year-old high school student Walter Gadsden being attacked by dogs in Birmingham, Alabama, June 1963

- The desegregation of lunch counters would go ahead.
- An ongoing programme of upgrading black employment was to be formulated, under which downtown businesses would desegregate and eliminate discriminatory hiring practices.
- A biracial committee to monitor the progress of the agreement would be formed.
- All protestors who were jailed were to be released.

It was not a total victory, since the desegregation was to be achieved in stages, and there was no mention of desegregating schools or public places. As expected, white supremacists responded to this news with violence. That night there was an explosion near the motel where King and SCLC leaders had previously stayed, and King's brother's home was bombed the following day.

President Kennedy ordered 3,000 federal troops into Birmingham and declared that he was prepared to federalise the Alabama National Guard. Most tragically of all, on 15 September, the local Ku Klux Klan bombed Birmingham's Sixteenth Street Baptist Church. Four girls were killed instantly. King delivered the eulogy at the joint funeral of three of the victims, and in his speech said that the children were martyred heroines of a holy crusade for freedom and human dignity.

But the 1963 SCLC Birmingham campaign was a major success. It had focused on one issue – the desegregation of Birmingham's downtown merchants – and not advocated a wider agenda as in Albany, that of total desegregation. The local police in Birmingham, led by Commissioner 'Bull' Connor, were a major contrast to Albany's police response, and the non-violent civil disobedience of the Birmingham activists was also notable. The massive publicity and public opinion meant that King had retained the moral high ground for the SCLC and had really judged the situation correctly. He had shown himself a leader in the front ranks who could act effectively to bring about desegregation. The mass protests in the south throughout the summer of 1963 owed much to King and Birmingham, and persuaded Kennedy to push through the bill that eventually became the 1964 Civil Rights Act.

QUESTION

What does **Source H** tell us about the impact King had on those who saw him and heard him? Does this source support the idea once expressed that being involved with King 'tended to free you'? What is meant by this phrase?

SOURCE H

King articulated, and helped to bring to articulation in others, much that was essential to the collective experiences of southern black people of whatever class or station. To be 'representative' in this way is neither to be typical nor is it to be superhuman. But King was able to capture the attention, even devotion of black southerners and then move them to a new place psychologically and politically, because what he said and the way he said it resonated so powerfully with their own experience and aspirations.

R.H. King (1992) *Civil Rights and the Idea of Freedom*, Athens, GA: University of Georgia Press, p. 88.

Washington

On 28 August 1963, more than 200,000 demonstrators participated in the March on Washington for Jobs and Freedom. The march aimed to encourage passage of a Civil Rights Bill and executive action to increase black employment. Initially, nether Roy

Wilkins of the NAACP nor President Kennedy were supportive. This alarmed King, who had staked much on the success of this march; and he feared that many blacks were becoming frustrated and embittered by the relatively slow pace of change. King hoped that the March on Washington would demonstrate multiracial support and justify the effectiveness of non-violent protest.

It succeeded tremendously and pressured Kennedy to initiate a strong federal Civil Rights Bill in Congress – although historians do vary in their interpretation over the extent to which the emotions of the day facilitated the passage of legislation, with Fairclough (1987) suggesting that its impact was minimal. But it also produced an iconic moment in civil rights history when King delivered his 'I Have a Dream' speech, widely considered to be one of the most eloquent speeches of all time, and King at his finest moment. Christian churches were prominent in this event and displayed a unity that was not always inherent in other issues. Other faiths were also very much in evidence. His 'dream' not only acknowledged Christian unity, but called for religious solidarity across the spectrum.

Further significance lies in the aptness of the date. Bayard Rustin (see section 4.1, The key groups), King's adviser, noticed that 1963 was one hundred years since the Emancipation Proclamation by President Abraham Lincoln. This had promised the abolition of slavery once the northern states had won the Civil War. The symbolism was there for all to see, especially when the rally at the end of the march was to take place at the Lincoln Memorial. It was also significant because it was a march for 'jobs and freedom', which showed a concern for black economic and social conditions, and not just a focus for segregation and racial bias.

Perhaps the march gave Kennedy extra leverage to gather cross-party support in Congress for the reforms King wanted. The bad publicity and media attention following events in Birmingham had caused the president to make civil rights an urgent issue; the March on Washington had swung the climate of opinion. After Washington, Kennedy arranged an immediate meeting for leaders from religious groups, labour unions and business groups to discuss the implications of civil rights reform. In September 1963, just after the bombing of the Baptist church in Birmingham where four black girls were killed, Kennedy got his proposed bill through its first hurdle – the Judiciary Committee.

It was then due to come before the whole of Congress for debate at the end of November: but on 22 November, Kennedy was assassinated in Dallas, Texas. It would fall to his successor, Lyndon Johnson, to pick up the negotiations with King. But Kennedy's killing had created a popular wave of sympathy, a desire to support the programme of the dead president, and to encourage the successor so tragically pitched into office. The assassination at Dallas played no small part in persuading some doubtful senators and congressmen to join those who were pledged to pass the legislation.

The March on Washington did provide the momentum SCLC strategists hoped to push through the 1964 Civil Rights Act and the 1965 Voting Rights Act. The march had succeeded beyond the organisers' hopes, and King's reputation was at its zenith. If black radicals were not totally enchanted by King and his peaceful warm-hearted biblical rhetoric then the march had definitely helped to solidify moderate Americans behind the cause.

Fact: Martin Luther King's 'I Have a Dream' speech was delivered on 28 August at the Lincoln Memorial in Washington, in front of nearly 250,000 marchers. King's 'dream' included many eloquent phrases, visions and great imagery. He mixed political text with fine biblical text and used his skills as a preacher to the full. His dream became prophetic and extensive, for example: '*On the red hills of Georgia, sons of slaves and former slave owners will be able to sit down together at the table of brotherhood. I have a dream today… my four little children will one day live in a nation where they will not be judged by the colour of their skin, but by the content of their character… I have a dream today… Every valley will be exalted and every mountain and hill laid low, the rough places made plain and the crooked place made straight… All of God's children, black men and white men, Jews and Gentiles, Catholics and Protestants, will be able to join hands. I have a dream today.*'

ACTIVITY

Look at **Source I** and the extract from King's speech in Washington. Using the library and internet, find and read the whole speech. Watch it on TV, DVD or YouTube. When you have done this, answer the following questions:

What techniques does King use in this speech to promote peace and unity?

In the aftermath of his speech, why does his vision of an integrated, peaceful community of Americans seem to be an attainable reality?

SOURCE I

King… made it clear that the movement's aim was not only to integrate blacks and whites, but also to reintegrate the South into the wider nation. 'I have a dream,' he intoned… 'that one day on the red hills of Georgia, sons of former slaves and sons of former slave-owners will be able to sit down together at the table of brotherhood. I have a dream that one day, even the state of Mississippi, a state sweltering with the heat of injustice, sweltering with the heat of oppression, will be transformed into an oasis of freedom and justice…' His stirring peroration confirmed his position as the most visible leader of the Civil Rights Movement in America.

R. Cook (1998) *Sweet Land of Liberty,* Harlow: Longman, p. 136.

Conclusions and opinions on Martin Luther King

King was often caught between militant student activism, such as the Freedom Riders, and more cautious national civil rights leaders, and his differences over SNCC tactics had emerged in Albany. At this point, his commitment and the value of his dominant role within the southern protest movement was seriously questioned. He was also censured over his apparent willingness to compromise the movement by courting unpopularity for speaking out about what he believed in. His support for other minorities, such as Mexican-Americans, irritated many in the SCLC, who felt it was a diversion from their aims and goals. There was also concern about King's anti-Vietnam pronouncements when US involvement increased after 1964. Many were worried that King would alienate President Johnson to the point where the president might 'go cool' on passing more civil rights legislation. Indeed, nearly 50 per cent of black Americans disagreed with King over this and felt that he had harmed the long-term prospects for the Civil Rights Movement.

Ella Baker commented that 'the movement made King, he didn't make the movement' – although most historians now credit King with the success of the Selma to Montgomery March in 1965 and how it led to the speedy passing of the Voting Rights Act. But King has been criticised for secretly agreeing with the federal government that the marchers would not confront the police, but turn back at the bridge (see Chapter 3, section 3.4, The Selma to Montgomery March). Manning Marable (1991) speaks of King's betrayal of his brothers, saying that he became an 'accomplice of the white power structure'. Not surprisingly, King has also been compared to Malcolm X (see section 4.1, The nature of the Civil Rights Movement). There were similarities: both were powerful speakers and gifted debaters. Both were fearless in championing black rights. Both believed that black people should be proud of their identity, should assert themselves and confront racism. However Marable believed that while King saw himself primarily as an American, albeit an African American, Malcolm X saw himself primarily as a black man. King showed that blacks were prepared to protest non-violently or even die to realise the ideals of 'life, liberty and the pursuit of happiness' in the American Declaration of Independence. Conversely, Malcolm X claimed that the oppressed had a natural right to armed self-defence.

Coretta King described her late husband as a guilt-ridden man who felt unworthy of the adoration he drew, by virtue of his many human failings. He was a renowned philanderer and had many sexual liaisons while preaching monogamy from the pulpit. He was even bugged by the FBI in the belief that he was a national security threat, not least because of his predilection for short, intense, romantic affairs with many different women. But this did not make him a bad civil rights leader. King was the most charismatic and effective leader of the Civil Rights Movement and he transcended racial and denominational barriers. It enabled him to engage in debate with the federal government to an extent hitherto unimaginable for blacks. He was also well-skilled at playing to the media and bringing regional and local conflicts into a national arena. Martin Luther King was neither a good King nor a bad King: he was a human King. All great leaders in history have had definite flaws; but their residual brilliance compensates. So did King's.

End of section activities

1   Draw a mind-map to illustrate the life and achievements of Martin Luther King. Remember to use your notes, this book and resources in the library and on the internet. Consider his strengths and his weaknesses, his triumphs and his failures.

2   Research further into the Albany Movement and Birmingham, Alabama. Imagine it is June 1963. Write a report for President Kennedy summarising Martin Luther King's role in these events, together with the position and attitude of the four main civil rights groups. Comment on the strengths and weaknesses of all parties, and recommend to Kennedy what you consider his next course of action should be. Share your findings with the class.

3   To what extent are the actions and personal qualities of Martin Luther King the main reason for the passage of civil rights legislation in 1964 and 1965? Draw up a table of arguments for and against, and then prepare to debate this in class.

4   What does the March on Washington tell us about the nature of the Civil Rights Movement at the end of 1963? Explain your answer carefully.

4.3 What influence did the mass media have on developments in the struggle for civil rights?

The Civil Rights Movement in the USA can be viewed in three distinct phases in relation to the influence of television media.

The first phase between 1954 and 1960 followed the *Brown v. Topeka* Supreme Court decision of 1954, via the Montgomery Bus Boycott and the stand-off at Little Rock, Arkansas. These key events occurred against a backdrop of battles over school desegregation and the rise of Martin Luther King and the SCLC.

Phase two was ushered in by the Greensboro sit-ins in 1960 and witnessed a change of emphasis towards mass public demonstrations pushing for integration in public facilities, including transport. These demonstrations were highlighted by the 1963 March on Washington and the signing of the Civil Rights Act of 1964, which outlawed segregation in public facilities in places such as hotels, restaurants and cinemas.

During the third phase after 1965, the Civil Rights Movement pushed for social and economic equality for African Americans, as it spread quickly from the south into other parts of the USA. The word 'black' began to replace 'negro' as the Black Power Movement came to the fore, with leaders such as Malcolm X and Stokely Carmichael challenging Martin Luther King's methodology.

Theory of knowledge

History and Communication: Martin Luther King's birthday is now a public holiday in the USA. How ought it to be commemorated? What purpose does this commemoration serve for students of history?

The media, especially television, was probably most successful and effective in covering the Civil Rights Movement during the second phase from 1960 to 1965.

In the first period, the media clearly reported on events such as Montgomery and Little Rock, but there is a perception that they just 'covered it' as part of their duty, as part of the expected coverage for the growing television network across the USA and its four time zones. There is little evidence that reporters analysed what was taking place or undertook much investigative reporting as to 'why' these stand-offs, boycotts and protests had developed.

In the third phase after 1966, coverage of civil rights issues became much more problematic for television, as many black Americans began to view the white-dominated media with increasing mistrust. The growth in black militancy, combined with an increased need for TV journalists to focus on Vietnam and the anti-war protests, meant that civil rights issues were pushed slightly backwards.

But the middle period, from 1960 to 1965, is viewed as the most crucial, where TV broadcasters and journalists were seen as supporters and allies of the Civil Rights Movement. In-depth coverage of such events as the Freedom Rides, the incidents in Birmingham, Alabama and, above all, mass coverage of the March on Washington, led one retired presenter to declare that television was virtually the chosen instrument of the Civil Rights Movement, and that the growing medium of television had an incalculable importance for King and the other civil rights activists.

Growth of television in the USA

During the mid-1950s, the struggle for civil rights escalated, just as television began to appear in most American homes. In 1950, television was accessible to relatively few people. But by the early 1960s almost 90 per cent of American homes had a set, meaning that news of events surrounding the Civil Rights Movement could be delivered faster and to a larger audience than ever before.

The use of 16mm handheld cameras and the arrival of satellite broadcasting all enabled more immediate and 'on the scene' coverage of breaking news. Consequently, civil rights marches and protests obtained far greater public exposure than previously, as seen by the national networks' unprecedented coverage of the 1963 March on Washington, which was screened all day long.

Northern viewers could now see what was happening in the south, and vice versa. TV truly became a 'window on the world', and not only did it play a major role in unifying southern blacks, but it gave a wider public, black or white, access to national newscasts that were witnessing and documenting this revolution.

Transatlantic and world news coverage developed too with the launch of the Telstar satellite. There were now fewer hiding places for the perpetrators of unjust policies, and a growing worldwide audience who were instant recipients of news coverage of their injustices.

John Lewis, a participant in the 1960 sit-ins and later a member of Congress in Georgia, stressed the importance of media coverage to the Civil Rights Movement in an interview in 1989: 'we felt that the media was necessary to help educate people, to convince people that our cause was right and just. The media became an ally' (quoted in Margaret A. Blanchard (ed.) (1998) *History of the Mass Media in the United States: An Encyclopedia*, London: Routledge, p. 374).

Figure 4.10 Veteran broadcasters Richard Dimbleby from the BBC (London) and Walter Cronkite from CBS (New York) discuss the impact of Telstar in 1962

TV was also helpful in revealing the non-violent nature of the movement in the early 1960s. When confrontations occurred between peaceful demonstrators and police or white supremacist crowds, TV news footage demonstrated that it was usually the police or onlookers who triggered the violence.

Equally, the civil rights demonstrators used the presence of TV cameras and press photographers to their advantage. An often repeated story by US TV journalists concerns a group of demonstrators praying in the streets in Alabama. They saw a TV reporter beside a camera pointing a microphone at them, trying to pick up the sound as well as the picture. So they all began to pray in louder voices. This was not an isolated event, as members of the media realised.

SOURCE J

Television newsmen, local and national, are accustomed by now to phone calls from civil rights groups with the details on when and where demonstrations are to be held. The civil rights groups quickly became sensitive to the possibilities of television… by the early 1960s… it was no longer certain whether these demonstrations were protests against injustice or extravaganzas for the mass media. A second consequence was the silent, implicit pressure by the media on various civil rights organisations to put on bigger and better shows. Whereas 100 arrests once attracted our collective attention, we began to look for 500.

Lawrence Fanning of the *Chicago Evening News*, quoted in M.A. Blanchard (ed.) (1998) *History of the Mass Media in the United States: An Encyclopedia*, London: Routledge, p. 374.

QUESTION

Are you surprised by this source? Explain your answer carefully. What does **Source J** suggest about the relationship between the press and Civil Rights Movements?

Television also afforded the civil rights groups and the captive TV audience 'visualisation' of what was happening, whereas many newspapers in the south, hostile to the Civil Rights Movement, ignored stories or relegated them to inside pages. Many newspaper editors were placed in a difficult position as well. If they were pro-civil rights, and their paper reported accordingly, the paper faced cancelled subscriptions, advertising boycotts and personal threats. This could put editors on a collision course with the paper's owner who, even if they sympathised, could not afford the economic consequences and so toned down or removed support. But the medium of television could overcome this.

QUESTION

Look at **Source K**. How does this suggest that the Civil Rights Movement had difficulties with the press that were not present with television? Now reread **Source J**. Compare and contrast both sources for evidence about the relationship between civil rights organisations and the media. How do they differ?

SOURCE K

Images of young black protesters being hit with fire hoses and police dogs in 1963 Birmingham, Alabama, are considered iconic. Hank Klibanoff saw them too. He was a fourteen-year-old paperboy when the Children's March took place. He's a Pulitzer Prize winner now. And what strikes him is where civil rights coverage wound up in the daily paper… 'My home town newspaper and all of the national media are very much focusing attention, page one attention and lead news item attention on the Children's Crusade and Commissioner Bull Connor's decision to unleash the dogs and the hoses on the administrators,' says Klibanoff. 'It makes page one news everywhere except in Birmingham.' Not only was the Children's March relegated to lesser news it was delivered without many pictures. 'You know 43 Negroes were arrested yesterday… and no images of the dogs and the hoses. I couldn't help but notice the newspaper I'm delivering didn't put that on page one.' That raises a question among critics of newspapers in the 1960s. Did the Birmingham papers not cover these events, or did they have the stories and chose not to run them?

C. Squires (2009) *African Americans and the Media,* Cambridge: Polity Press, p. 89.

Years later in Birmingham, news photographers discovered that thousands of photographs and their negatives had been put away into a filing cabinet and marked 'confidential'. So the iconic images of the movement were not published by the *Birmingham News*. This suggests strongly that if they took those photographs but deliberately did not publish them then a lot of the narrative behind these events was also ignored or neglected. But many on the paper recollected that when Martin Luther King took his movement to Birmingham in 1963, the local paper responded. Reporters were apparently given an open assignment, instructed that they needed to be on round-the-clock standby in case the paper needed them to cover a march or a rally or a bombing. The *Birmingham News* staff clearly went out to almost everything every event, but outside influences forced editors to dilute coverage.

Many believe that one of the turning points came when an NBC TV news reporter from New York broadcast his film about Birmingham and described the atmosphere: the tension he felt, the hatred, the segregation and the social problems in the city. This was also supported by a New York newspaper writer, although many people in Birmingham were shocked because that wasn't the image that they got from reading their local papers. Ultimately it was television coverage, combined with some brave reporting, that helped to precipitate change.

Southern and northern journalists who covered events in the south were often victims of violence. Richard Valeriani of NBC News was beaten with a wooden club by

Figure 4.11   The Fire Department aims high-pressure water hoses at civil rights demonstrators, Birmingham, Alabama, June 1963

white segregationists while they sprayed the NBC camera lens with black paint; yet even though reporters and cameramen placed themselves at considerable personal risk to obtain these stories, many in the Civil Rights Movement remained critical of the coverage. They faulted the media for ignoring the problems facing African Americans that led to the protests, and argued that even though they were being supported increasingly by the media, the media did not understand the roots of the problem. Such lack of understanding led to growing mistrust in the third phase of the Civil Rights Movement after 1966, when the movement itself had become more radical. When the urban riots of the mid-1960s struck, the honeymoon between the media and the black community was over. The 'good guys' taking the high moral ground against the 'bad guys' of segregation and white supremacy were easy to film, interview and sympathise with. But when attention changed towards access to housing, jobs and a demand for greater social and economic justice – in both the north and the south – the 'good guys' and the 'bad guys' became less visible. TV coverage of the race riots in Los Angeles' Watts District, followed in successive years by coverage of the same in Newark and Detroit, proved much more complex and emotive to report on, and to flash into people's sitting-rooms every night.

In conclusion, it can be affirmed that the mass media had a significant influence on developments in the struggle for civil rights. Thanks to the arrival of international satellites and the wise anticipation of the US television networks, Martin Luther King's March on Washington in August 1963 was the first event to be broadcast live to six countries around the world.

NBC broadcast special reports throughout the day, and CBS covered the whole event. More than 3,000 police or press passes were given to journalists on the scene, and one TV commentator called the march part of the 'American Revolution of 1963'. Then

Figure 4.12   An American family watching President Kennedy address the nation about civil rights in 1963

on 7 March 1965, ABC interrupted its TV premiere of the 1961 Oscar-winning film *Judgment at Nuremberg* with footage from Selma of state forces beating peaceful marchers, which made an acute impression on millions of Americans.

Squires made an interesting point, suggesting the mainstream news media looked for 'camera-ready leaders' but forgot about the less flashy contributions from people who provided the bedrock of the Civil Rights Movement. This might seem unjust to the many TV cameramen and reporters who were passionate about bringing the truth – however unpalatable – into the homes of Middle America, but it does let historians see just how ambivalent and at times confused the relationship was between the media and the Civil Rights Movement.

As television became the dominant visual medium throughout the 1960s, it increasingly vitally documented the civil rights struggle and became the lens through which millions of Americans, black or white, could witness the African American protests and actions. It was also the catalyst for awakening a nation to face the problems it had chosen to ignore.

End of section activities

1   Think of a significant event in your country's history that has been televised in recent years. It could be a music concert, the inauguration of a president, a sporting event, an important religious meeting or a major funeral. Did it have long-term impact by being shown on television? How different would it have been to listen to this event on radio or only read about it in the paper? Consider the visual impact of TV. Think now about how it impacted on the Civil Rights Movement – even in the days of black-and-white TV – and to what extent the campaigners used the media. How far did the media use the civil rights groups?

End of chapter activities

Summary

You should now understand the role and significance of key groups and people in the struggle for civil rights in America from 1956 to 1965. You have studied the involvement of the NAACP, CORE, the SCLC and the SNCC and considered the relationship between these groups; where they worked together and where they were at odds.

The role of churches has been considered and you have seen the crucial connection between the indigenous black churches and the Civil Rights Movement. The role and significance of Martin Luther King has also been evaluated, as has historiography relating to his effectiveness, his leadership role and his personal characteristics. Finally, you have observed how the developing role of television benefitted the Civil Rights Movement as TV rose to dominate the media by the mid-1960s, as well as how the medium of television later fell afoul of the civil rights groups.

Summary activity

Copy the diagram below then, using the information in this chapter and from any other available sources, make brief notes under the headings shown. Remember to include information on historical debate/interpretations – including names of historians – where appropriate.

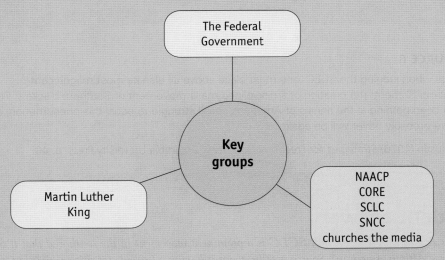

113

4

Paper 1 exam practice

Question

Compare and contrast the views expressed in **Sources A** and **B** about the significance of the SCLC in the Civil Rights Movement. **[6 marks]**

Skill

Cross-referencing.

SOURCE A

NAACP was a national organisation, but SCLC concentrated on the South, which had very specific problems that needed addressing… poor organisation and the lack of salaried staff and of mass support hampered SCLC's 'Crusade for Citizenship', which aimed to encourage Southern blacks to vote… in 1959 King admitted that the SCLC had achieved little in its first 36 months. He therefore gave up his Montgomery ministry and moved to Atlanta to concentrate on SCLC.

V. Sanders (2006) *Race Relations In the USA 1863–1980,* London: Hodder Murray.

SOURCE B

Thus when judging the SCLC, one must place above all else its most magnificent accomplishment: the creation of a disciplined mass movement of Southern blacks… There has been nothing in the annals of American social struggle to equal this phenomenon, and there probably never will be again.

B. Rustin (1976) *Strategies for Freedom,* New York: Columbia University Press, p. 40.

Student answer

Sources A and B both agree that SCLC is a prominent movement in the south and that it tried to encourage African Americans. Source A talks about it having a 'crusade for citizenship', but achieved little in its first three years. Source B says that SCLC created a 'disciplined mass movement of southern blacks'. So this is a difference between the sources.

Examiner's comments

The answer mainly paraphrases both sources, although there is a basic identification of similarity and difference between them. But there is little attempt to develop this comparison and contrast, and is no real attempt to link the sources. The student has thus only done enough to get into Band 3, and so be awarded three marks.

Activity

Look again at the two sources, the simplified mark scheme in Chapter 8 and the student answer above. Now try to rewrite the answer, linking the two sources by developing further the similarities and differences between them, and commenting on the sources without simply paraphrasing them.

Paper 2 practice questions

1 Compare and contrast the success of television and the press in drawing the attention of ordinary Americans to the civil rights campaigns between 1955 and 1965.

2 Discuss the contribution to African American civil rights in the 1960s by the SCLC and the SNCC.

3 'The ordinary people who made up the Civil Rights Movement in their thousands were more significant in improving the rights of African Americans than Martin Luther King or the US government.' To what extent do you agree with this statement?

4 Examine the importance of churches in the campaign for civil rights in the decade after 1955.

5 Evaluate the role of Martin Luther King in the campaign for civil rights between 1954 and 1965.

TIMELINE

1910 May: Formation of the Union of South Africa.

1948 May: National Party wins election and introduces apartheid.

1949 July: Prohibition of Mixed Marriages Act.

1950 May: Immorality Act.

June: Suppression of Communism Act.

July: Population Registration Act; Group Areas Act.

1951 July: Bantu Authorities Act.

1952 June: Native Laws Amendment Act.

July: Abolition of Passes Act.

1953 Mar: Public Safety Act; Criminal Law Amendment Act.

April: Bantu Education Act.

Oct: Separate Amenities Act; Native Labour (Settlement of Disputes) Act.

1954 Aug: Natives Resettlement Act.

1956 May: Separate Representation of Voters Act.

1959 June: Promotion of Bantu Self-government Act; Separate Universities Act.

KEY QUESTIONS

- What were the origins of racial discrimination in South Africa?
- How was the population divided and segregated?
- Why and how was communism suppressed?

South Africa was another country in which there was a struggle for human rights and political freedom in the mid-20th century. Like the United States after the Second World War, there were also policies of discrimination and segregation in South Africa. But unlike the United States, where civil rights campaigners succeeded in getting legal recognition of the equality of all Americans, in South Africa the opposite happened. In spite of sustained protests, discrimination based on race intensified. This was due to the victory of the National Party in the 1948 election and the introduction of the policy of apartheid. This was a strictly enforced system of racial segregation that lasted until 1994. Although there was discrimination based on race in other parts of the world, apartheid South Africa was unique in that nowhere else did a minority of the population discriminate against the indigenous majority in such a systematic way and with such ruthless determination. For more than forty years, it used repressive methods to enforce policies based on racial discrimination. This chapter explains the nature and characteristics of discrimination in South Africa after the National Party came to power in 1948 and implemented the policy of apartheid.

Overview

- Discrimination based on race was rooted in the early days of colonialism in South Africa. The mineral discoveries (diamonds and gold) of the late 19th century laid the foundations of a formal system of segregation.

- When the Union of South Africa was formed in 1910, white people had political and economic control. Between 1910 and 1948 they set up a system of segregation that discriminated against the 80 per cent of the population who were not white.

- Segregation laws affected all aspects of people's lives, especially those of 'Africans'; pass laws controlled their movement; a colour bar denied them access to skilled work; they had to live in townships on the outskirts of town; and they could own land only in the 'native reserves'.

- During the Second World War (1939–45) segregation began to break down and black workers began to demand more rights; opposition groups voiced their criticisms of segregation more openly.

- But the white electorate feared the increasing worker militancy and more outspoken protests; they blamed the government for not upholding white interests; they turned instead to the National Party.

- The National Party won the 1948 election with a promise of introducing a policy of strict separation of the races, under white domination, called apartheid.

- The new government banned mixed marriages and sexual relations between people of different races and classified the whole population into four racial groups (white, coloured, Indian and African); the effects of all subsequent apartheid laws were determined by this classification.

- Apartheid laws demarcated separate living areas for each race group; strengthened the system of control over the movement of Africans; set up separate – but not equal – facilities and services for 'whites' and 'non-whites', and created separate state-controlled schooling systems and universities.

- 'Influx control' laws prevented the free movement of Africans between rural and urban areas; the limited numbers allowed into urban areas had to live in outlying townships that lacked services and amenities.

- Whole communities were destroyed and torn apart when thousands of people were forced to move from mixed race areas (such as Sophiatown in Johannesburg and District Six in Cape Town) when they were declared to be white areas.

- Under the policy of 'separate development', the reserves were turned into 'homelands' – one for each 'national group' – which theoretically were to become self-governing states; the homelands were geographically fragmented, lacked infrastructure and were never economically viable.

- Three and a half million people were forcibly removed to the homelands where unemployment, poverty and malnutrition caused high death rates, especially among children.

- The right of 'coloured' males to vote, a remnant of the 1910 Union constitution, was removed, ensuring that whites had total political control.

- The government outlawed communism, and used the Suppression of Communism Act to crush opposition, workers' movements and criticism; it strengthened its own position by 'banning' political opponents and giving itself extra powers to suppress resistance.

Figure 5.1 These signs show the reality of everyday life under apartheid in South Africa. These two men enter a railway station under a sign that divides the staircase into two sections – one for whites only and one for non-whites. Photograph by Ernest Cole

5.1 What were the origins of racial discrimination in South Africa?

segregation: a system of laws to separate people, based on race.

migrant labour: workers from rural areas who signed contracts to work on the mines for a fixed period and then returned home again; they had to live in 'compounds' that provided basic accommodation and strict controls over labour.

Afrikaners: South Africans of Dutch and French Huguenot descent who speak Afrikaans.

Discrimination based on race did not start with apartheid in 1948. It had been present right from the early days of colonialism, when parts of Southern Africa were colonised, first by the Dutch and then by the British. The discovery of diamonds (in 1867) and then gold (in 1886) had a profound effect on the economy. It led to an industrial revolution and the potential for rapid economic growth. But it also laid the foundations for a formal system of **segregation,** by introducing strict systems of control over black mineworkers. Under the system of **migrant labour,** black workers from rural areas did the manual labour on the mines for low wages, living in strictly controlled 'compounds'. Their movement to the mines was controlled by a system of 'passes'. This system formed the basis for much of the segregation and apartheid legislation during the 20th century.

South Africa as a country was established in 1910, when four British colonies united to form the Union of South Africa. It was part of the British Empire but had the right to make its own laws. Right from the start, white South Africans (who at that stage made up about 20 per cent of the population) controlled the government and

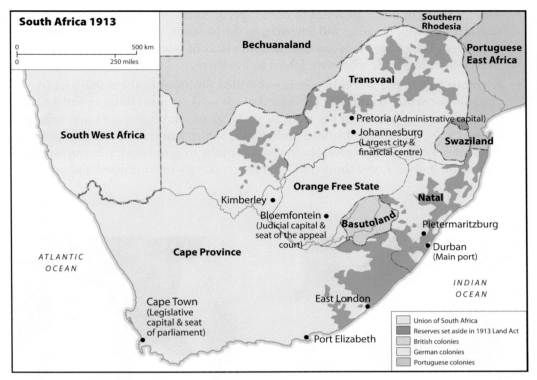

Figure 5.2 A map of South Africa in 1913

Theory of knowledge

History and language: In what ways can terminology be an extremely sensitive issue in history? Most people today would avoid using a term like 'coloured'. However, it is impossible to understand South African history without referring to race. In this chapter, we use the terms 'black', 'white', 'coloured' and 'Indian', which were the main racial divisions used by the apartheid system. The term 'black' had two uses: it was used to refer specifically to 'Africans', but was also used collectively for anyone who was not white. 'Coloured' was the official term used to label people of mixed descent. They formed about 9 per cent of the population. 'Indians' were the descendants of labourers brought from India in the 19th century to work on sugar plantations. In 1960, they formed about 3 per cent of the population.

the economy. Most of them were immigrants from Britain or descendants of Dutch settlers (called **Afrikaners**) who had colonised the Cape in the 17th century. In three of the four provinces of the Union of South Africa, only white males had the right to vote. Only the Cape had a 'non-racial' franchise, which allowed some 'coloured' and African males to vote. This right was supposedly protected by a special clause in the constitution.

Between 1910 and 1948 a succession of governments introduced segregation laws that protected the privileged position of the white minority and discriminated against anyone who was not white. The people who were most negatively affected by these segregation laws were 'Africans' who made up about two-thirds of the total population. The lives of the 'coloured' and 'Indian' minorities were also affected, but not to the same extent.

The effects of segregation on people's lives

Segregation laws affected all aspects of people's lives, especially those of Africans:

- The **pass laws** controlled where they could live and work. The aim behind the pass laws was to limit and control the movement of people from rural areas to the towns and cities. Every African male had to carry a 'pass' (or reference book) that stated where he lived and where he worked. Any changes had to be officially recorded. A pass had to be carried at all times, and those caught without one could be arrested and jailed.

Fact: When the Cape Colony was granted representative government by Britain in 1954, the vote was given to all males who qualified, regardless of race. The Cape refused to join the Union unless its non-racial franchise was retained. In the other three provinces blacks had no voting rights. In the British colony of Natal theoretically all males had been able to qualify for the vote but the criteria were so stringent that in reality fewer than ten Africans qualified. The constitutions of the former Boer Republics of the Transvaal and Orange Free State (which had been established by Afrikaners who moved into the interior after Britain took over the Cape) stated quite bluntly that only whites had political rights.

Fact: Before the Second World War, racism and segregation were not unique to South Africa. In the European colonies in Africa and Asia, people had no political rights, such as the vote, except in very limited circumstances. Economic and social discrimination favoured white settlers above local people for jobs, education and housing. There was also widespread prejudice and discrimination against black people in many European countries, including Britain.

pass laws: these laws controlled the movement of Africans from the reserves to the cities; failure to carry a pass could mean imprisonment. Passes had been used as a form of control over slaves in the early Cape Colony; they were first used systematically on a large scale at the Kimberley diamond mines.

colour bar: segregation in the workplace; the reservation of certain categories of work for white workers.

- Africans living in urban areas had to live in special 'locations' or townships on the outskirts of towns. Housing and amenities in the locations were inferior to those in other areas. They were often situated far from places of work, causing great expense and hardship to people who were forced to live there.

- A '**colour bar**' in the workplace reserved skilled positions in the mines and in factories for white workers. It prevented black workers from training for skilled positions, and denied them the right to strike or to join registered trade unions. In the 1920s, the 'civilised labour' policy gave white workers a protected place in the economy. They were given preference for jobs in government departments, such as the railways, and thousands of black workers were dismissed and replaced by whites.

Figure 5.3 A policeman checking a pass book

- The 1913 Land Act set aside certain areas as '**reserves**', which were the only places where Africans could own land. They covered only 7 per cent of the country. The Land Act caused great hardship to many thousands of people who were forced off their land. It destroyed the independence of black peasant farmers and forced them onto the cheap labour market, as workers on white-owned farms or in the mines. The Land Act was extended in 1936, and many more people were forced off the land and removed to the overcrowded reserves. Separate tribal councils were set up to administer the reserves. Traditional chiefs were given limited powers, and a separate system of 'native law' was applied, ensuring that Africans had segregated legal and administrative systems.

- In the constitution of the Union of South Africa, only whites had the right to vote (except in the Cape Province, where men of other races could qualify to vote) and only whites were allowed in parliament or government. In 1936, Africans in the Cape lost the right to vote. After that they were represented in parliament by elected white representatives. The government set up a Natives' Representative Council (NRC) to represent Africans, but it had limited advisory powers only. This meant that from then on all Africans lost the opportunity to gain political rights.

The impact of the Second World War

When the Second World War broke out in September 1939, the ruling United Party government was divided over the issue of whether to join in the war. About half of the cabinet wanted to remain neutral, while the rest favoured supporting Britain by declaring war on Germany. The issue caused a split in the governing United Party. With the support of a narrow majority in parliament, **Jan Smuts** formed a wartime **coalition** government that declared war on Germany. It was supported by most English-speaking voters, as well as many moderate Afrikaners. Many radical Afrikaners, who bitterly opposed South Africa's participation in the war on the British side, regarded Smuts as a traitor and tried to sabotage the war effort.

During the war, segregation began to break down. As industry grew rapidly to meet the wartime demand for weapons, vehicles and uniforms, there was a shortage of labour to fill positions in the factories. So the colour bar was relaxed and black workers took up skilled positions in the workplace. The pass laws too were temporarily relaxed and large numbers of people moved from the reserves to the towns, where there was an acute shortage of housing. Many of them built **informal settlements**, especially around Johannesburg. It seemed as though segregation was no longer working, and many people hoped that positive changes were imminent. Even members of the government hinted at the need for change after the war.

The stronger position of black labour resulted in increasing demands and strikes by black workers after the war. The biggest of these was the 1946 Mineworkers' Strike, involving 75,000 workers on the gold mines of the Witwatersrand. They were demanding the official recognition of their union and their right to strike, a minimum wage, safer working conditions and improved living conditions. The government took forceful action to crush the strike, and 12 miners were killed and over 1,000 injured before it

reserves: the only areas where Africans could own land. By the 1950s the reserves formed 13 per cent of the land and became the basis of the homeland system under apartheid.

Figure 5.4   Jan Smuts (1870–1950)

A former Boer general, he served as prime minister from 1939 until 1948. He was highly regarded in Allied circles and was made a field marshal of the British Empire, but many Afrikaners regarded him as being too pro-British and he was defeated by the National Party in the 1948 election.

coalition: a government formed by two or more political parties.

informal settlements: also called squatter camps – are places on the outskirts of towns and cities where people build their own houses; they are a common feature of developing countries at times of rapid urbanisation.

Figure 5.5 During the Second World War, segregation began to break down as black workers filled skilled positions in factories

Fact: The Indian nationalist movement fought a non-violent struggle for independence from British rule. It used methods of civil disobedience (or passive resistance) devised by Mahatma Gandhi. Gandhi had first developed this policy during a twenty-one-year stay in South Africa (1893–1914) where he organised protests about discrimination against Indians.

was over. But the size of the strike and the temporary closure of the mines alarmed the mining companies and also white voters.

After the war, the Indian community launched a passive resistance campaign in protest against a new law preventing Indians from living and trading freely except in certain restricted areas. They were inspired by the success of the nationalist movement in India. The campaign brought Africans and Indians together in a more broadly based opposition movement.

The demands of the extra-parliamentary opposition, the breakdown of segregation laws, the growth of informal settlements and the actions of black workers worried white voters. They criticised the government too for postwar economic problems such as food and housing shortages. Many white ex-soldiers were angry too when they returned from the war to find that their jobs had been taken by black workers, and they blamed the government for neglecting their interests.

The 1948 election

After the war, as more white voters lost confidence in the United Party government, they began to think that a change of government was necessary to protect their interests. They turned increasingly to the National Party, which promised to do so with a policy of 'apartheid'. Apartheid meant the complete separation of all races in South Africa, under white domination.

The ideology of apartheid had been developed by Afrikaner intellectuals during the 1930s. It became the core of the National Party's appeal to the predominantly white electorate in its campaign for the 1948 election. It shamelessly played on white fears of being outnumbered by a militant black majority. Not for the first time in South African politics, it referred repeatedly to the 'Black Peril' (in Afrikaans the *Swart Gevaar*) in its election campaign. It presented apartheid as the solution to this perceived threat.

In the general election of 1948, the National Party won a majority of seats, although they received only 37 per cent of the total vote. This was because they had strong support in the rural, mainly Afrikaner areas, where fewer votes were needed to win a parliamentary seat. The National Party remained in power for the next 46 years and based its rule on the policy of apartheid.

Fact: Louis Botha (1910–19), Jan Smuts (1919–24 and 1939–48) and J.B.M. Hertzog (1924–39) were the first three prime ministers of the Union of South Africa. All three were Boer generals who had fought against the British in the South African War (1899–1902). This was the war between Britain and the Boer Republics for control of the gold mines. D.F. Malan was the leader of the National Party that came to power in 1948.

SOURCE A

The general election of 1948, which excluded as voters all South Africans of African or Indian origin, was won by the National Party (NP). It was supported primarily by white Afrikaans-speaking descendants of those defeated by the British in the bitter war of 1899–1902, and campaigned on a new concept of 'apartheid' or 'separateness'. For some, looking at the racism, segregation and control of black labour embedded in the South African political economy, apartheid was nothing new, simply a continuation – with one more turn of the capitalist screw, perhaps – with policies that had been relentlessly pursued by white colonists ever since they had landed on the shores of Table Bay three centuries previously. But for others the election results of 1948 were a disaster – a moment when white South Africa turned its back on the new world opening up after the Second World War to pursue instead a naked, legalised racism that drew its ideals from the Nazis. With hindsight, it is possible to see that both views contained elements of truth.

F. Wilson (2009) *Dinosaurs, Diamonds and Democracy: A Short, Short History of South Africa*, Cape Town: Umuzi, p. 81.

KEY CONCEPTS ACTIVITY

Change and Continuity: Compare and contrast the views expressed in **Sources A** and **B** about whether the result of the 1948 election represented change or continuity.

SOURCE B

The 1948 election has often been viewed as a watershed in South African history. It was certainly significant in as far as it brought about a change of government. Beyond that, its importance can easily be exaggerated. It has often been labelled as the apartheid election. Yet despite the National Party's black peril tactics, it did not have a fully formulated blueprint apartheid policy ready to implement. Much of it was ad hoc and had to be negotiated in the face of competing Afrikaner and other interests. It also has to be seen in the light of what went before. Apartheid was not so much a change in policy as a change in emphasis.

Certainly, for the majority of the voteless South Africans at the time, the election was not seen as particularly crucial. Admittedly, some feared an intensification of discriminatory measures, but they also realised that the issue was more deep-seated and wide-ranging than any white election could reveal.

A. Grundlingh (2004) 'Afrikaner Nationalism in the 1930s and 1940s' in B. Nasson (ed.), *Turning Points in History Book 4: Industrialisation, Rural Change and Nationalism*, Johannesburg: STE Publishers, p. 60.

ACTIVITY

Source C offers a different perspective about the significance of the election result. Explain what it is and suggest why this writer would have a different view of this event.

SOURCE C

Albert Luthuli was the president of the African National Congress during the 1950s.

For most of us Africans, bandied about on the field while the game was in progress and then kicked to one side when the game was won, the election seemed largely irrelevant. We had endured Botha, Hertzog and Smuts. It did not seem of much importance whether the whites gave us more Smuts or switched to Malan. Our lot had grown steadily harder.

A. Luthuli (1962) *Let My People Go,* London: Collins, p. 97.

End of section activities

1 Draw up a table to summarise the impact of early segregation laws on the lives of black South Africans. Be sure to include the following aspects: pass laws; townships; colour bar; reserves; voting rights.

2 Explain how the consequences of the Second World War contributed to the victory of the National Party in the 1948 election.

3 Do some research on the ideology of the National Party's policy of apartheid and explain whether it 'drew its ideals from the Nazis' as **Source A** suggests.

5.2 How was the population divided and segregated?

After winning the election, the new government put the policy of apartheid into practice. Its supporters believed that each race had its own distinct identity, which would be destroyed in an integrated society, and therefore, they believed, the population should be strictly divided along racial lines. Most of the legislative framework of apartheid was in place within five years. Apartheid was a much stricter system of discrimination than the segregation laws that already existed, and it was applied far more harshly. It affected every aspect of people's lives.

Supporters of apartheid believed that social contact and, more especially, sexual contact between the races should be prevented. Accordingly, two of the first apartheid laws were the Prohibition of Mixed Marriages Act (1949) and the Immorality Act (1950), which made marriages and sexual relations between whites and people of other races illegal. The police went to extraordinary lengths to convict people under the Immorality Act, using binoculars, tape recorders and cameras to obtain evidence, and even bursting into bedrooms to do so. By the time the Act was repealed in 1985, more than 11,000 people had been convicted of offences under the Immorality Act.

But for the government to implement these laws comprehensively, the whole population had to be classified into specific race groups.

Figure 5.6 This cartoon by David Marais, published in the *Cape Times* on 24 November 1959, makes fun of the Population Registration Act and the Separate Amenities Act. ['Net vir blankes' means 'Whites only']. The caption reads: 'When I ask you to produce proof, I mean your identity card.'

The Population Registration Act (1950)

The Population Registration Act (1950) classified all South Africans into race groups – white, coloured, Indian and African. Some groups were further subdivided – into, for example, 'Zulu' or 'Xhosa', 'Malay' or 'Griqua'. Everyone had to have identity cards that stated their racial classification. A Race Classification Board was set up to review cases where the race classification was unclear or where it was challenged.

The racial classification on an identity card determined what opportunities people had in life. It determined where they could live and what sort of work they could do, as well as which schools or hospitals they could attend. This classification into racial categories affected many aspects of people's private lives and caused misery for families and relationships, especially in the Cape, where mixed marriages were more common than in other parts of the country. Some mixed families were torn apart when members of the same family were classified in different race groups.

The segregation of the population

The apartheid laws aimed to enforce the total separation of blacks and whites – politically, socially and culturally. The Group Areas Act (1950) demarcated separate residential areas for each race group. This meant that if an area was set aside for one race

> **QUESTION**
>
> Why was the Population Registration Act fundamental to applying all other apartheid laws?

Figure 5.7   Police lorries line up to move the possessions of residents who have been forced out of Sophiatown

group, all others living there would have to move out. Sometimes whole communities were destroyed when they were forced to move from places where they had lived for generations. Two of the best known examples of this are Sophiatown in Johannesburg and District Six in Cape Town, from where black and coloured families were forced to move when these suburbs became white 'group areas'. (You will read more about these later in this chapter.)

Fact: Historians Hermann Giliomee and Bernard Mbenga note that the average number of pass law offences in the early 1950s was 318,700 cases per year. This figure rose to over half a million per year in the early 1970s (Giliomee and Mbenga (2007) *New History of South Africa*, Cape Town: Tafelberg, p. 321). The pass laws were finally abolished in 1985.

The Abolition of Passes Act (1952), despite its contradictory name, strengthened the pass system by consolidating all existing forms of passes and permits into a single pass or reference book. The underlying aim of the pass system was to control the movement of Africans from the reserves to other parts of the country. All African men had to have a 'pass' that recorded their name, address and the name of their employer. Any changes had to be recorded by officials of the Native Affairs Department. These passes had to be carried with them at all times, and they could be arrested and imprisoned if they were caught without a pass by the police. In the Transvaal, prison farms were established and men convicted under this act were forced to work on these farms. The system of passes was extended to African women in 1957.

Regular police raids resulted in the arrest and conviction of millions under the pass laws. The law courts and prisons were congested as a result, and the pass laws made criminals of large numbers of people, whose sole offence was to be unable to produce a pass book on request.

SOURCE D

This is an extract from Blame Me on History *by Bloke Modisane. He was a journalist, actor and writer who grew up in Sophiatown and went into exile in 1959. This autobiography was published in 1963. It is partly an account of the destruction of Sophiatown and also an examination of the effects of apartheid on the self-esteem of educated black people. The book was banned in South Africa.*

This is the essence of the Pass Law.

I cannot sell my labour to the highest bidder.

I cannot live in the residential area of my choice; I am committed by the colour of my skin to live in segregated ghettos or locations or slums.

Freedom of movement is restricted by the reference book [pass].

The right to live in peace in my house is subject to the pleasure of any superintendent or Native Commissioner who is empowered to endorse me out of the municipal area if, in his opinion, my presence is a danger to public peace and good order.

That is the law.

Quoted in *Understanding Apartheid*, 2006, published by the Apartheid Museum and Oxford University Press, p. 26.

ACTIVITY

Source D is written in an unemotional and factual way, and yet it conveys anger and frustration. How does the writer achieve this?

How reliable is this as a source about the effects of the apartheid laws?

Segregation of amenities

Apartheid was extended to every aspect of daily life by the Separate Amenities Act (1953). Facilities and services were allocated for 'whites' or 'non-whites'. There were separate buses, trains and taxis, separate entrances to government buildings, separate counters in post offices, separate parks, toilets, benches and beaches. Hotels, cinemas, theatres and restaurants could serve one 'race group' only. There were signs everywhere to remind people that virtually everything in South Africa was divided by race. Sporting activities were strictly segregated: no interracial competitions were allowed, no multiracial teams could represent South Africa, and no multiracial teams from other countries were welcome.

Segregation of education

The Bantu Education Act (1953) specified a separate curriculum for African children. It was designed to prepare them to be manual labourers. The curriculum was limited and strictly controlled by the government. Mission and church schools that refused to teach the Bantu Education curriculum were forced to close down. This meant that many independent institutions that until then had offered the opportunity of a wide-ranging and sound education to future leaders such as Nelson

Figure 5.8 A crowded classroom in a Bantu Education school

Mandela were forced to stop teaching. Historian Nigel Worden, in *The Making of Modern South Africa*, notes that these schools had 'previously led the field in African education and were viewed as breeding grounds for African independent thinking and protest' (2000, p. 106).

The system of Bantu Education led to a drastic decline in the quality of education available to African children. Far less money and fewer resources were set aside for their education than for the education of other 'race groups'. The result of this was that the schools were understaffed and overcrowded, and had few resources, such as libraries, science laboratories or sports fields. Black children were barred from attending any other schools – government or private – that were set aside for other 'race groups'.

The Separate Universities Act (1959) forced students to study at separate universities. The 'open' universities, such as Cape Town (UCT), Natal, and the Witwatersrand (Wits), were forced to accept white students only (with very few exceptions, where special permits were issued). Separate universities were established for other 'race groups' – for example, the University of the Western Cape (UWC) for coloured students, Durban-Westville for Indian students, the University of the North for Sotho students, the University of Zululand for Zulu students and the University of **Fort Hare** for Xhosa students.

Townships and forced removals

Under apartheid, a number of laws were introduced to prevent Africans who lived in the reserves from becoming permanent residents in urban areas. The most notorious of these was Section 10 of the Native Laws Amendment Act (1952). This prevented Africans from staying in an urban area for more than seventy-two hours unless they had been born there, or had worked continuously for one employer for ten years or more, or had proof of having lived there continuously for more than 15 years. People who did not fall into these categories had to register as jobseekers at a government labour bureau. If no jobs

Fort Hare: was established by missionaries in 1916 and developed into what was regarded as the best institution of higher education for black students in southern and eastern Africa. Until 1959, when the apartheid government forced it to become a college for Xhosa-speaking students only, it had welcomed students of different race and language groups. Many prominent South Africans studied at Fort Hare, including Nelson Mandela, Oliver Tambo, and Robert Sobukwe, as well as future leaders of other African countries, such as Julius Nyerere (Tanzania), Kenneth Kaunda (Zambia) and Robert Mugabe (Zimbabwe).

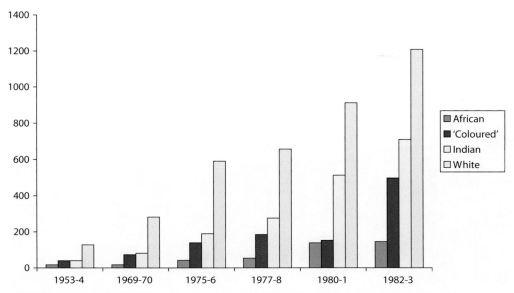

Figure 5.9 This graph shows how much money (in Rands) the government spent on the education of each child according to their racial classification under the system of apartheid)

were available, they would be 'endorsed out' and sent to the reserves. This practice was referred to by the government as 'influx control'.

The influx control laws were only partially successful in preventing the movement of people to the towns. They required a massive bureaucratic system and police effort to enforce them. Although regular police raids resulted in the arrest and conviction of millions of people, many more risked arrest and came to the towns illegally, rather than starve in the homelands.

The authorities built more townships on the outskirts of towns and cities to house the limited numbers of Africans who were legally entitled to live there. Many of these townships were situated a considerable distance from places of work, forcing township residents to spend long hours and inadequate incomes on transport costs. Most houses were small, uniform and lacked basic facilities, such as electricity or running water. Many workers were housed in hostels for single men. The townships lacked infrastructure and adequate public transport, or services and amenities such as tarred roads, sanitation and refuse removal, or shops and banks.

Under apartheid laws such as the Group Areas Act, as well as the Natives Resettlement Act (1954), people were forced to leave mixed areas, where they had owned land and houses, and move to the townships. The most well-publicised forced removals of the 1950s occurred in Sophiatown, a multiracial suburb near central Johannesburg, which was one of the few urban areas where Africans had been allowed to own land. In 1955, despite a vigorous protest campaign and worldwide publicity, the government sent in heavily armed police to force residents out of their homes and load their belongings onto government trucks. The 60,000 residents were taken to Meadowlands, now part of Soweto (an acronym for South Western Township). Sophiatown was destroyed by bulldozers, and a new white suburb named Triomf (Triumph) was built in its place.

QUESTIONS

In what ways was apartheid a more extreme system of discrimination than the segregation laws had been?

In what ways would apartheid have had an impact on every aspect of people's lives?

Figure 5.10 The new township of Meadowlands where the residents of Sophiatown were forced to move after the destruction of their homes close to central Johannesburg

The government also destroyed other black suburbs that it felt were too close to city centres. Cato Manor (Mkhumbane), near Durban, was an informal settlement of about 50,000 households. Living conditions there were poor, but it was conveniently close to job opportunities in Durban. In 1957, the government began moving the people of Cato Manor to a new township called KwaMashu, 25km from the centre of Durban.

The 'coloured' community of Cape Town was forced to leave the centrally situated suburb of District Six to move to new townships on the Cape Flats outside Cape Town, where violence and crime had devastating effects. District Six was destroyed by bulldozers. Many other parts of Cape Town were similarly affected by the Group Areas Act. Families that had lived for generations in places like Mowbray, Newlands, Claremont and Simon's Town were also forced to move, and all that remained of once vibrant communities were their mosques and churches. In Port Elizabeth, the mixed-race suburb of South End was demolished to make way for white housing and other developments, and thousands of people were forced to move to new townships.

When the National Party came to power in 1948, it continued the policy of previous governments by trying to encourage South African Indians to move to India. The policy was not successful, however, and the government abandoned it in 1961. Instead, the government established a Department of Indian Affairs and, later, the South African Indian Council, to accommodate Indians within the framework of separate development. Although partially elected, this council was a purely advisory body that had no effective

Fact: It has been estimated that nearly 600,000 coloured, Indian and Chinese people, and a further 40,000 white people, were moved in terms of the Group Areas Act. The historians Giliomee and Mbenga (2007, p. 318) note that one out of every four coloured people, and one out of every six Indian people, were forced to move (as opposed to only one out of every 666 whites).

Figure 5.11 District Six after 66 000 people were forced to move to make way for a white group area. Virtually all that remained were the churches and mosques

Fact: The apartheid laws that enforced the strict segregation of all aspects of daily life, and which were introduced in the early 1950s, were sometimes referred to as 'petty apartheid', while the policy of separate development (the Bantustan system) was referred to as 'grand apartheid'.

Hendrik Verwoerd (1901–66)

He was born in the Netherlands and came to South Africa with his family as a child. As Minister of Native Affairs during the 1950s, he was responsible for the framing and implementation of many apartheid laws. He served as prime minister from 1958 to 1966, during which time South Africa became a republic and withdrew from the Commonwealth. A few weeks after the Sharpeville shootings in 1960 (see Chapter 6, section 6.2.8), he survived an assassination attempt by a white farmer. However, he was assassinated in 1966, when he was stabbed to death by a parliamentary messenger, who seems to have had no clear political motive.

powers, and it failed to satisfy the demands of the Indian population for proper political representation.

Most of the South African Indian population lived in Durban, and as a result of the Group Areas Act, thousands of Indians were forced to move out of the central areas to the new township of Chatsworth. In many other towns and cities, thousands of Indian-owned shops and businesses were forced to close and move out of the central business districts. This caused economic ruin for many Indians, who were often forced to sell their property and businesses cheaply.

Homelands and forced removals

A further extension of the policy of apartheid was the concept of 'separate development'. This was based on the idea that every black South African belonged to a separate 'national' group, each with its own language and traditions. Each group should have its own 'homeland' (or Bantustan), which would be politically separate from the rest of South Africa. The driving force behind the policy was **Hendrik Verwoerd**, the Minister of Native Affairs. The groundwork for the homelands policy was the Bantu Authorities Act (1951), which abolished the Natives' Representative Council and gave more power to traditional chiefs in the reserves. No provision was made for any form of political representation for Africans in urban areas.

The government appointed the Tomlinson Commission (1950–6) to investigate how the homelands could become economically self-sufficient. The commission recommended that they should be substantially enlarged and consolidated geographically, and that significant economic investment would be needed for them to become economically viable. The government ignored these recommendations and it went ahead with its homelands policy.

Verwoerd's master plan for the policy was outlined in the Promotion of Bantu Self-Government Act (1959). The reserves were to become 'self-governing' states (or 'Bantustans'), in which black people could exercise their political rights, rather than in 'white' South Africa. They would be stripped of their South African citizenship and

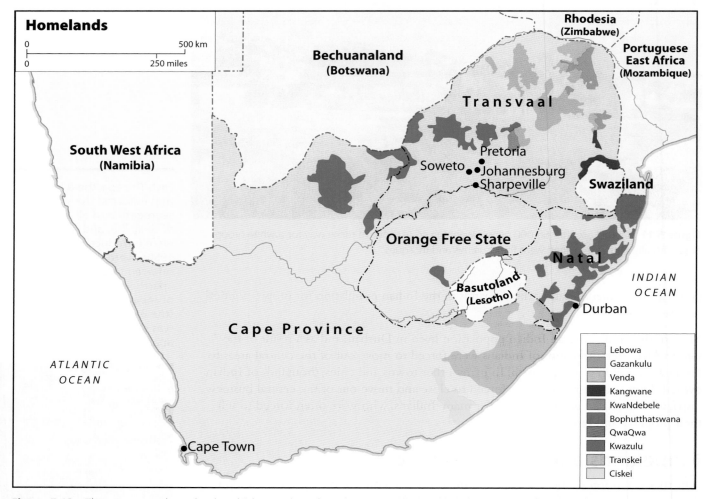

Figure 5.12 There were ten homelands, which were based on the reserves set aside in the 1913 Land Act. Four of them – Transkei, Bophuthatswana, Venda and Ciskei – subsequently opted for 'independence', which was never officially recognised by the rest of the world

forced to become citizens of one of the homelands, even if they had never lived there. The homeland authorities would control education, agriculture and roads, but crucially the South African government would control key elements such as foreign affairs, defence and internal security.

The government saw the homeland system as a means of maintaining white control by creating divisions among the black majority – the principle of 'divide and rule'. Another aim of the homeland system was to provide a cheap source of labour for the mines, industries and farms of 'white' South Africa. The homelands were geographically fragmented and lacked adequate infrastructures as well as health and education facilities. They were not economically viable and were maintained by substantial, yet inadequate, financial grants from the South African government.

Over the next three decades, about three and a half million people were forced to move to the homelands, which were overcrowded, undeveloped and desperately poor, and could not support the number of people who were forced to live there. As a result, many men were forced to become migrant workers, leaving the homelands populated mainly by women, children and the elderly or sick. Separated families, severe malnutrition and high infant mortality rates were features of life for the millions of people living there. Critics of the system referred to the homelands as 'dumping grounds'. The millions of people living there grew poorer and poorer.

Figure 5.13 The homelands lacked basic services and infrastructure and were populated mainly by women and children, while the men worked as migrant labourers in 'white' South Africa

The disenfranchisement of voters

Before the Union of South Africa was formed in 1910, the Cape was the only colony in which black people had any political rights. The Cape had refused to join the Union unless its non-racial franchise was guaranteed. This was done in what was called an 'entrenched' clause in the constitution (which could only be changed by a two-thirds majority in a joint sitting of both houses of parliament). As a result, African and coloured males in the Cape could qualify to vote. In 1936, this clause was amended and Africans lost the right to vote in general elections. But coloured voters retained their right to vote, and it was assumed that most of them voted for the United Party and against the National Party in the 1948 election.

In the early 1950s, the government was determined to remove coloured voters from the common voters' roll, partly because it wanted to strengthen its own position in the next election: coloured voters held the balance of power in several marginal constituencies. Another reason was that the concept of a common voters' roll went against the National Party's ideology of apartheid. The methods it used to disenfranchise coloured voters caused the most heated parliamentary struggle over the new apartheid policy.

The government first introduced a Separate Representation of Voters Bill in parliament in 1951. When the act was passed by a simple majority, its validity was challenged in the courts by a group of voters, supported by the United Party. The Appeal Court declared the act to be invalid (on the grounds that it had not fulfilled the requirements for the changing of an entrenched clause – namely a two-thirds majority in a joint sitting of both houses of parliament). Determined to succeed despite this setback, the government then introduced the High Court of Parliament Bill, which gave parliament the power to overrule decisions of the court. This too was declared invalid by the courts.

Theory of knowledge

History, ethics and bias:
Many people at the time felt that the National Party government had used immoral tactics by tampering with the constitution to ensure that it got what it wanted. What is the role of the historian when writing about issues such as this? Should historians make moral judgements about the past, or should they adopt a neutral stance and record what happened impartially? Is it possible to describe historical events in an unbiased way?

However, the government was still determined to continue with its quest to disenfranchise coloured voters. In 1955 it prepared the way for the reintroduction of the first bill. It increased the number of judges in the Appeal Court from five to eleven, and ensured that pro-government judges were appointed to fill the new places. In addition, the Senate Act (1955) increased the size of the Senate (the upper house of parliament) from forty-eight seats to eighty-nine, and the method by which senators were chosen was altered in such a way that the National Party controlled seventy-seven of the seats in the enlarged senate. Finally, in a joint sitting of the two houses of parliament, the Separate Representation of Voters Act (1956) was passed. An appeal against the validity of the Senate Act was rejected by the Appeal Court.

The 1956 Act removed coloured voters from the common voters' roll in the Cape and established a separate voters' roll for them. Coloured voters could now elect four white MPs to represent them in parliament. The government established a Department of Coloured Affairs and later a Coloured Persons' Representative Council. This was an advisory body that had limited legislative authority, depended on the white-controlled parliament for funding and needed the approval of the (white) minister of coloured affairs before any of its decisions could be implemented. It therefore had little support or credibility amongst the coloured community.

By these controversial means, the National Party government succeeded in its aim of separating white and coloured voters in the Cape, and ensuring that, in effect, only white voters had a say in determining the political future of South Africa.

End of section activities

1   Explain these terms in the context of the policy of apartheid: townships; influx control; forced removals; homelands; separate development.

2 Copy this table and fill in the missing information as a summary of the apartheid laws and how they affected people's lives:

Aims of the government	Laws passed	Negative effects on people's lives
To prevent interracial relationships		
To classify into race groups		
To prevent mixed-race suburbs		
To prevent movement to urban areas		
To produce manual labourers		
To prevent social, cultural and sporting contact between races		
To restrict political power to whites only		
To prevent Africans from being in an urban area for more than seventy-two hours		
To give Africans some form of substitute for political representation in the homelands		

3 Anthony Butler has written that the early apartheid legislation 'was not designed to reshape South Africa's structures of economic opportunity but was distinguished by its undisguised racial malevolence [meanness or spite]' (Butler (2009) *Contemporary South Africa*, Basingstoke: Palgrave Macmillan, p. 17). Explain what he means by this and comment on this view.

4 Write a report to explain why the homeland system was never viable, either politically or economically.

5.3 Why and how was communism suppressed?

The Communist Party of South Africa (CPSA) was formed in 1921, mainly by radical white workers and socialists from Europe, who were inspired by the success of the Bolshevik Revolution in Russia. It also attracted a large group of coloured members at its founding meeting in Cape Town. The CPSA focused on organising African workers around issues concerning worker's rights and trade unions, and by 1925 it had a predominantly black membership. It established early links with the African National Congress (ANC), but the relationship between the two groups was not always close and there were groups within the ANC leadership who were strongly opposed to communism.

As South Africa industrialised during the 1930s and 1940s, the CPSA was active in organising workers in the new factories, among them thousands of Afrikaner men

Fact: About 125,000 black South Africans volunteered for military service during the Second World War, but they were not supplied with weapons. Instead they worked as unarmed drivers, cooks, guards, orderlies and stretcher-bearers. The government thought that giving military training to blacks would undermine white domination in South Africa. About 25 per cent of the 5,500 South Africans killed during the war were black.

and women. During the Second World War, the CPSA demanded the arming of black soldiers, the recognition of black trade unions, the scrapping of the pass laws and the vote for all. But although its membership grew during the war years, the CPSA never won widespread support.

However, as a result of the CPSA's work among Afrikaner factory workers, the National Party saw communism as a threat to Afrikaner unity. Afrikaner nationalists were further angered by the CPSA's role in organising black workers and the part it played in organising the 1946 strike by black mineworkers. Above all, they rejected the CPSA's support for non-racialism and internationalism, both of which they viewed as a threat to the interests of the Afrikaner people. The National Party accused Jan Smuts and the United Party of being too tolerant of communists and used their own anti-communist stance as a means of attracting voters.

QUESTIONS

What imagery does the pamphlet use to get its message across?

How effective do you think this is as an example of political propaganda?

Historical debate:
Historians point out the link between the timing of the Suppression of Communism Act and the Cold War in Europe, suggesting that the National Party wanted to show its support for the West in the Cold War that was emerging between Western capitalism and Soviet communism at the time. Robert Ross, in *A Concise History of South Africa* (1999, p. 116) sees it as a *'reaction to international trends at the start of the Cold War'*. Irina Filatova and Apollon Davidson go further and suggest, in *The Hidden Thread: Russia and South Africa in the Soviet Era* (2013, p. 201), that the National Party's idea of a communist threat *'conveniently fell into the framework of the Cold War'* and that the *'international context gave the NP's anti-communist campaign the mantle of respectability'*.

Figure 5.14   This anti-communist pamphlet was produced by D.F. Malan, the leader of the National Party and future prime minister. The words mean: 'The Communist Threat! The National Party stands up against Communists! The South African Party defends them!' (The South African Party was a former name for the United Party.)

In 1950, the National Party government introduced the Suppression of Communism Act, which banned the Communist Party and made it an offence to promote communist ideas. The Act defined the term 'communism' so broadly that the law was used to suppress any opposition to the government's policies, even if it had nothing to do with communism.

The Act also gave the state the power to use 'restriction orders' or house arrest to silence its critics. People under restriction orders could not leave a certain district, and those under house arrest had to stay in their homes. 'Banned' people were barred from holding office in any trade union or political organisation, and they could not attend meetings. They could not be quoted in newspapers, and anything they had previously written was banned. Other people had their passports withdrawn. The law was used to restrict many political leaders and activists who opposed the government. Eleven of the twenty-seven members of the ANC executive at the time were the objects of banning orders. Among them were Albert Luthuli, the president of the ANC, Oliver Tambo (see Chapter 6, section 6.4, The banning of the ANC and PAC) and Nelson Mandela. The government used the Suppression of Communism Act to ban any newspaper, organization or meeting that 'promoted communist ideology'.

The government was also determined to close the Soviet Consulate in Pretoria. Shortly before the 1948 election, the National Party leader, D.F. Malan, had promised his supporters: 'We shall break diplomatic relations with Russia… Russia has been planning to export communism here and to incite to revolution, and the next fertile field for its activity is the non-white population' (reported in *Die Burger*, the National Party newspaper, on 16 March 1948; quoted in Filatova and Davidson, 2013, p. 194.) After the Suppression of Communism Act was passed, the government imposed restrictions on the number of staff allowed in the consulate, and kept a careful watch and record of all visitors to it. Further restrictions included a ban on the distribution of periodicals by the consulate. The government blamed it for spreading communist propaganda and inciting revolution, and suspected it of setting up links with African and Indian leaders and trade unionists, many of whom were banned. Finally, in 1956, the government forced the consulate to close down altogether.

The government targeted communists in other ways too. The historian Robert Ross, in *A Concise History of South Africa* (1999, p. 119) suggests that one reason for its determination to destroy Sophiatown was because the Communist Party had strong support there.

Steps were also taken by the government to weaken any organised labour movements. In the early 1950s African workers had used stayaways and strikes to protest against apartheid laws. The government introduced the Native Labour (Settlement of Disputes) Act (1953). This made it illegal for employers to recognise African trade unions or to negotiate with them. This meant that these unions were powerless to improve working conditions for their members. African unions were also excluded from bargaining negotiations with unions representing other race groups.

The government also introduced other new laws that gave it extra powers to enforce apartheid and weaken opposition. The Criminal Law Amendment Act (1953) provided for terms of imprisonment, fines or floggings for people who broke laws as a means of protest or in support of any campaign against the law. (This was the government's response to the Defiance Campaign, which you will read about in Chapter 6, section 6.2, The Defiance Campaign) The Public Safety Act (1953) gave the state the power to declare an emergency and use harsh measures to suppress opposition, including the use of detention without trial. The government used the police, and in some cases the army, to enforce apartheid laws. The police had considerable powers in arresting and detaining people, enforcing the

5

Apartheid in South Africa, 1948–64

Pondoland revolt: In 1960, peasant farmers in Pondoland in the Eastern Cape refused to pay taxes and murdered several chiefs who supported government policies. The revolt was crushed with great force by the police and the army.

QUESTION

In what ways was the government's declared intention of suppressing communism a convenient cover for crushing all opposition?

pass laws and implementing forced removals. The army was also used to crush widespread resistance, such as the **Pondoland revolt** in 1960, where 5,000 people were arrested.

After the Communist Party was disbanded at the time of the passing of the Suppression of Communism Act, some of the more active members formed an underground organisation, the South African Communist Party (SACP) in 1953. Others continued to be actively involved in the resistance movement that developed during the 1950s, as members of other organisations, such as the African National Congress, the South African Indian Congress, the Coloured People's Congress and the largely white Congress of Democrats. Together these organisations formed what was known as the Congress Alliance.

These two sources give different perspectives on the National Party's attitude towards communism. The first is an analysis by academic historians and the second is from an apartheid-era school history textbook.

SOURCE E

Whatever their original reaction to the Bolshevik revolution, Afrikaner nationalists had regarded socialists and communists as their worst enemy from the moment the Socialist movement had first appeared in South Africa… Marxism as an ideology, and communism as a political system, were seen as adversaries of the very existence of the Afrikaner nation. The class struggle – the basic tenet of Marxism – meant division within the Afrikaner nation, 'Die Volk', in the face of the 'black peril', the main threat to their existence. The communists' internationalism and their support for the exploited and downtrodden turned them into allies of the black population. Moreover, Afrikaner nationalist politicians thought that communist propaganda worsened race relations in the Union, inciting the black population against the whites. Worse still, communists were 'godless', a notion completely unacceptable to deeply religious Afrikaners.

I. Filatova and A. Davidson (2013) *The Hidden Thread: Russia and South Africa in the Soviet Era*, Cape Town: Jonathan Ball Publishers, pp. 200–1.

SOURCE F

After the war the national and political awareness of the Blacks was expressed in different ways. They began to voice their ideals and ambitions in no uncertain manner. They also began to pose more and more as the injured party and proudly called themselves 'Africans'. They referred to the fact that they were not given the vote in spite of being in the majority, and were ruled by a White minority who approved discriminatory laws which were to the detriment of the Blacks.

Communism made an increasingly strong impact on Blacks. Communist methods, namely incitement, strikes and riots, were also in evidence, with an eye to creating chaos if possible. The once-reasonable passive ANC changed completely…

The Government had however previously taken precautionary measures to maintain law and order. Thus the Suppression of Communism Act was steered through in 1950, and the Criminal Law Amendment Act as well as the Public Safety Act were placed on the statute book in 1953. As a counter-reaction against these laws, the Non-Whites tried to form a united front…

The Government was, however, not intimidated. The Russian Consulate in Johannesburg was closed down to put an end to the communist-inspired revolt movement.

E.H.W. Lategan and A.J. De Kock, *History in Perspective: Standard 10*, Johannesburg: Perskor, pp. 186–7; quoted in J. Pampallis (1997), *Foundations of the New South Africa*, Cape Town: Maskew Miller Longman, pp. 212–13.

End of section activities

Use **Sources E** and **F** to answer these questions:

1 Use the information in **Source E** to list the reasons why the National Party was opposed to communism.

2 In what ways does **Source F** give a different perspective of the issue?

3 Which of the two sources is a more reliable source of information? Explain your choice.

4 Why are both sources useful to historians?

5 Why might some people consider the title of the textbook *History in Perspective* to be ironic?

6 Design a spider diagram to illustrate the different laws and methods used by the National Party to enforce its policies and suppress opposition.

End of chapter activities

Summary

You need to be able to explain the context of the struggle for rights and freedoms in South Africa by clarifying the policy of apartheid and its application. You should understand the causes and consequences of the National Party victory in the 1948 election and be able to discuss whether the policy of apartheid represented change or continuity in a long tradition of discrimination and segregation. You should be able to explain how the lives of people were affected as the population was classified and segregated in every aspect of their daily lives. You also need to be able to clarify the connections between townships, homelands and forced removals.

Summary activity

Copy the diagrams below. Use the information in this chapter, and from other sources, to make brief notes under each heading.

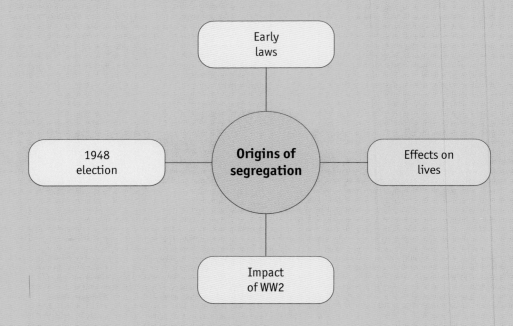

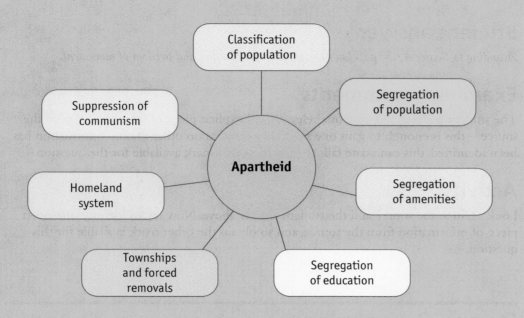

Paper 1 exam practice

Question

What message is conveyed by Bloke Modisane about the pass laws in **Source A**?

[2 marks]

Skill

Comprehension of the message of a source.

SOURCE A

This is the essence of the Pass Law.

I cannot sell my labour to the highest bidder.

I cannot live in the residential area of my choice; I am committed by the colour of my skin to live in segregated ghettos or locations or slums.

Freedom of movement is restricted by the reference book [pass].

The right to live in peace in my house is subject to the pleasure of any superintendent or Native Commissioner who is empowered to endorse me out of the municipal area if, in his opinion, my presence is a danger to public peace and good order.

That is the law.

This is an extract from an autobiography called *Blame Me on History* by Bloke Modisane, who was a journalist, actor and writer who lived in Sophiatown in the 1950s.

Student answer

According to Source A, the pass laws limited job opportunities and freedom of movement.

Examiner's comments

The student has selected only one relevant and explicit piece of information from the source – this is enough to gain one mark. However, as no other reason/information has been identified, this candidate fails to gain the other mark available for the question.

Activity

Look again at the source and the student answer above. Now try to identify one other piece of information from the source, and so obtain the other mark available for this question.

Paper 2 practice questions

1   'Apartheid was nothing new. It was based on decades of discrimination and segregation laws in South Africa.' With reference to the situation in South Africa after 1948, to what extent do you agree with this statement?

2   Examine the impact of the apartheid laws on the lives of black South Africans.

3   Evaluate the significance of the Population Registration Act as the basis of the whole system of apartheid.

4   Examine the causes and consequences of the Suppression of Communism Act.

Protest and action

6

KEY QUESTIONS

- What protests and actions against segregation happened before 1948?
- What non-violent protests against apartheid took place in the 1950s?
- How significant were international protests during this period?
- How did government repression affect the protest movements?

Figure 6.1 On 9 August 1956, 20,000 women of all races marched to Pretoria to protest against the pass laws. Here the leaders carry petitions to present to the government

TIMELINE

1912 Jan: Formation of the African National Congress (ANC).

1944 April: Formation of the Congress Youth League (CYL).

1946–8 Indian Passive Resistance Campaign.

1948 May: National Party wins election and introduces apartheid.

Dec: UN adopts Universal Declaration of Human Rights.

1949 Dec: ANC adopts CYL's Programme of Action.

1950 May: May Day Strike.

1952 June: Start of Defiance Campaign.

1955 June: Congress of the People adopts Freedom Charter.

1956 Aug: Women's March to Pretoria.

1956–61 Treason Trial.

1959 April: Formation of Pan Africanist Congress (PAC).

Dec: Formation of Anti-Apartheid Movement in Britain.

1960 Mar: Anti-pass demonstrations; Sharpeville massacre; Cape Town march; government declares state of emergency.

April: UN Security Council Resolution 134; Unlawful Organisations Act bans ANC and PAC.

1961 Mar: All-In Africa Conference in Pietermaritzburg.

June: ANC establishes Umkhonto we Sizwe (MK).

Sept: PAC forms Poqo.

Dec: MK launches sabotage campaign.

1962 Nov: UN Resolution 1761 establishes Special Committee Against Apartheid.

1963 July: Police raid MK headquarters in Rivonia.

Aug: UN Security Council Resolution recommends arms embargo.

Oct: Start of Rivonia Trial.

1964 June: Rivonia Trialists sentenced to life imprisonment.

6

Introduction

There was opposition to segregation laws right from the beginning. During the 1950s, resistance to apartheid grew in intensity, although it remained non-violent. The resistance was encouraged by worldwide opposition to racial discrimination and the growth of an international anti-apartheid movement. The government responded with repression, which drove the movement underground in the early 1960s and turned it into an armed struggle against the government. This chapter traces the development of protest against apartheid during this period.

Overview

- From its establishment in 1912, the African National Congress (ANC) supported non-violent forms of protest that tried, unsuccessfully, to bring about change.

- The Second World War brought expectations of change after the war; the Congress Youth League injected new energy into the ANC; and community protests revealed the extent of dissatisfaction with existing conditions.

- After the war, the new mood was reflected in greater worker militancy as well as non-violent resistance by the Indian community against the extension of segregation laws.

- The 1950s were a decade of determined yet non-violent protests and actions against the implementation of apartheid.

- The ANC adopted the more assertive approach advocated by the Congress Youth League, using strikes, boycotts and civil disobedience.

- The ANC and other opposition groups organised the 1952 Defiance Campaign, which increased awareness of the situation in South Africa and increased mass support for the ANC.

- Opposition groups formed the Congress Alliance to organise a national conference – the Congress of the People. It adopted the Freedom Charter, which spelled out its vision for a non-racial, democratic South Africa; 'Charterism' was adopted as official ANC policy.

- The government responded by charging the leaders of the Congress Alliance with high treason; but all were acquitted after a four-year trial.

- Women were active in protest actions, in organisations such as the Federation of South African Women (FEDSAW) and the Black Sash, and in community protests in Cato Manor; a notable event was the 1956 Women's March to Pretoria to protest against the pass laws.

- Grass-roots community resistance included protest actions against Bantu Education, forced removals and conditions in the reserves; the Torch Commando protested against plans to disenfranchise coloured voters.

- In 1959 'Africanists' within the ANC broke away to form the Pan Africanist Congress (PAC); its slogan was 'Government of Africans, by Africans, for Africans'.

- In 1960 the ANC and PAC organised peaceful anti-pass demonstrations; the police responded with violence and sixty-nine protesters were killed at Sharpeville.

- The government responded to further protests around the country, including a peaceful march into central Cape Town, with a policy of harsh repression.

- Even before Sharpeville there had been international protests against apartheid, which was at odds with the greater respect for human rights in other parts of the world after the Second World War.

- The Anti-Apartheid Movement, formed in Britain in 1959, stepped up its campaign after Sharpeville; it organised protest marches, demonstrations, petitions and boycotts, and promoted sanctions and cultural and sporting isolation to force South Africa to end apartheid.

- The United Nations passed resolutions calling on South Africa to abandon apartheid; Resolution 1761 (1962) urged diplomatic isolation and economic sanctions and set up a Special Committee Against Apartheid. But Resolution 1761 was not binding and South Africa's main trading partners ignored it, limiting its effectiveness.

- As repression in South Africa increased, the UN Security Council passed Resolution 181 (1963) calling for an arms embargo, which was supported by the USA but not Britain and France.

- The UN also called for the release of political prisoners and helped initiate an international campaign to release Nelson Mandela and others who faced the death penalty in South Africa, after their arrest in 1963.

- The effectiveness of international calls for economic sanctions was limited by the attitude of Western governments; South Africa had vital minerals and was seen as a strategically placed ally of the West in the Cold War.

- 1960 was a turning point that marked the change from non-violent to violent forms of protest; the Sharpeville massacre had shown the failure of non-violent protests in the face of violent repression.

- After the banning of the ANC and PAC, they formed underground military wings to overthrow the government; they also sent representatives abroad to set up headquarters in exile.

- Umkhonto we Sizwe (MK), the military wing of the ANC, planned a sabotage campaign and a guerrilla war; Poqo, the military wing of the PAC, planned a mass uprising; the Armed Resistance Movement (ARM) also adopted an armed struggle.

- The government uncovered Poqo's plot and arrested its leaders, effectively destroying it as an organisation.

- The leaders of MK were arrested at their secret headquarters in Rivonia and put on trial in the 'Rivonia Trial'; they faced the death penalty.

- The ANC used the trial to inform South Africa and the world why it had adopted an armed struggle, and outlined the history of oppression and non-violent resistance.

- After a sustained international campaign, the Trialists were sentenced to life imprisonment and not death.

- By the end of 1964, it seemed that all resistance had been crushed; but both inside and outside South Africa the liberation movements continued to plan to end the system of apartheid.

6.1 What protests and actions against segregation happened before 1948?

From the early years there was resistance to segregation, but for many years most of it was cautious and conservative in its approach and ineffective in its methods. This only changed after the Second World War.

Early resistance to segregation policies

One of the organisations formed to lead resistance to early segregation laws was the South African Native National Congress (SANNC, later renamed the African National Congress or ANC), established in 1912. Its main aim was to overcome the ethnic, language and regional differences between Africans so that they could present a united front against discrimination and win equal political rights. The early ANC was a moderate organisation that supported non-violent methods of protest, such as petitions or appeals to the authorities. For example, it sent a delegation to London in 1914 to appeal – unsuccessfully – to the British government to overturn the Land Act. It sent another unsuccessful delegation to the Paris Peace Conference in 1919, hoping to get support from the British government for self-determination for black people in South Africa. In the early years, the ANC did not have mass appeal. Its leaders were mainly moderates who did not want confrontation with the authorities, and most of its members were educated, middle-class, urban blacks who did not support the use of more forceful methods of resistance.

In contrast to this, an organisation called the Industrial and Commercial Workers' Union (ICU) attracted the support of the working class after its formation in 1919. It started as a trade union among dockworkers in Cape Town but became a national political organisation, with a membership of 160,000, mainly in rural areas, and branches throughout Southern Africa. During the 1920s it played a leading role in organising protests against the segregation policies of the government. However, by the end of the 1920s it had ceased to function effectively, partly because of internal tensions over policy and also as a result of strong reactions against it by police and white farmers.

The Atlantic Charter (August 1941): This was an agreement between Roosevelt and Churchill, the leaders of the US and Britain during the Second World War. It was a statement of Allied war aims and principles, and confirmed their support for the rights of all people to choose their own form of government. African nationalists welcomed this as a sign that colonialism would end after the war.

During the 1930s, the ANC worked with other organisations, such as the African People's Organisation, to protest against further segregation laws. Together they formed the All-African Convention (AAC) in 1935 to fight against proposed legislation to disenfranchise Africans in the Cape, who up until that stage still had the right to qualify for the vote. The AAC called on the British parliament to intervene on its behalf, sent a delegation to Cape Town to present a petition to the government, and organised protest meetings throughout the country. Despite its efforts, the 1936 legislation was passed: Africans in the Cape lost the right to vote and a Natives' Representative Council (NRC) was set up, with advisory powers only. After this, there was increasing disillusion with the ineffective moderate approach of the ANC and other organisations.

Resistance politics during the Second World War

In 1940, Dr Alfred Xuma became president of the ANC and injected new energy into the organisation through his strong, active style of leadership. He favoured cooperation with coloured and Indian leaders to present a united front against discrimination, and he called for the abolition of the NRC. The ANC also granted full membership rights to women for the first time, and established the ANC Women's League, with Madie Hall Xuma, Xuma's American-born wife, as its first president.

The war had a significant impact on black expectations about the future. Allied claims that the war was being fought for freedom and democracy encouraged black people to hope that the postwar world would see an end to discrimination and oppression. In 1941, they were encouraged in this view when the Allied leaders issued the **Atlantic Charter**, promising support for self-determination.

At its 1942 congress, the ANC set up a committee to study the recently published Atlantic Charter, and its implications for Africa. The result was the adoption in 1943 of a document called 'African Claims in South Africa', which called for the vote for all adults; a fair distribution of land, and the right for Africans to own land in urban areas; an end to discrimination in the workplace; and the right to a good education and adequate medical care for all.

In 1944, younger members of the ANC formed the Congress Youth League (CYL), with Anton Lembede as its first president, and Nelson Mandela, Walter Sisulu and Oliver Tambo among the founder members. Impatient with the conservative attitude and lack of success of the older generation of leaders, they wanted to turn the ANC into an active organisation that would play a more assertive role in bringing about change. Although Lembede was an '**Africanist**', not all members of the CYL shared this view.

Another feature of resistance politics during the 1940s were community protests resulting from grass-roots dissatisfaction with existing conditions. These protests were not organised by political parties but by the communities themselves. They were often triggered by economic factors, such as the high cost of living or housing shortages. Two of these community protests were the Alexandra Bus Boycotts and the Sofasonke Movement.

In a series of bus boycotts between 1940 and 1945, the residents of Alexandra township in Johannesburg refused to pay the increased fares proposed by the local bus company. Instead they walked to work, sometimes leaving home at 3am to get there on time. The government tried to stop the boycotts by arresting pass offenders among the walkers, and banning processions or meetings of more than twenty people. But the boycotts continued and were successful in keeping the bus fares down, because the government finally approved a subsidised fare system. These events demonstrated the potential power of boycotts as an economic and political weapon.

As a result of the rapid growth of the black urban population during the war, there was a severe housing shortage in Johannesburg. Towards the end of the war, thousands of homeless people, tired of waiting for the municipal authorities to act, built their own houses on open land. The largest of these informal or squatter settlements was organised by James Mpanza, the founder of what became known as the Sofasonke Movement.

Africanism: was the view that Africans should rely on their own efforts to achieve freedom and equality; it stressed the assertion of African identity and rejected the influence of 'foreign' ideologies and leaders. These ideas later formed the basis of the ideology of the Pan Africanist Congress, which was established as a breakaway group from the ANC in 1959.

Fact: Sofasonke movement 'Sofasonke' means 'We shall die together'. In return for a small weekly fee from each household, families were given a site on which to build their own home. They were provided with a system of laws, administration and discipline, which were enforced by 'police' recruited from the population themselves. James Mpanza (1889–1970) had a colourful background. He had been convicted of murder and spent thirteen years in prison, where he became a devout Christian. After his release he worked as a teacher before moving to Johannesburg and experiencing the hardships of living in crowded urban slums. Although he ran his camp like a dictator, he was regarded as a hero for highlighting the situation of homeless workers, and is remembered today as the 'Father of Soweto'.

The authorities tried to demolish the shacks, and crush the movement, but did not succeed. Mpanza's example was followed by others, and similar settlements were built on open land around Johannesburg and elsewhere. The movement exerted pressure on the authorities to provide more housing, leading to the construction of modern Soweto.

By the end of the war, many people hoped that the shifts that were already happening in the economy and the changing attitudes that the war seemed to promise would lead to an end to discrimination and segregation in the postwar period. But their hopes for and expectations of change did not happen after the war, as the government, with the support of the conservative white electorate, moved towards stricter forms of labour control and segregation.

Figure 6.2 A cartoon by Zapiro, South Africa's best-known contemporary political cartoonist, published in *The Sowetan* on 9 May 1995 to commemorate the 50th anniversary of VE Day and the end of the Second World War in Europe. It comments wryly on the contrast between heightened expectations and reality in postwar South Africa

The postwar situation

During the war, black workers had been in a stronger position because of the wartime demand for labour, and the number and power of trade unions had increased. Among them was the African Mineworkers Union, which persuaded the government to appoint a commission of enquiry in 1943 to investigate the wages and working conditions in the mines. In its submission to the enquiry, the union called for a minimum wage and an end to the compound system and the system of migrant labour.

Between 1942 and 1944 there was a series of strikes, as a result of which there were some improvements in wages and working conditions. The end of the war, however, had an adverse effect on the position of black workers. They were no longer in such a strong position, especially when white soldiers returned and expected their jobs back. When the government commission of enquiry recommended improvements in wages and working conditions for workers in the gold mines, the mining companies rejected their recommendations. The result of these deteriorating conditions was the 1946 Mineworkers' Strike, which was brutally suppressed by the police. The government did not even consult the Natives' Representative Council, the body it had established in 1936 to represent African opinion, and the NRC ceased to function at all from then onwards.

The government also introduced stricter forms of segregation for Indians. In 1946, a new law, the Asiatic Land Tenure and Indian Representation Act, barred Indians from living and trading freely except in certain restricted areas. Calling it the 'Ghetto Act', the Indian community launched a passive (or non-violent) resistance campaign to resist the new law, using the tactics that the Indian Nationalist Movement had used so effectively against British rule in India. Thousands of people deliberately broke the law and invited arrest. The campaign went on for two years, and during this time 2,000 people were arrested.

The resistance campaign did not result in a change in government policy towards the Indians, but it attracted overseas attention and the matter was discussed at the United Nations. In South Africa, the campaign brought Africans and Indians together into a more broadly based black opposition movement when, during the campaign, leaders of the African and Indian communities signed an agreement to act together to oppose oppression. The campaign also played a role in impressing upon the ANC leadership the need to adopt a more forceful approach.

After the death of Anton Lembede in 1947, the CYL moved away from the Africanist view that he had supported to one that accepted the need for cooperation between Africans, coloureds and Indians. At the same time, the CYL began to play a more decisive role in the ANC. In 1948, the CYL proposed a 'Programme of Action' to the ANC National Conference, advocating the use of more active forms of protest. But conservative older leaders in the ANC were still wary of this approach and it was only the following year that the programme was formally adopted by the ANC – after the victory of the National Party in the 1948 election.

The views of the Congress Youth League on issues such as African nationalism and the position of whites in South Africa were outlined in a policy document in 1948.

SOURCE A

Now it must be noted that there are two streams of African nationalism. One centres around Marcus Garvey's slogan 'Africa for the Africans'. It is based on the 'Quit Africa' slogan and on the cry 'Hurl the white man into the sea.' This brand of African Nationalism is extreme and ultra-revolutionary.

There is another stream of African Nationalism (Africanism) which is moderate and which the Congress Youth League professes. We of the Youth League take account of the concrete situation in South Africa, and realize that the different racial groups have come to stay. But we insist that a condition for inter-racial peace and progress is the abandonment of white domination, and such a change in the basic structure of South African society that those relations which breed exploitation and human misery will disappear. Therefore the goal is the winning of national freedom for African people, and the inauguration of a people's free society where racial oppression and persecution will be outlawed...

The majority of Europeans share in the spoils of white domination in this country. They have a vested interest in the exploitative caste society of South Africa. A few of them love Justice and condemn racial oppression, but their voice is negligible, and in the last analysis counts for nothing. In their struggle for freedom the Africans will be wasting their time and deflecting their forces if they look up to the Europeans either for inspiration or for help in their political struggle.

The ANC Youth League Basic Policy Document issued by the National Executive Committee of the ANC Youth League, 2 August 1948. Marcus Garvey (1887–1940) was a Jamaican political thinker and activist who is regarded as one of the founders of African nationalism. *www.anc.org.za/show.php?id=4448.*

QUESTION

In what ways did the Congress Youth League bring about a change in the attitude and tactics of the ANC?

During the 1940s there had been a shift in black resistance politics, from the ineffective protests of the 1930s to the decade of mass – yet still peaceful – protests that followed in the 1950s. The trigger for the increased resistance was the election of the National Party in 1948 and the introduction of apartheid.

End of section activities

1   Use the information in the text and do some further research to compile a table to summarise the role of each of these groups in the resistance to segregation policies before 1948: ANC; Industrial and Commercial Workers' Union (ICU); African People's Organisation (APO); All-African Convention (AAC); Congress Youth League (CYL).

2   Do some research on the Atlantic Charter and write a brief report to explain why it was such a significant document.

3   Explain how and why the Second World War had a significant effect on expectations about the future among black South Africans.

6.2 What non-violent protests against apartheid took place in the 1950s?

The 1950s was a decade of determined yet peaceful protest and resistance. Many political groups and communities demonstrated their rejection of the discriminatory laws of apartheid that were introduced by the new National Party government.

The ANC's Programme of Action

Previously the ANC had resisted discrimination by attempting to negotiate with the government, but now it adopted a more assertive style. This was due to the growing influence of the CYL, which wanted to build the ANC into a mass resistance movement. In 1949, six members of the CYL were voted onto the national executive of the ANC. Also in 1949, the ANC adopted its Programme of Action, which put into practice this more forceful approach. The Programme of Action called for strikes, boycotts and other forms of **civil disobedience** to oppose white domination.

In 1950, the ANC formed alliances with the South African Indian Congress (SAIC), the African People's Organization (APO) and the Communist Party (CPSA) to organise a general **May Day** strike. The purpose of this one-day stayaway was to protest against low wages, the banning of communist leaders and government plans to ban the Communist Party. In Johannesburg, there were clashes between the protesters and police, and eighteen strikers were killed. In reaction to the shootings, the ANC called for a National Day of Protest and Mourning on 26 June 1950. The strongest support for it came from black workers in the Eastern Cape and Indian workers in Durban.

The Defiance Campaign

In 1951, the ANC, SAIC and APO established a Joint Planning Council to organise a campaign of peaceful resistance against six laws that people considered to be particularly unjust. These were the pass laws, the proposed Separate Representation of Voters Act, the Group Areas Act, the Suppression of Communism Act, the Bantu Authorities Act and the limitation of stock laws (a measure that was deeply resented in the reserves). On 6 April 1952, they held mass meetings around the country to plan the Defiance Campaign, as it was called. This date was chosen to coincide with the start of the government-sponsored Van Riebeeck Festival, held to celebrate the 300th anniversary of white settlement in South Africa.

Participants in the Defiance Campaign, which started on 26 June 1952, purposely broke the law by, for example, using 'whites only' entrances or refusing to carry passes. When they were arrested, they refused to apply for bail or to pay fines. They hoped that so many people would be arrested that the jails would be full and the government would be forced to reconsider its policies.

The campaign lasted for three months and more than 8,000 people were arrested, some spending many months in overcrowded jails. It had the strongest support in the Eastern Cape. Although it did not succeed in getting the government to change its policies, it had significant results. It increased political awareness inside and outside South Africa and turned the ANC, a key organiser of the campaign, into a mass-based organisation: its membership rose from 7,000 to 100,000 paid-up members as a result. Another significant factor was the fact that Albert Luthuli, the newly elected president of the ANC, supported the principle of mass action, which was a clear change from the more

civil disobedience: (sometimes referred to as passive or non-violent resistance) is a form of peaceful protest in which people simply refuse to obey certain laws rather than opposing them with violent protests. It was based on Gandhi's philosophy of *satyagraha* (or soul force), which the Indian Nationalist Movement used effectively against British rule in India.

May Day: also known as Labour Day or International Workers' Day in many countries, where it is a public holiday celebrating workers' rights. It was a day commonly chosen for demonstrations by workers all over the world, and also a day on which communist regimes, such as the Soviet Union, held elaborate military parades.

KEY CONCEPTS QUESTION

Causes and Consequences: What were the causes and consequences of the formation of the Congress Youth League?

Figure 6.3   Lilian Ngoyi, one of the founder members of the Federation of South African Women, addressing a public meeting in Johannesburg during the Defiance Campaign in 1952

QUESTION

In what ways was the Defiance Campaign a significant event, even though it did not succeed in its objectives?

conservative views of previous ANC leaders. World attention was focused on the situation in South Africa and the United Nations set up an enquiry into apartheid. The campaign also helped create greater unity between resistance groups. Among the groups that joined to form a united front against apartheid were the Liberal Party and the Congress of Democrats, both of which had a predominantly white membership.

The Congress Alliance and the Freedom Charter

In 1953, Dr Z.K. Matthews, the Cape leader of the ANC, proposed that the ANC arrange a national meeting (a 'Congress of the People') to which all resistance groups would be invited to plan for a future democratic South Africa. A National Action Council (later called the Congress Alliance) was formed to coordinate this. It included representatives from the ANC, the SAIC, the Coloured People's Congress, the Congress of Democrats and, later, SACTU (the South African Congress of Trade Unions).

Volunteers travelled around the country speaking to people in their communities, writing down their concerns and their demands. Using these as a basis, the organisers drew up a 'Freedom Charter', which spelled out their vision for a future non-racial South Africa. On 26 June 1955, the Congress of the People was held at Kliptown near Soweto, and attended by more than 3,000 delegates from around the country. Many more people were prevented from attending because of banning orders and police roadblocks. The delegates unanimously adopted the Freedom Charter, but shortly afterwards the meeting was broken up by police action.

Among other things, the Freedom Charter called for a non-racial South Africa, where human rights would be upheld, with political rights for all, an equal distribution of wealth and social security and education for all. It is seen as a significant step, as it gave the resistance movement a vision of what sort of society they were fighting for. It pledged support for non-racialism, and this philosophy, which became known as 'Charterism', became the foundation of ANC ideology. From then on, the Freedom Charter was used by the ANC as the guideline for a future non-racial South Africa. But Africanists within the ANC were critical of aspects of it, as well as of the multi-racial composition of the Congress Alliance. Radicals were critical of the Freedom Charter because it set out no clear guidelines for meaningful social and economic transformation.

Fact: There were different perspectives on the significance of the Freedom Charter. Mandela described it as a revolutionary document, but not a blueprint for a socialist state. But left-wing members in the Congress Alliance believed that it held the promise of a transitional stage on the road to a communist state.

Fact: When apartheid ended in 1994, a new democratic constitution was drawn up. It included many of the demands made in the Freedom Charter, including all those relating to equality and human rights. But the constitution said nothing about the nationalisation of industry or redistribution of land, both of which were specifically mentioned in the Freedom Charter.

SOURCE B

We, the people of South Africa, declare for all our country and the world to know:

that South Africa belongs to all those who live in it, black and white, and that no government can justly claim authority unless it is based on the will of the people;

that our people have been robbed of their birthright to land, liberty and peace by a form of government founded on injustice and inequality;

that our country will never be prosperous or free until all our people live in brotherhood, enjoying equal rights and opportunities;

that only a democratic state, based on the will of the people, can secure to all their birthright, without distinction of colour, race, sex or belief;

And therefore we, the people of South Africa, black and white together – equals, countrymen and brothers – adopt this Freedom Charter. And we pledge ourselves to strive together, sparing neither strength nor courage, until the democratic changes here set out have been won.

Preamble to the Freedom Charter, *www.sahistory.org.za/archive/74-freedom-charter-1955*.

QUESTIONS

Read the preamble to the Freedom Charter (**Source B**). Explain how it contradicted the Africanist viewpoint. How would Africanists have wanted to adapt it to reflect their views?

Suggest why the apartheid government rejected the Freedom Charter and accused the leaders of the Congress of the People of treason, or of being inspired by communist ideas.

In what ways was the Freedom Charter a very idealistic document?

Which of the clauses do you think were a response to each of these aspects of apartheid: forced removals; the Bantu Education Act; the Separate Representation of Voters Act; the Land Act; the Suppression of Communism Act; the pass laws?

high treason: the crime of betraying one's country, especially by plotting to overthrow the government

SOURCE C

The Freedom Charter

1 The people shall govern! Every man and woman shall have the right to vote for and stand as a candidate for all bodies which make laws…; the rights of the people shall be the same regardless of race, colour or sex.

2 All national groups shall have equal rights!… All apartheid laws and practices shall be set aside.

3 The people shall share in the country's wealth! The national wealth of our country, the heritage of all South Africans, shall be restored to the people; the mineral wealth beneath the soil, the banks and monopoly industry shall be transferred to the ownership of the people as a whole…

4 The land shall be shared among those who work it! Restrictions of land ownership on a racial basis shall be ended, and all the land re-divided amongst those who work it…

5 All shall be equal before the law! No one shall be imprisoned, deported or restricted without a fair trial…

6 All shall enjoy equal human rights! The law shall guarantee to all their right to speak, to organize, to meet together, to publish, to preach, to worship, and to educate their children… Pass laws, permits and all other laws restricting these freedoms shall be abolished.

7 There shall be work and security! All who work shall be free to form trade unions… Men and women of all races shall receive equal pay for equal work…

8 The doors of learning and culture shall be opened!… Education shall be free, compulsory, universal and equal for all children…

9 There shall be houses, security and comfort! Rent and prices shall be lowered, food plentiful, and no one shall go hungry;… free medical care… shall be provided…; slums shall be demolished;… the aged, orphans, the disabled and sick shall be cared for by the state…

10 There shall be peace and friendship!… Let all who love their people and their country now say, as we say here: 'THESE FREEDOMS WE SHALL FIGHT FOR, SIDE BY SIDE, THROUGHOUT OUR LIVES UNTIL WE HAVE WON OUR LIBERTY'.

www.sahistory.org.za/archive/74-freedom-charter-1955.

The Treason Trial

In 1956, the government responded to the Congress of the People and the Freedom Charter by arresting 156 of the leaders and charging them with **high treason**, a crime that carried the death penalty. They were charged with 'conspiracy to use violence to overthrow the present government and replace it with a Communist state'. The accused included 105 Africans, twenty-three whites, twenty-one Indians and seven coloureds, and they represented almost the entire leadership of the ANC, the Congress of Democrats, the SAIC, the Coloured People's Congress and SACTU. The 'Treason Trial' dragged on for more than four years, and all of the accused were eventually found not guilty and acquitted by 1961.

Historians have interpreted the Treason Trial as an attempt by the government to weaken the resistance movement by removing the most experienced leaders at a crucial time. It also caused financial hardship to those who were charged, as many of them lost their jobs or could not work during the long trial. Certainly the organisational structures of many groups were weakened by the long trial.

Figure 6.4   Because of government interference, no photograph of all the trialists together could be taken. This one is assembled from a number of different photographs, but it does include all 156 of the accused. Nelson Mandela is the tall figure in the middle of the third row from the front

Women's resistance

Women were actively involved in the resistance movement in several ways. In 1954, when the government announced plans to extend the pass laws to African women as well as men, a group of women formed the Federation of South African Women (later called FEDSAW). It was linked to the Congress Alliance. FEDSAW organised a series of peaceful anti-pass demonstrations. The most famous of these was a march on 9 August 1956 by 20,000 women of all races to the Union Buildings in Pretoria to deliver thousands of protest letters

Figure 6.6 The Black Sash held regular protests about the unjust laws and actions of the apartheid government. This protest was outside the City Hall in Johannesburg

Figure 6.5   Helen Joseph (1905–92)

A social worker from the UK, she was shocked when she saw the conditions under which black women in South Africa were forced to live. She became a leading anti-apartheid activist, was a founder member of FEDSAW, a leader in the Women's March, helped to draft the Freedom Charter and was one of the Treason Trialists. She was placed under house arrest by the government, faced other kinds of intimidation and harassment, and remained banned until she was eighty years old.

and petitions to the office of the prime minister. The leaders of the Women's March were Rahima Moosa, Lilian Ngoyi, **Helen Joseph** and Sophie Williams (see Figure **6.1**). These leaders were symbolically chosen to represent the four 'race groups' in South Africa, to demonstrate to the government that people of different races could work together. The government never responded to the women and went ahead with the extension of the pass laws. In the late 1950s, women's organisations continued to protest against the extension of the pass laws, and there were pass-burning campaigns in several areas.

Another women's organisation was established in 1955 to defend human rights issues. It was called the Women's Defence of the Constitution League, but it came to be known as the Black Sash, as its members wore a black sash over one shoulder as a symbol of mourning for the constitution. Their members were predominantly white, middle-class, English-speaking women. Their first campaign was to oppose the government's plans to disenfranchise coloured voters in the Cape. Members staged silent protests outside parliament and in other public places, wearing black sashes. They regularly protested outside parliament whenever particular discriminatory legislation was introduced (until 1962 when the government banned all demonstrations near parliament). Throughout the apartheid years, the Black Sash protested against discrimination and injustice. They wrote letters to the press, petitioned parliament, and monitored court hearings (so that people would know what had happened to activists). They also ran legal advice offices that helped millions of people, especially with legal problems linked to the pass laws.

In 1959, women's protests of a different kind took place in Natal, where women were involved in fierce battles with the police in many areas. It started when the authorities decided to act against the illegal liquor trade in Cato Manor (Mkhumbane) outside Durban, where women supplemented their income by brewing and selling beer in home-based *shebeens*, or informal bars. But this infringed on a government monopoly on the control and sale of alcohol in black areas, where the authorities had built municipal beerhalls, the proceeds of which were used to finance the administration of the townships. When the police destroyed the *shebeens* and the home-brewing operations of the women, the women reacted. The local ANC Women's League organised a boycott of the beerhalls, and the women of Cato Manor attacked the beerhalls and destroyed equipment belonging to the authorities. Violent clashes between the police and the women in Cato Manor continued for several weeks, and similar protests spread to other parts of Natal.

Community resistance

There were several instances of peaceful protests by whole communities in the 1950s. The fact that some of these took place at a time when most of the leaders were involved in the Treason Trial was an indication that protests against apartheid policies were continuing at a grass-roots level:

- When the Bantu Education Act (see Chapter 5, section 5.2, segregation of education) was passed in 1953, many parents in townships on the Witwatersrand and in the Eastern Cape at first refused to send their children to school. Although the ANC tried to set up independent alternative schools, these schools lacked equipment, money and sufficient trained teachers. In addition, official threats that children who did not enrol in government schools by a certain date would be excluded for life and that teachers would be blacklisted, made many parents conclude that poor education was better than no education at all, so they reluctantly sent them to the Bantu Education schools.

- In Cape Town, ex-servicemen who had fought in the Second World War formed the War Veterans' Torch Commando. Its aim was to protest against the government's plans to disenfranchise coloured voters. Members believed that this action would violate the values they had fought for in the war. Its leader was Adolph 'Sailor' Malan, a much-decorated pilot who had fought in the Battle of Britain. The Torch Commando had the support of about 250,000 ex-servicemen. They held rallies and spectacular torchlight processions in the early 1950s, in Johannesburg, Port Elizabeth and Durban, as well as Cape Town. It supported the United Party in the 1953 election, hoping that the National Party would be voted out of power. But when this did not happen, the movement lost some momentum. Ironically, the movement was torn by internal disagreements over whether coloured people could become full members.

- The residents of Sophiatown tried to resist their forced removal and the destruction of their homes. They adopted the slogan 'We won't move' and refused to move voluntarily to Meadowlands in Soweto. Among those who played a prominent role in mobilising this resistance were Nelson Mandela, Helen Joseph and Father Trevor Huddleston.

- There were bus boycotts in several urban areas, including Port Elizabeth and Pretoria. In 1957, the people of Alexandra staged a successful bus boycott that stopped another proposed increase in bus fares.

- In 1955, the first non-racial trade union, the South African Congress of Trade Unions (SACTU), was formed. It allied itself with the Congress Alliance and fought against racism and exploitation in the workplace. It organised worker stayaways, demanding a minimum wage and better working conditions.

- In rural areas, widespread discontent – fuelled by land shortages, the migrant labour system and the Bantu Authorities Act – resulted in sustained protests. There was particular resentment at government 'betterment' schemes, designed to improve agriculture in the reserves, which involved cattle culling and restrictions on grazing. Chiefs who were forced to collect taxes and implement these unpopular policies were often targeted. In 1960, peasant farmers in Pondoland in the Eastern Cape refused to pay taxes and murdered several chiefs who supported government policies. The revolt was crushed with great force when the government sent in the army to assist the police, and 5,000 'rebels' were arrested.

QUESTION

The 1950s are usually referred to as a decade of non-violent rather than violent protest against apartheid. To what extent is this accurate?

Figure 6.7 A defiant slogan on a wall in Sophiatown before the forced removals

The formation of the Pan Africanist Congress

Peaceful resistance to government policies reached a peak in 1960 in protests against the pass laws. Some of these protests were led by a new organisation called the Pan Africanist Congress.

Not all members of the ANC supported the non-racial approach of the Freedom Charter. They accused the ANC of abandoning the ideals of the Congress Youth League of the 1940s by moving away from 'Africanism' in favour of a broad multi-racialism. They felt that only Africans should lead the resistance movement, and they rejected the ANC's willingness to cooperate with other race groups to oppose apartheid. The Africanist slogan was 'Government of Africans, by Africans, for Africans' – in other words, black African interests had to come first and there should be no power-sharing.

This view was in conflict with the principles of the Freedom Charter, which called for a democratic government for all South Africans, regardless of race, which the ANC had adopted as its official policy in 1955. ANC leaders such as Mandela, Sisulu and Tambo strongly opposed this Africanist view because they felt that the support of Indian and coloured people, as well as liberal whites, should be encouraged. The Africanists also disagreed with the ANC leadership about the most effective way of organising resistance. They believed that the ANC approach, which focused on careful organisation and planning, was too cautious, and that more effective mass action could be generated by inspiring leadership and bold initiatives.

In March 1959, a group of Africanists, led by **Robert Sobukwe** and Potlako Leballo, broke away to form the Pan Africanist Congress (PAC). Sobukwe wanted the PAC to take its inspiration from countries to the north, where Africans were gaining independence from colonial rule. At its first meeting, formal greetings were sent to the new PAC from Kwame Nkrumah and Ahmed Sékou Touré, leaders of the recently independent West African states of Ghana and Guinea respectively. Within a short time, PAC membership rose to 27,000. The strongholds of the PAC were in the Vereeniging district south of Johannesburg and in the Western Cape, especially in Langa township.

Figure 6.8   Robert Sobukwe (1924–78)

He became interested in politics while attending Fort Hare University. He joined the ANC and was influenced by the Africanist views of Anton Lembede. He later became a lecturer in African Studies at the University of the Witwatersrand. In 1960s he was sentenced to three years' imprisonment for leading a protest against the pass laws. Before his sentence was completed, the government introduced a new law giving itself the power to extend a prison term annually. This became known as the 'Sobukwe clause'. He spent much of his term of imprisonment in solitary confinement on Robben Island. After his release in 1969 he was placed under house arrest in Kimberley where he lived until his death in 1978.

SOURCE D

At the present moment the A.N.C. leadership regards anybody and everybody who is against the Nationalist government (for whatever reasons) as allies.

This latter attitude is the result of a mentality that continues to speak of South Africa as though it were an island, completely cut off from the continent and, therefore, able to fashion its own policies and programmes, unrelated to and unaffected by those of the other African States. We, on the other hand, have always been acutely aware of the fact that ours is a particular front in a battle raging across the continent. We claim Africa for the Africans; the A.N.C. claims South Africa for all. To the A.N.C. leadership the present Nationalist government is the properly elected government of South Africa whose policies, however, it does not approve of. And the A.N.C.'s main struggle is to get the National Party out of power...

We, however, stand for the complete overthrow of white domination.

Robert Sobukwe explains the Africanist view in 'Future of the Africanist Movement', in *The Africanist*, January 1959, *www.sahistory.org.za/archive/future-africanist-movement-questions-and-answers-yrm-sobukwe-africanist-january-1959.*

QUESTION

Compare Sobukwe's view (**Source D**) with the views of the Congress Youth League (**Source A**) and the Freedom Charter (**Sources B** and **C**).

Figure 6.9 The PAC logo symbolised its links with a broader African nationalism. The colours (black, green and gold) are the colours associated with Pan-Africanism, and the star and lines of light radiating out from it symbolise the belief that Ghana, as the first sub-Saharan colony to gain independence, was a source of inspiration to the rest of Africa

The anti-pass campaigns and the Sharpeville massacre

The pass laws, which forced Africans to carry a 'pass' or identity document with them at all times, were among the most hated of the apartheid laws. Hundreds of thousands of people had been put in jail each year because they did not have the proper stamp in their pass books, or because they did not have their passes with them.

In March 1960, both the ANC and PAC organised campaigns against the pass laws. According to the historian Robert Ross, in *A Concise History of South Africa* (1999, pp. 128–9), the two organisations were 'driven largely by their need to compete with each other, and seriously underestimated the power and ruthlessness of the white-run state'. The ANC planned a series of one-day anti-pass marches. The PAC plan was more dramatic: protestors would march to police stations, burn their passes and hand themselves over for arrest. They hoped that mass arrests would affect the economy and force the government to suspend the pass laws. Sobukwe informed the Commissioner of Police in advance that the PAC campaign would be 'non-violent, disciplined and sustained'.

On 21 March 1960, large crowds gathered in the townships around Vereeniging (south of Johannesburg), and in other places such as Langa and Nyanga outside Cape Town. At Vanderbijlpark, a crowd of 4,000 was dispersed by a police baton charge, and at Evaton 20,000 protesters were forced to disband by low-flying aircraft. At Sharpeville, outside Vereeniging, unarmed protesters gathered outside the police station, until by midday there were about 5,000 protesters facing 300 policemen. Facing a situation that they could not control, the police panicked and opened fire, killing sixty-nine people and injuring 180 more. Investigations later showed that nearly all those killed or injured had been shot in the back. On the same day, two people were shot by police at an anti-pass protest at Langa.

Figure 6.10 The funeral of the people who were shot by the police at Sharpeville

Theory of knowledge

History, evidence and emotion:
How reliable is eye-witness testimony as a primary source? How can the perceptions and emotions of an eyewitness distort the value of a primary source? Do you think that **Source E** can be taken at face value as an account of what happened at Sharpeville?

Robert Sobukwe was arrested on the day of the Sharpeville massacre when he led an anti-pass demonstration in Orlando, Soweto. He was subsequently charged with incitement to defy the pass laws and given a three-year sentence, which was subsequently extended for another six years.

SOURCE E

We came to a large square compound in the centre, a police station surrounded by wire fences, with fields on two sides and roads on the other two. The armed vehicles went into the compound and we drove on to the waste ground beside, unobserved… I got out to see what was happening. Not much, it seemed; my guess was that there were two to three thousand there, but they were spread over a large area and with people no more than three or four deep at the fence, it didn't seem an enormous crowd. The demonstrators I talked to showed no hostility.

The cops were some distance away inside the compound, and there wasn't much to photograph… so I walked back across the waste ground to… the car. Suddenly there was shouting from the crowd.

I turned and started to walk back towards the compound. The cops were now standing on top of their armoured cars waving Sten guns, and when I was fifty yards away from the compound they opened fire into the crowd. I can't say for sure that nobody lobbed a stone at the police, but I do not believe a threatening situation had built up in the time it took me to walk the two sides of the compound and back. The cops were in no danger. I can only assume that they came out with the intention of showing the crowd, and in the process black South Africa, a dreadful lesson.

An eyewitness account of the Sharpeville massacre from Ian Berry, a photographer with *Drum magazine, www.sahistory.org.za/eyewitness-accounts-sharpeville-massacre-1960*

QUESTION

What evidence is there that, even before the shootings at Sharpeville, the South African government was prepared to sanction police brutality to enforce apartheid and crush protests?

The Cape Town march

A week later a young PAC leader, **Philip Kgosana**, led a peaceful march of 30,000 people from Langa and Nyanga townships to police headquarters in central Cape Town to protest against police actions at Sharpeville and Langa. With parliament currently in session in the city, there were official concerns that there would be violence with so many protesters in the centre of the city. Kgosana met the police at their headquarters at Caledon Square and, in return for an offer of a meeting with the Minister of Justice the next day, he agreed to lead the marchers peacefully out of the city centre and back to the townships. On his return for the promised meeting, he was arrested, and the meeting never took place. A military blockade was set up around the two townships.

The government's reaction to the anti-pass demonstrations and the tragedy at Sharpeville seemed indecisive at first: the pass laws were temporarily suspended (although they were reimposed ten days later). But after some initial indecision, the government went ahead with a policy of total repression.

Philip Kgosana (1936–)

He was a 23-year-old student and local PAC leader when he led the march. After the march he was arrested and charged with incitement to commit violence. He fled from South Africa while on bail, and completed his university studies and military training in Ethiopia. He went on to work as a development officer for the United Nations, attached to UNICEF, before his return to South Africa in 1996 to work for the PAC.

The shootings at Sharpeville brought to an end a decade of peaceful protest. The resistance organisations had failed in their attempts to bring about change through non-violent means. The government had suppressed all resistance and used violence and police brutality to crush protests.

Figure 6.11 Philip Kgosana leading the march of 30,000 people into central Cape Town to protest about the police shootings at Sharpeville

End of section activities

1 Copy this table and fill in the missing information as a summary of the non–violent protests against apartheid during the 1950s:

	Causes	Consequences	Significance
Defiance Campaign			
Congress of the People			
Torch Commando			
Black Sash			
Women's March to Pretoria			
Pondoland Revolt			

2 In groups, hold a debate between ANC and PAC supporters on the options facing the liberation movement in 1960. First you will need to do some research on the non-racial views of the ANC (as outlined in the Freedom Charter) and the Africanist viewpoint of the PAC.

3 Do some research on two of the following people to find out some biographical details about their background which help to explain why they became involved in the protests against apartheid: Lilian Ngoyi, 'Sailor' Malan, Oliver Tambo, Helen Joseph, Robert Sobukwe, Philip Kgosana.

Fact: Three of the public holidays celebrated in post-apartheid South Africa commemorate events during the protests of the 1950s: 1 May (the day of the 1950 May Day protest) is Workers Day; 9 August (the day of the 1956 Women's March to Pretoria) is National Women's Day; and 21 March (the day of the Sharpeville shootings in 1960) is Human Rights Day. Some PAC supporters thought that it should have been called Sharpeville Day instead.

Historical debate: Nigel Worden, in *The Making of Modern South Africa* (2007, p. 114) refers to the 1950s as *'a decade of heightened defiance, but also of lost opportunities'*, a time in which the resistance movement failed to realise its full potential in challenging the state. He says that the reasons for this are much debated by historians. Some argue that the middle-class leaders of the ANC were still too detached from a popular base, and that communication and coordination of actions was poor. Others argue that the urban leaders of the ANC realised too late the potential of mobilising support in rural areas.

6.3 How significant were international protests during this period?

In many parts of the world there was a greater awareness of human rights issues after the Second World War, when the actions of the Nazis in Germany had shown the shocking consequences of state-sanctioned racism and the abuse of power. In 1948, the newly formed United Nations drew up a Universal Declaration of Human Rights, which signified a greater recognition of the importance of people's rights. During the 1950s, the start of the Civil Rights Movement in the United States and the nationalist struggle for independence in Africa were both indications that attitudes about rights and freedom were changing. The success of the Civil Rights Movement ended centuries of legal discrimination against African Americans. In Africa, the struggle against colonialism gained increasing momentum, and resulted in the independence of most African colonies by the early 1960s.

In contrast to these successes, the policies of the National Party government in South Africa went against the worldwide trend away from racism and discrimination. As the National Party entrenched its hold on power, enforced the laws of apartheid and suppressed all opposition, the rest of the world became increasingly concerned about the situation in South Africa.

The Anti-Apartheid Movement

Protests such as the 1952 Defiance Campaign made the rest of the world aware of the apartheid laws and their effects, but there was no major campaign against apartheid until 1959, when a Boycott Committee was formed in Britain by South African exiles and their supporters to encourage the British public to refuse to buy South African products. This committee was the forerunner of a larger movement, the Anti-Apartheid Movement (AAM), which was launched in December 1959. A key factor leading to the formation of the AAM was a statement issued by Albert Luthuli, the banned president of the ANC, calling for sanctions against the apartheid government, to bring about change and avert what he referred to as 'the greatest African tragedy of our time'.

The AAM received support from the British Labour and Liberal Parties and from the Trades Union Congress, but the ruling Conservative Party government of Harold Macmillan was critical of the concept of sanctions. The boycott campaign started with a rally of 15,000 people in Trafalgar Square in London, where the South African High Commission was based. The initial aim of the AAM was to create awareness about what was happening in South Africa, but after Sharpeville it called for a change of government, not simply of policy, in South Africa. When the ANC and PAC were banned, the AAM stepped up its protests and called for support for the banned organisations. The AAM was strengthened when members of the liberation organisations went into exile in London.

Figure 6.12 More than 15,000 people marched through central London on 27 March 1960 to protest about the Sharpeville massacre. This march marked the beginning of the Anti-Apartheid Movement's campaign against the apartheid government, which went on for more than thirty years

The Sharpeville shootings focused world attention far more directly on what was happening in South Africa, and strengthened public support for a boycott. The South African government was widely criticised, both by Western governments and by the United Nations. Protest demonstrations were held in many countries, and calls were made for the sporting and cultural isolation of South Africa, as well as for economic sanctions. The award of the 1960 Nobel Peace Prize to ANC president Albert Luthuli for his role in the struggle for peace and freedom in South Africa was in many ways symbolic of world opinion in the wake of Sharpeville.

In 1964, the AAM organised an International Conference on Economic Sanctions against South Africa, with delegates from forty countries attending. After the Rivonia Trial (see section 6.4, The arrest of resistance leaders), the AAM established the World Campaign for the Release of South African Political Prisoners, and launched an international petition that was signed by 194,000 people. The AAM also worked with the South African Non-Racial Olympic Committee (SANROC) to get South Africa excluded from the 1964 Tokyo Games and later expelled from the Olympic movement altogether. The AAM worked tirelessly to maintain support from the British public and, as a result, many people refused to buy South African products such as fruit and wine. It organised demonstrations outside the offices of British companies with investments in South Africa, such as Barclays Bank, and also organised sustained protests outside South Africa House in London. One of the people who played an important role in sustaining the work of the AAM was Father **Trevor Huddleston**.

Trevor Huddleston (1913–98)

He was an Anglican priest from the UK who went to South Africa in 1943, where he became a determined opponent of discrimination and apartheid. He lived in Sophiatown and campaigned against the Sophiatown removals and the imposition of Bantu Education. He worked closely with other activists such as Nelson Mandela and Oliver Tambo. After his recall to the UK by his religious order, he continued to play an active role in the struggle against apartheid, as a founder member of the Anti-Apartheid Movement, of which he was president for many years. At his request, he was buried at Christ the King Church in Sophiatown.

KEY CONCEPTS QUESTION

Causes and Consequences: What were the causes and consequences of the international protests against apartheid?

There were student protests in Ireland during the Rivonia Trial, and in 1964 the Irish Anti-Apartheid Movement was formed. Anti-apartheid organisations were established in several other European countries as well, and some European governments, such as Sweden and the Netherlands, supported the ANC with financial aid.

There was also opposition to apartheid in the United States. In December 1962, Martin Luther King and Albert Luthuli issued a joint statement denouncing the actions of the apartheid government and calling on people to support anti-apartheid initiatives. It was signed by many prominent Americans. However, the attention of concerned Americans in the early 1960s was focused more on the Civil Rights Movement rather than on external issues such as apartheid. The heated anti-apartheid protests on US campuses, the stringent measures passed by the US Congress, and the disinvestment from South Africa by American companies, came much later.

United Nations involvement

South Africa was a founder member of the United Nations (UN) in 1945, and the South African prime minister at the time, Jan Smuts, had played a significant role in drafting the UN Charter. However, even before 1948 there were concerns about South Africa's segregation policies. During the 1946–8 Indian Passive Resistance Campaign against the Asiatic Land Tenure and Indian Representation Act, or 'Ghetto Act' as it was called by its critics, the government of India had raised the issue of the treatment of Indians in South Africa for discussion in the General Assembly of the UN. As a result of concerns about discriminatory policies in South Africa, the UN rejected South Africa's request to annex South West Africa.

After the election of the National Party in 1948, relations between South Africa and the UN became more strained. When the UN adopted the Universal Declaration of Human Rights in 1948, South Africa was one of only three countries that abstained (the other two were the Soviet Union and Saudi Arabia). The clause in the Declaration that stated that all people, regardless of 'race, colour, sex, language, religion, political or other opinion', were entitled to the same rights and freedoms, was obviously in direct conflict with the National Party's belief in white supremacy.

As the National Party government started introducing discriminatory legislation, the UN General Assembly declared in 1950 that apartheid was based on doctrines of racial discrimination. In 1952, the UN established a 'Commission on the Racial Situation in the Union of South Africa', to investigate the issue. The Commission produced detailed annual reports, which included information about new legislation as well as protest actions. However, the Commission lacked support from the United States and most other Western governments and so its activities were discontinued after 1955, despite the deteriorating situation in South Africa.

After the Sharpeville massacre in March 1960, the twenty-nine African and Asian governments represented at the UN requested an urgent meeting of the UN Security Council to discuss the grave situation. As a result, the Security Council passed Resolution 134, voicing its disapproval of the policies and actions of the South African government, and calling on it to abandon apartheid. The fact that the Security Council noted that, if unresolved, the situation in South Africa might pose a threat to international peace and security was a significant step, and this resolution

Fact: South West Africa was a German colony until the First World War, when Germany's colonies were taken away and given to Allied countries as mandates under the League of Nations. South Africa was given control of South West Africa. After the National Party came to power in 1948, South Africa administered South West Africa as part of South Africa, and even implemented apartheid policies there. The South West African People's Organisation (SWAPO) fought a long resistance against the continued South African occupation and in 1990 the territory became the independent country of Namibia.

was a powerful inspiration to the Anti-Apartheid Movement. But the South African government ignored it: on the very day on which the Security Council was meeting, it declared a state of emergency and mobilised more troops to assist the police and army.

UN Resolution 1761

In November 1962, the UN General Assembly passed Resolution 1761, which declared that apartheid was a threat to international peace and security. It called on South Africa to abandon its policies of apartheid and racial discrimination, and it urged UN members to break off diplomatic relations; to boycott South African goods; to stop exporting goods, including all arms and ammunition, to South Africa; and to deny passage to South African ships and aircraft. It called on the Security Council to ensure that South Africa complied with the resolution, and to apply economic sanctions if necessary. In order to keep apartheid policies under review, it also established the UN Special Committee Against Apartheid, which would report to the General Assembly and the Security Council.

The resolution was adopted by a vote of sixty-seven to sixteen, with twenty-three abstentions. Many African, Asian and socialist countries broke off diplomatic relations, and African countries closed their airspace to South African aircraft, forcing them to fly the long route round the coast of West Africa on flights between South Africa and Europe. However, no Western state voted in favour of the resolution. All of South Africa's main trading partners, including Japan, voted against it. As a result, the economic impact of the resolution was limited because the main trading partners took no action. According to Dr Enuga S. Reddy (a political activist, author and head of the UN Centre Against Apartheid), a spokesman for the South African government at the time claimed that the states that voted for General Assembly Resolution 1761 'accounted for less than one-sixth of South Africa's foreign trade, while those opposed to it accounted for nearly two-thirds' (E.S. Reddy (2014) 'The United Nations and the struggle for liberation in South Africa', in South African Democracy Education Trust, (ed.), *The Road to Democracy in South Africa, Volume 3: International Solidarity*, Pretoria: UNISA Press, p. 54).

The Western countries did not make any nominations to serve on the Special Committee Against Apartheid either, and the eleven who were nominated were from African, Asian, Central American and Eastern European countries. The Special Committee, which started meeting in April 1963, received memoranda from organisations and individuals, and held meetings at which people could deliver testimonies. The ANC and PAC, as well as many individuals, submitted either written submissions or testified in person before the Committee.

During 1963 the international situation changed. The Organisation of African Unity (OAU) was formed, and it became an important pressure group, urging sanctions against the apartheid government. By then, more African countries had become independent, and the African, Asian, non-aligned and socialist countries had a comfortable majority at the UN. But although the anti-apartheid bloc could rely on a majority vote to pass resolutions in the General Assembly, the same did not apply in the Security Council, which was the only UN body that could impose sanctions that would be binding on all members. There, three of the permanent member states – Britain, France and the United States – which were opposed to sanctions at that stage, used their veto to block any decision.

As South Africa increased its expenditure on military equipment designed to suppress further resistance – violent or non-violent – the Special Committee urged the General Assembly and the Security Council to respond to the mounting crisis. It pointed out that South Africa's military expenditure had increased fourfold between 1960 and 1964,

Fact: The General Assembly, at which all member states are represented, serves as the main discussion forum at the UN. Although it has the power to pass resolutions, these resolutions are not binding on its members, and it cannot commit the UN to action. Only the Security Council can do this.

Fact: The Security Council is the most powerful body within the United Nations, with the power to commit the UN to action in situations that threaten international peace and security. It can impose economic sanctions and order military action, and its decisions are binding on member states. It has fifteen members, five of which are permanent (the USA, Russia, Britain, France and China). These five have the right to veto any decision. This means that unless all of them agree on an action, it cannot be implemented.

Figure 6.13 Miriam Makeba, an exiled South African singer with a successful international career, testified before the UN Special Committee Against Apartheid in March 1964. As a result, the government cancelled her citizenship and banned her records in South Africa

and expressed concerns about the continued supply of arms and military equipment to South Africa, as well as outside assistance to enable the government to set up a local arms industry. A significant victory for the Special Committee was an announcement by the United States that it would support and apply an arms embargo.

In August 1963, Security Council Resolution 181 called for all UN member states to stop the sale and shipment of arms, ammunition and military vehicles to South Africa. Nine members of the Security Council voted in favour of the resolution, but Britain and France abstained. This was a significant step, as it was the first time that the Security Council had called for measures against the apartheid government. However, as the Security Council had not determined that the situation in South Africa was a 'threat to international peace and security', the resolution was regarded as a recommendation rather than a binding decision, meaning that the arms embargo was voluntary.

When the Rivonia Trial started in October 1983, the General Assembly passed Resolution 1881, calling on South Africa to stop the trial and release all political prisoners. This resolution helped to initiate an international campaign to release the Rivonia prisoners, who faced the death penalty. In a further resolution, the General

Assembly agreed to provide support and financial aid to the families of political prisoners. The Special Committee kept up the pressure on the government. It appealed to the governments of all member states, organisations and prominent people to use whatever influence they had to persuade the South African government not to execute the trialists, to release all political prisoners and to abandon apartheid. During the duration of the Rivonia Trial, the UN made several appeals to the South African government about the fate of the trialists, including Security Council resolutions demanding their release.

In November 1963, General Assembly Resolution 1899 urged all countries to stop supplying oil to South Africa. This was the first of many similar resolutions over the years.

QUESTION

How effective were UN actions calling for change in South Africa?

The attitude of Western governments towards apartheid

South Africa was a member of the Commonwealth and a former British colony, and, in the late 1950s, the UK was its biggest trading partner, with more than 30 per cent of South Africa's imports coming from there, and nearly 30 per cent of its exports going to Britain. There were also close family and cultural ties between the two countries, and 113,000 British immigrants had settled in South Africa since the Second World War. But with an Afrikaner nationalist government in power implementing a policy that was attracting critical reactions from the rest of the world, these relations became strained. Just a few weeks before the Sharpeville massacre, the British prime minister, Harold Macmillan, ended a month-long tour of Africa in Cape Town, where he addressed the South African parliament. In it he described the strength of African nationalism, which he had witnessed elsewhere in Africa, and hinted that South Africa's racial policies were going against the trend of what was happening and would not get British support.

SOURCE F

The wind of change is blowing through this continent and whether we like it or not, this growth of national consciousness is a political fact. And we must all accept it as a fact, and our national policies must take account of it... it has been our aim in the countries for which we have borne responsibility, not only to raise the material standards of life, but to create a society that respects the rights of individuals, a society in which men are given the opportunity to grow to their full stature – and that must in our view include the opportunity of an increasing share in political power and responsibility, a society finally in which individual merit and individual merit alone, is the criterion for a man's advancement, whether political or economic... As a fellow member of the Commonwealth we always try I think and perhaps succeeded in giving to South Africa our full support and encouragement, but I hope you won't mind my saying frankly that there are some aspects of your policies which make it impossible for us to do this without being false to our own deep convictions about the political destinies of free men to which in our own territories we are trying to give effect. I think therefore that we ought, as friends, to face together, without seeking I trust to apportion credit or blame, the fact that in the world of the day, today, this difference of outlook lies between us.

Harold Macmillan's speech to the South African parliament, Cape Town, 3 February 1960, *www.africanrhetoric.org/pdf/J%20%20%20Macmillan%20-%20%20the%20wind%20of%20 change.pdf.*

The speech was significant in two ways: not only was it a public acceptance by Britain that the days of empire in Africa were over, but it also openly voiced international opposition to apartheid at government level. But Nationalist Party politicians were outraged by the speech and it spurred on their determination for South Africa to become a republic and to sever ties with Britain. At the Commonwealth Conference in 1961, South Africa was criticised for the Sharpeville shootings and for its apartheid policies. In response to this criticism, South Africa withdrew from the Commonwealth and became increasingly isolated internationally.

At first, the Sharpeville massacre had a negative impact on the economy, as multinational companies began to review their investment in South Africa, and huge amounts of capital left the country in the following months. However, during the 1960s, the South African economy grew steadily at an annual growth rate of between 5 and 7 per cent, one of the highest in the world. Other countries were eager to do business in this booming economy so they continued to invest in South Africa, despite calls for sanctions. Initially, the biggest investor was Britain, followed by the United States, Germany and Japan. The increasing international criticism of apartheid did not deter investors, who still saw South Africa as a profitable business opportunity.

When the Labour Party won the general election in Britain in 1964, the new prime minister, Harold Wilson, announced that Britain would stop all arms sales to South Africa. But the British government failed to cancel existing contracts and continued to supply naval spares to South Africa. It was clear that the call for sanctions was a threat to the financial interests of some sectors of the British economy, and the government was unwilling to risk losing their support. However, trade between Britain and South Africa declined during the 1960s, while trade between South Africa and West Germany picked up rapidly. This was helped by the fact that West Germany was not yet a member of the UN and so was not constrained by UN resolutions. France became the major supplier of weapons to South Africa, including helicopters, submarines and fighter jets, as well as the expertise to develop future nuclear capability. South Africa also successfully built up its own arms industry, Armscor, which in time became an exporter of arms. In these ways, South Africa was able to continue to suppress the resistance movement. It was only in the 1980s that official government sanctions were applied more comprehensively.

There were two main reasons – South Africa's strategic minerals and the climate of the Cold War – why Western governments were reluctant to apply full economic sanctions, as Martin Roberts explains.

SOURCE G

South Africa possessed more valuable minerals than any other country other than the Soviet Union. New gold fields were discovered in the Orange Free State and more diamonds were found in South West Africa. But this was only part of the story. South Africa was the major producer of rare minerals… [which] were vital to American and European industries.

Consequently, however much American and European companies and governments said that they disliked apartheid, they would not back schemes put forward by the UN or the OAU to overthrow the white government. They themselves had too much to lose in investments and in vital mineral supplies. Many of them argued that the richer South Africa grew, the better-off the blacks would become. Slowly but surely, they said, white governments would listen more carefully to business leaders and gradually bring to an end the apartheid system…

The global Cold War between the two superpowers, the capitalist United States and the West against the communist Soviet Union and the East, was another important reason why white South Africa was able to ignore the anger of the UN. Both superpowers wanted to strengthen their positions in Africa. Whatever Britain and the United States might say about the horrors of apartheid, when it came to the crunch, they believed that they needed white South Africa too much in their struggle against world communism to let it be seriously threatened…

Geographically, South Africa seemed important in the Cold War since it commanded a vital sea route, that taken by tankers carrying oil – the essential fuel of modern industry – from the Persian Gulf to the West. Under no circumstances would America and Britain allow South Africa to fall under the control of a government which was more friendly to the Soviet Union than to them.

M. Roberts (1996) *South Africa 1948–1994*, Harlow: Longman, pp. 59–60.

End of section activities

1 Do some research on the activities of the international anti-apartheid movement in Britain, the United States, the Commonwealth and other European countries. You can start your research by looking at www.aamarchives.org.

2 Design a spider diagram to show the different measures adopted by the UN to put pressure on the South African government to end apartheid.

3 Write a summary to explain why the apartheid government was able to remain in power for thirty years after the Sharpeville massacre, despite the activities of the Anti-Apartheid Movement and the actions of the UN.

6.4 How did government repression affect the protest movements?

The year 1960 was a turning point in South African history: it marked the switch from non-violent to violent forms of protest. Until then, opposition groups had protested peacefully against the policies of the apartheid government, but all protests had been violently suppressed by the state. The Sharpeville massacre had been the culmination of this and had shown the failure of non-violent resistance in the face of ruthless oppression. It forced the opponents of apartheid to adopt a new approach and so, after 1960, the nature of resistance to apartheid in South Africa changed.

The banning of the ANC and PAC

A week after the Sharpeville massacre, and on the same day as the Cape Town march, the government declared a nationwide state of emergency, giving the police and army extra powers to crush resistance. It arrested and detained more than 2,000 of its opponents under the emergency regulations, most of them members of the Congress Alliance and the PAC. A week later it outlawed the ANC and PAC in the Unlawful Organisations Act (1960). This meant that they could no longer operate legally. The state of emergency remained in force for five months, making it difficult for them to maintain any organisational structures.

Before being outlawed, the ANC sent representatives out of the country to establish offices in exile. Among them was **Oliver Tambo**, who crossed over the border into Bechuanaland (Botswana) to set up the ANC's external mission abroad. The aim was to mobilise international support and to set up links with other African national liberation movements. Other leaders decided to operate underground in South Africa. The PAC and SAIC also sent leaders out of the country and, for a while, the liberation movements tried unsuccessfully to form a united front, which collapsed largely as a result of the PAC's unwillingness to work with the ANC.

In March 1961, a year after Sharpeville, the remaining members of the Congress Alliance held the All-In Africa Conference in Pietermaritzburg, which was attended by 1,400 delegates from all parts of the country. A highlight of the conference was the unexpected appearance of Nelson Mandela, who had been banned for eight years and been unable to speak in public. At the conference, he made his first public speech since the Defiance Campaign in 1952. The conference called for a National Convention representing all South Africans to draw up a non-racial and democratic constitution. It also planned to hold countrywide demonstrations on 31 May 1961, the day on which South Africa would become a republic. After the conference, Mandela went underground and managed to avoid arrest, travelling round the country and organising the planned protests, which would take the form of a three-day stayaway.

The police made urgent efforts to prevent the planned demonstrations, by detaining leaders, arresting thousands of people under the pass laws, banning meetings and confiscating leaflets. In spite of these repressive measures, hundreds of thousands of people participated in the stayaway, although it was not as successful as the organisers had hoped it would be, due largely to government intimidation. As they had expected, the government ignored the request to hold a national convention, and instead concentrated on building up its forces to meet any future challenges to white domination.

The start of the armed struggle

After this, the resistance groups decided on a radical shift in policy. Up until that point they had used non-violent methods of protest. But the Sharpeville shootings had served as a stark reminder of the ineffectiveness of these methods against a government that did not hesitate to use violence.

In June 1961, the ANC and its allies in the Congress Alliance established a military wing, Umkhonto we Sizwe ('Spear of the Nation' or MK), to conduct a sabotage campaign, targeting infrastructure such as government buildings, railway installations and power lines, to try to force the government to negotiate with the ANC. As far as possible, they would avoid targets that would cause bloodshed and endanger civilians. At the same time, MK would plan a guerrilla campaign to overthrow the government. Not all ANC leaders agreed with this strategy, and ANC president Albert Luthuli steadfastly

Figure 6.14   Oliver Tambo (1917–93)

He became involved in politics while he was at Fort Hare University, and he was one of the founder members of the Congress Youth League. Together with Nelson Mandela he established the first black law firm in South Africa. After Sharpeville and the banning of the ANC, the ANC president Albert Luthuli asked him to head the ANC in exile. From London and later Lusaka in Zambia, he coordinated resistance and kept the ANC intact, 'holding it together with quiet dignity and great political skill' according to historian Robert Ross (1999, p. 131). He returned to South Africa in 1990 after the ANC was unbanned.

DRAGON'S TEETH

Figure 6.15 This cartoon from the British magazine *Punch* suggests that the continuation of apartheid will provoke armed resistance. The apartheid government has sown the seeds of resistance, which are now starting to grow in the form of spears

maintained his commitment to non-violent forms of protest, while at the same time understanding what had driven the decision.

MK began its campaign in December 1961 with a series of explosions in Durban, Johannesburg and Port Elizabeth, and in the next eighteen months attacked more than 200 targets around the country. MK operations were directed by a National High Command, which was based at Liliesleaf Farm at Rivonia, on the outskirts of Johannesburg. The leadership of MK included members of the SACP and the Congress of Democrats as well as the ANC, and it was technically a separate organisation from the ANC. On the same day that it started its sabotage campaign, MK issued a manifesto, outlining the reasons for its formation (see **Source H**).

Nelson Mandela remained underground and managed to avoid arrest for the next eight months, during which time he travelled to other parts of Africa to organise military training for MK recruits. After his return to South Africa he was finally arrested and charged with organising strikes and leaving the country without permission. He was

SOURCE H

It is, however, well known that the main national liberation organisations in this country have consistently followed a policy of non-violence. They have conducted themselves peaceably at all times, regardless of government attacks and persecutions upon them, and despite all government-inspired attempts to provoke them to violence. They have done so because the people prefer peaceful methods of change to achieve their aspirations without the suffering and bitterness of civil war. But the people's patience is not endless.

The time comes in the life of any nation when there remain only two choices: submit or fight. That time has now come to South Africa. We shall not submit and we have no choice but to hit back by all means within our power in defence of our people, our future and our freedom. The government has interpreted the peacefulness of the movement as weakness; the people's non-violent policies have been taken as a green light for government violence. Refusal to resort to force has been interpreted by the government as an invitation to use armed force against the people without any fear of reprisals. The methods of Umkhonto we Sizwe mark a break with that past.

Extract from the Manifesto issued by Umkhonto we Sizwe (MK), 16 December 1961, *www.sahistory.org.za/article/manifesto-umkhonto-we-sizwe.*

given a five-year jail sentence with hard labour and sent to Robben Island, the prison island off the coast of Cape Town.

At about the same time as the ANC adopted the decision to embark on an armed struggle, the PAC launched an armed wing, Poqo (meaning 'pure' or alone' in Xhosa) in September 1961. It planned a mass uprising by black people in South Africa. Most of its supporters came from the Transkei and the Western Cape. Poqo targeted chiefs and headmen whom they accused of working with the government, and several of them were assassinated. It was also responsible for the deaths of suspected informers, policemen and a small number of random white civilians. Historian Tom Lodge, in *Black Politics in South Africa since 1945* (1983, p. 241), describes Poqo as the first political movement in South Africa 'to adopt a strategy that explicitly involved killing people and it was probably the largest active clandestine organisation of the 1960s'. Poqo set up its headquarters in Maseru in Basutoland (Lesotho) and planned a countrywide uprising for April 1963. The organisation in Maseru was led by Potlako Leballo, because Sobukwe was in prison serving a three-year sentence for inciting people to break the pass laws. After his sentence was served, the government used what was referred to as the 'Sobukwe clause' in the General Laws Amendment Act to keep the PAC leader on Robben Island for a further six years.

In addition to Umkhonto we Sizwe and Poqo, the African Resistance Movement (ARM) also adopted an armed struggle against the state. It was a small organisation, consisting mainly of white radicals and intellectuals, which had been established in October 1961. Its members were based in Cape Town and Johannesburg. They were responsible for bombing installations, including Johannesburg Railway Station in 1964, in which a passenger was killed and others injured. One of its members, Frederick John Harris, a school teacher, was arrested, convicted and executed for this. As well as being a member of the ARM, Harris was also chairman of the South African Non-Racial

Olympic Committee (SANROC). The ARM collapsed when its other members were either jailed or left the country.

By the end of 1961, therefore, a complete change had occurred in resistance politics. In contrast to the non-violent protests of the 1950s, and the peaceful anti-pass campaigns of March 1960, the resistance groups were now prepared to use sabotage and violence to overthrow the government.

The arrest of resistance leaders

While the armed wings of the resistance movements were planning and launching their campaigns to overthrow the apartheid state, government forces were working to uncover and destroy them. They made use of spies and police informers and both organisations were 'crippled by government infiltration', according to historian Robert Ross (1999, p. 131).

The government increased its powers by introducing even harsher security laws. In June 1962, the Sabotage Act gave the state wide-ranging powers to restrict the liberty of opponents of the government. Anyone labelled a 'communist agitator' could be placed under twenty-four-hour house arrest. The Act's definition of sabotage was very wide, and included tampering with water and electricity supplies, disrupting postal or telephone services, or interrupting the flow of traffic. The act made sabotage as serious an offence as treason, with a minimum sentence of five years and a maximum penalty of death. Later in 1962, the Congress of Democrats, another organisation that had been part of the Congress Alliance, was also banned.

The General Law Amendment Act (1963) introduced detention without trial. It gave police the power to arrest anyone suspected of sabotage, without a warrant of arrest, and to detain such a person for ninety days before bringing the suspect to trial. During this ninety-day period, the suspect was not allowed legal advice or visitors. The detention order could be renewed at the end of the ninety days, making it, in effect, indefinite detention without trial. In the eighteen months after it was introduced, more than 1,000 people were detained under this law. In September 1963, a political prisoner, Looksmart Khulile Ngudle, died in police detention while being interrogated. Other deaths followed, and over the years dozens more people died in police detention under suspicious circumstances. The official causes of death were given as 'suicide', 'slipped in the shower', 'fell out of a tenth-floor window', 'fell down the stairs' and other improbable reasons.

Poqo's plan to launch a mass uprising in April 1963 was uncovered by the police. More than 3,000 Poqo members were arrested and detained, and more than 1,000 sentenced. This had a severe impact on the PAC and put an end to Poqo's attempt to overthrow the government. As historian John Pampallis (1997, p. 223) comments: 'The crackdown on the PAC was a devastating blow which all but destroyed it as an organized force in South Africa, and from which it was never to recover fully.'

The secret headquarters of MK were at Liliesleaf Farm in Rivonia, outside Johannesburg. In July 1963, the police launched a raid on the farm and arrested almost the entire high command of MK, as well as taking important documents. It is suspected that the police had inside information from an informer. One of the documents discovered during the raid was Operation Mayibuye, which contained detailed plans for guerrilla warfare. The government used this as the basis for charges against the MK leadership in the subsequent Rivonia Trial.

KEY CONCEPTS QUESTION

Causes and Consequences: What were the causes and consequences of the change in philosophy and tactics by the resistance movement in 1960?

SOURCE I

In Detention

He fell from the ninth floor

He hanged himself

He slipped on a piece of soap while washing

He hanged himself

He slipped on a piece of soap while washing

He fell from the ninth floor

He hanged himself while washing

He slipped from the ninth floor

He hung from the ninth floor

He slipped on the ninth floor while washing

He fell from a piece of soap while slipping

He hung from the ninth floor

He washed from the ninth floor while slipping

He hung from a piece of soap while washing

This powerful protest poem 'In Detention', by Chris van Wyk, satirises the improbability of police denials of the torture and murder of political prisoners.

QUESTION

Besides poetry, what other forms of art can be used as forms of political protest? How effective can art be in protest politics?

Bram Fischer (1908–75)

A member of a prominent conservative Afrikaner family, he was a brilliant lawyer who was attracted by the ideology of communism and joined the CPSA. When the party was banned, he joined the Congress of Democrats and later the underground SACP. He represented ANC leaders in trials during the Defiance Campaign, at the Treason Trial and was leader of the defence team in the Rivonia Trial. He was later arrested under the Suppression of Communism Act but went underground while on bail to continue his political work for the Communist Party. He was rearrested, charged with sabotage and sentenced to life imprisonment. Many Afrikaners regarded him as a traitor because of his communist beliefs.

The Rivonia Trial and the imprisonment of the ANC leaders broke the power of MK and the ANC inside South Africa. After the trial, Wilton Mkwayi and **Bram Fischer** tried unsuccessfully to revive MK, but they too were arrested and imprisoned. Bram Fischer had led the team of lawyers who defended the accused in the Rivonia Trial. Soon after the trial he was arrested and charged with 'supporting communism' and sentenced to life in prison. Many people suspected that Fischer had been targeted because of the role he had played in providing such an able defence in the Rivonia Trial.

The Rivonia Trial

The Rivonia Trial lasted from October 1963 until June 1964. Nelson Mandela was brought from Robben Island to join the other MK leaders who had been arrested at Liliesleaf Farm. The main charge against them was they had been 'recruiting people for training in the preparation and use of explosives and in guerrilla warfare for the purpose of violent revolution and committing acts of sabotage'. They were also charged with conspiring to aid foreign military units when they invaded South Africa, furthering the aims of communism and receiving money for these purposes from sympathisers abroad. The prosecution demanded that the accused be given the death penalty. One of the state's key witnesses was an MK operative from Natal, Bruno Mtolo, who was a police informer.

According to Mandela, in his autobiography *Long Walk to Freedom*, the Rivonia Trialists were charged with conspiracy and sabotage rather than treason, because in cases involving high treason the prosecution had to prove its case beyond reasonable doubt, whereas under the Sabotage Act, the onus was on the defence to prove the accused innocent of the charges. In either case, the supreme penalty was death by hanging.

SOURCE J

'We were charged with sabotage and conspiracy rather than high treason because the law does not require a long preparatory examination (which is highly useful to the defence) for sabotage and conspiracy. Yet the supreme penalty – death by hanging – is the same. With high treason, the state must prove its case beyond a reasonable doubt; under the Sabotage Law, the onus was on the defence to prove the accused innocent.'

N. Mandela (2001) *The Illustrated Long Walk to Freedom*, London: Little, Brown, p. 110.

The trial gave the ANC an opportunity to tell South Africa and the world why it had adopted the armed struggle. The accused used it as an opportunity to outline the history of discrimination and repression, non-violent resistance and the state's violent response. The most memorable part was Mandela's four-hour address to the court, at the opening of the defence case on 20 April 1964. In it he re-affirmed the Charterist view of non-racialism embedded in the Freedom Charter.

SOURCE K

Above all, we want equal political rights, because without them our disabilities will be permanent. I know this sounds revolutionary to the whites in this country, because the majority of voters will be Africans. This makes the white man fear democracy.

But this fear cannot be allowed to stand in the way of the only solution which will guarantee racial harmony and freedom for all. It is not true that the enfranchisement of all will result in racial domination. Political division, based on colour, is entirely artificial and, when it disappears, so will the domination of one colour group by another. The ANC has spent half a century fighting against racialism. When it triumphs it will not change that policy.

This then is what the ANC is fighting. Their struggle is a truly national one. It is a struggle of the African people, inspired by their own suffering and their own experience. It is a struggle for the right to live.

During my lifetime I have dedicated myself to this struggle of the African people, I have fought against white domination, and I have fought against black domination. I have cherished the ideal of a democratic and free society in which all persons live together in harmony and with equal opportunities. It is an ideal which I hope to live for and to achieve. But if it needs be it is an ideal for which I am prepared to die.

Extract from Nelson Mandela's speech in court on 20 April 1964, *www.anc.org.za/show.php?id=3430.*

> **QUESTION**
> Explain why the last paragraph of Mandela's speech is so powerful.

Mandela's speech from the dock made a significant impression. Historians Giliomee and Mbenga (2007, p. 339) wrote: 'It would remain for decades to come the definitive expression of liberal African nationalism, cementing Mandela's iconic status in South Africa and – importantly for the ANC – internationally.'

Mandela's speech inspired anti-apartheid activists around the world to redouble their efforts to persuade the South African government to spare the trialists' lives and release all political prisoners. However, it did not result in their acquittal. In June 1964, eight of the trialists (Mandela, Walter Sisulu, Govan Mbeki, Raymond Mhlaba, Dennis Goldberg,

Ahmed Kathrada, Elias Motsoaledi and Andrew Mhlangeni) were found guilty and sentenced to life imprisonment. Much of it was served on Robben Island, before their release about twenty–five years later.

SOURCE L

The speech received wide publicity in both the local and foreign press, and was printed, virtually word for word, in the *Rand Daily Mail*. This despite the fact that all my words were banned. The speech both indicated our line of defence and disarmed the prosecution, which had prepared its entire case based on the expectation that I would be denying responsibility for sabotage. It was now plain that we would not attempt to use legal niceties to avoid accepting responsibility for actions we had taken with pride and premeditation.

Nelson Mandela describes the reaction to his speech, in N. Mandela (2001) *The Illustrated Long Walk to Freedom,* London: Little, Brown, pp. 113–14.

Historical debate:
Why did the Rivonia Trialists get a sentence of life imprisonment and not the death penalty? Some historians believe that it was the result of the worldwide campaign by, among others, the UN and the Anti-Apartheid Movement. Others suggest that it was through the efforts of a very able defence team at their trial. Some believe that it was a result of behind-the-scenes pressure from the British and American governments.

Figure 6.16   Women protest outside the court in Pretoria after life sentences had been imposed in the Rivonia Trial

SOURCE M

[T]he South African government must have been aware that the execution of Mandela or any of the defendants would hinder the ability of the United States and the United Kingdom to shield South Africa from further international sanctions. Did this have an effect on Pretoria? There is no documentation to prove that it did. But the instinct for self-preservation may have led the government to realise that its goals might be achieved without death sentences.

To execute the defendants would certainly rid white South Africa of some troublesome anti-government leaders forever. Yet the adverse international reaction would likely exceed by far anything that Pretoria had previously endured. On the other hand, life sentences would get these very troublesome men out of the way almost as effectively.

K.S. Broun (2012) *Saving Nelson Mandela: The Rivonia Trial and the Fate of South Africa,* New York: Oxford University Press, p. 113.

The situation at the end of 1964

Although Mandela and the other Rivonia trialists had been spared the death sentence, other political prisoners were executed in South Africa later the same year.

The state obviously had every intention of continuing to crush resistance. Further laws gave the police even more powers, and huge military spending increased the size and effectiveness of the security forces. Military conscription was introduced for all young white men, and the length of this military service was gradually extended to a compulsory two-year period.

By the end of 1964, it seemed as if the government had succeeded in silencing the resistance movements, using the law as well as the might of the security forces to do so. Nelson Mandela and the other Rivonia trialists were serving life sentences on Robben Island, and most other leaders of the resistance movements were in prison or in exile. Robert Sobukwe was on Robben Island too, but in solitary confinement, where he was allowed no contact with any of the other prisoners.

However, both inside and outside South Africa, the resistance movements continued to plan to end the system of apartheid. Protests against apartheid were to take new forms in the following decades, leading ultimately to its collapse in 1994, when Nelson Mandela became president of a democratic South Africa.

QUESTION

Why was the National Party confident that it had crushed all resistance by the mid-1960s?

End of section activities

1 Write a newspaper editorial on the decision by the liberation groups to adopt an armed struggle after their banning in 1960. You may either take the view that such a decision is understandable given the circumstances, or that violence is never justified.

2 In 1963, the leaders of MK were arrested at Liliesleaf Farm in Rivonia, which is now a museum and heritage site. Go to www.liliesleaf.co.za, read up on the 'The Liliesleaf Story – 1960–64' and then write a brief report outlining what happened there, the police raid itself, the consequences and its significance.

3 The years 1948 and 1960 have both been called important turning points in South African history. Compare the significance of each of these two dates and explain which you think can more accurately be described as a critical turning point.

End of chapter activities

Summary

You need to understand the history of protest against discrimination and be able to show why these protests intensified in the 1950s. You should be able to explain the various forms of non-violent protest that took place, culminating in the anti-pass protest at Sharpeville in 1960. You need to analyse the causes and consequences of the Sharpeville massacre and its significance in changing the nature of resistance to apartheid. You also need to pay attention to the actions of the government to suppress protest and opposition.

Summary activity

Copy the diagrams below. Use the information in this chapter, and from other sources, to make brief notes under each heading.

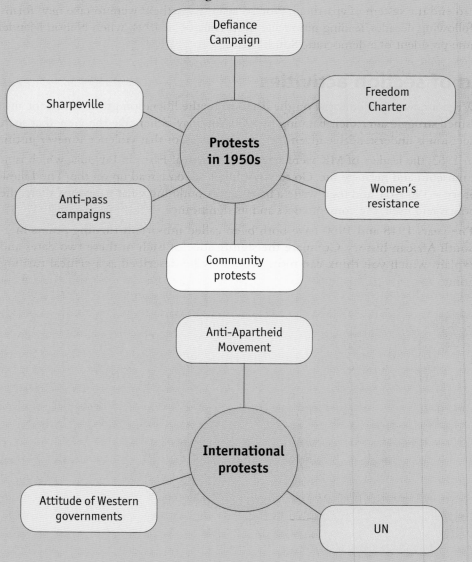

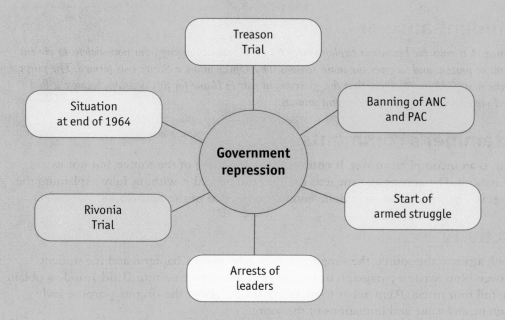

Treason Trial

Situation at end of 1964

Government repression

Banning of ANC and PAC

Rivonia Trial

Start of armed struggle

Arrests of leaders

Paper 1 exam practice

The terms 'origin', 'purpose', 'content', 'value' and 'limitations' are explained in Chapter 8.

Question

With reference to its origin, purpose and content, analyse the value and limitations of **Source A** for historians studying the decision by the ANC to adopt an armed struggle in 1961.   **[4 marks]**

Skill

Value/limitations (utility/reliability) of a source.

SOURCE A

The time comes in the life of any nation when there remain only two choices: submit or fight. That time has now come to South Africa. We shall not submit and we have no choice but to hit back by all means within our power in defence of our people, our future and our freedom. The government has interpreted the peacefulness of the movement as weakness; the people's non-violent policies have been taken as a green light for government violence. Refusal to resort to force has been interpreted by the government as an invitation to use armed force against the people without any fear of reprisals. The methods of Umkhonto we Sizwe mark a break with that past.

An extract from the manifesto issued by Umkhonto we Sizwe (MK), 16 December 1961, *www.sahistory.org.za/article/manifesto-umkhonto-we-sizwe*.

Student answer

Source A is valuable because it explains why the ANC was changing from non-violent to violent forms of protest, and so gives the main reasons why Umkhonto we Sizwe was formed. The purpose of the manifesto was to show that the government was to blame for this decision, because it had used violent methods to crush peaceful protests.

Examiner's comments

This is an incomplete answer. It comments on the value of the source, but not its limitations. The answer also suggests the purpose behind it without fully explaining the origins. The student has only done enough to get two of the four marks.

Activity

Look again at the source, the simplified mark scheme in Chapter 8 and the student answer. Now write a paragraph or two to push the answer up into Band 1, and so obtain the full four marks. Remember to make comments about the origins, purpose and content, *and* value and limitations of the source.

Paper 2 practice questions

1 Examine the impact of the Congress Youth League on the policies and actions of the African National Congress in the 1940s and 1950s.

2 Examine the reasons for the failure of non-violent forms of resistance to bring about meaningful change in South Africa in the 1950s.

3 Evaluate the significance of the Sharpeville massacre as a turning point in the history of resistance in South Africa.

4 'The South African state's willingness to use violence to crush peaceful protest was counterproductive.' To what extent do you agree with this statement?

The role and significance of key actors/groups

KEY QUESTIONS

- How did the National Party implement apartheid?
- What role did the ANC play in the protests against apartheid?
- What impact did the PAC have after its formation in 1959?
- What role did the underground Communist Party play?
- How effective was the armed struggle launched by Umkhonto we Sizwe (MK)?
- What was the significance of the role played by Nelson Mandela?
- What was the significance of the role played by Albert Luthuli?

Figure 7.1 Nelson Mandela played a significant role in the protests for rights and freedom in South Africa between 1948 and 1964. However it took thirty more years before these were achieved. In 1994 he was able to vote for the first time at the age of seventy-six

TIMELINE

1944 April: Formation of the Congress Youth League (CYL).

1948 May: National Party government comes to power.

1949 Dec: ANC adopts CYL's Programme of Action.

1950 May: May Day Strike.

1952 June: Start of Defiance Campaign.

1953 Underground South African Communist Party is formed.

1955 June: Congress of the People adopts the Freedom Charter.

1956–61 Treason Trial.

1959 April: Formation of Pan Africanist Congress.

1960 March: Anti-pass demonstrations; Sharpeville massacre; Cape Town march; banning of ANC and PAC.

1961 March: All-In Africa Conference in Pietermaritzburg.

May: SA becomes a republic.

June: ANC establishes Umkhonto we Sizwe (MK).

Sept: PAC establishes Poqo.

Dec: MK launches sabotage campaign.

1962 Aug: Nelson Mandela arrested.

1963 July: Police raid MK headquarters in Rivonia.

Oct: Start of Rivonia Trial.

1964 June: Rivonia Trialists sentenced to life imprisonment.

Introduction

Many organisations and individuals played a role in the protests against apartheid. In this chapter you will investigate the role played by the most prominent ones and also evaluate how significant they were. You will start off by examining the role of the National Party in implementing apartheid.

Overview

- The National Party supported the ideals of Afrikaner nationalism, which had emerged as a strong force in the 1930s and 1940s; after coming to power in 1948 it implemented its aims of strengthening its political position and of becoming a republic outside the Commonwealth.

- The strong position of the National Party, the weak parliamentary opposition and the suppression of protests and opposition enabled the National Party to implement apartheid ruthlessly.

- Before the 1940s, the ANC played a cautious and conservative role, but after the formation of the Congress Youth League it became more assertive in its approach.

- During the 1950s, the ANC played a significant role in non-violent protests, notably the Defiance Campaign and the Congress Alliance; but historians debate the effectiveness of its role in rural, community and mass-based protests.

- The banning of the ANC after the Sharpeville Massacre forced it to reassess its commitment to non-violent protest and adopt an armed struggle.

- Africanists within the ANC opposed collaboration with other organisations and rejected the non-racial policy of the ANC; in 1959 they broke away to form a separate organisation, the Pan Africanist Congress (PAC).

- The determination of the PAC to inject new energy into protest actions led to the shootings at Sharpeville, which had far-reaching consequences.

- An anti-pass march organised by the PAC ended in the Sharpeville massacre and subsequent banning of the PAC; it too formed an underground armed wing, Poqo, which planned a violent national uprising.

- The Communist Party played a key role in organising workers and became the first target of the National Party's suppression of opposition when it was banned in 1950; but it continued to operate as an underground organisation.

- Although small, the Communist Party played an active part in resistance to apartheid; members of the party frequently operated as members of other organisations, such as the ANC, SAIC, Congress of Democrats, SACTU and MK.

- The establishment of MK marked a significant change in ANC policy; but the subsequent sabotage campaign failed in its aim of forcing the government to negotiate.

- MK's plans for a guerrilla campaign had to be abandoned when its headquarters were discovered in a police raid and its leaders received life sentences in the Rivonia Trial.

- Nelson Mandela played a central role in the all the protest actions between 1948 and 1964; his views also had a significant impact on the decision to change from non-violent to violent forms of protest.

- Albert Luthuli became president of the ANC in 1952, but was 'banned' by the government because of his support for the 1952 Defiance Campaign. In spite of the difficulties that this caused, he was re-elected as president of the ANC. He was widely respected for his resolute support for non-violence and in 1960 was awarded the Nobel Peace Prize.

7.1 How did the National Party implement apartheid?

The National Party, which came to power in 1948, was the party associated with Afrikaner nationalism. As well as planning to introduce a stricter system of segregation to entrench white domination, the party also wanted to sever ties with Britain. After narrowly winning the election, the National Party gradually increased its majority in parliament and left the Commonwealth in 1961. At the same time it ruthlessly crushed all protests against apartheid.

The rise of Afrikaner nationalism before 1939

Afrikaner nationalism was an important force in 20th-century South African history. Afrikaners were the descendants of Dutch and French Huguenot settlers who first came to the Cape in the 17th century. Over the centuries they developed their own language – Afrikaans – and a fierce spirit of independence. When Britain took over the Cape during the Napoleonic Wars, many Afrikaners moved into the interior to escape British control. In the process they conquered the African tribes already living there and established two independent Boer Republics. However, the discovery of vast gold deposits in the Transvaal in 1886 sparked British interest and led to war between Britain and the Boer Republics for control of the gold mines. This was the South African War (or Anglo-Boer War) between 1899 and 1902. Britain eventually won, but British actions during the war (especially a **scorched-earth policy** and concentration camps for Boer civilians) left a legacy of bitterness among Afrikaners.

After the war, Britain was keen to conciliate Afrikaners by making concessions to them. One of these was the creation of the Union of South Africa as a self-governing dominion within the British Empire. The Union was also an attempt to unite English-speaking and Afrikaans-speaking South Africans into one nation. A political party called the South African Party, which formed the first elected government of the Union, was made up of English speakers and moderate Afrikaners (such as Louis Botha and Jan Smuts, see Chapter 5, section 5.1, The impact of the Second World War) who supported the concept of conciliation between the two white language groups. However, Afrikaner nationalists opposed this policy and in 1914 they formed the National Party to promote white Afrikaner interests. It was led by J.B.M. Hertzog, a former Boer general and Afrikaner politician. When the National Party was voted into power in 1924, Afrikaans was recognised as an official language and a South African flag was adopted, which included the flags of the former Boer republics.

During the crisis years of the Great Depression in the 1930s, the National Party merged with the South African Party to create a United Party government which it was believed would be better able to cope with the severe economic problems. However, not all Afrikaners supported this merger, and a small group, led by D.F. Malan, broke away to form the 'Purified' National Party. This party kept alive the aspirations of Afrikaner nationalists.

Afrikaner nationalists wanted to promote Afrikaner unity and political dominance and wanted South Africa to become a republic outside the British Commonwealth. They formed political and cultural organisations to promote a sense of Afrikaner identity

scorched-earth policy: is a military strategy to destroy all the resources that may be useful to the enemy; during the South African War, the British burnt Boer farmhouses, destroyed crops, shot horses and livestock and poisoned wells in order to deprive Boer forces of support; they also moved Boer women and children into the world's first concentration camps, where 30,000 of them died; black civilians who were displaced by the war were also put into concentration camps.

and unity, stressing the concept that white Afrikaners were a distinct people, with their own language, religion and history that needed to be promoted and defended. Afrikaans-speakers who were not white (such as many coloured people in the Cape) were excluded from this vision. This sense of racial exclusion formed the background to the policy of apartheid. During the 1930s the 'Purified' National Party gained increasing support with a revival of Afrikaner nationalism.

When the Second World War started in September 1939, the ruling United Party government was divided over the issue of whether to join in the war. About half wanted to remain neutral, while the rest favoured supporting Britain by declaring war on Germany. The issue caused a split in the United Party. With the support of a narrow majority in parliament, Smuts formed a wartime coalition government, supported by most English-speaking voters, as well as many moderate Afrikaners. Many other Afrikaners joined D.F. Malan's Purified Nationalists to form the Reunited National Party.

Afrikaner politics during the 1940s

Many Afrikaners, like Smuts himself, supported the war effort and about half of the white troops who volunteered for active service were Afrikaners. But other Afrikaners were deeply divided. Some favoured neutrality simply because the war did not directly affect South Africa. Afrikaner nationalists, however, were determined not to support Britain in any way, as their political goal was for South Africa to break all ties with Britain.

During the war there were also extremist right-wing organisations. The New Order wanted an Afrikaner republic, modelled on Hitler's Third Reich, free of both British and Jewish influences. Attracting more support, with about 300,000 members, was the Ossewabrandwag (OB). They conducted acts of sabotage to undermine South Africa's war effort. The government reacted strongly and about 2,000 OB leaders were detained in camps during the war.

After the war, there was a swing away from the United Party and more Afrikaner voters turned to the National Party. When this party was voted into power in the 1948 election, Afrikaner nationalism had triumphed. There was a government in power that was determined to break ties with Britain, to advance the economic and political power of white Afrikaners, and to introduce a strict system of segregation designed to ensure white domination.

QUESTION

How does this speech reflect the aspirations and prejudices of Afrikaner nationalists?

KEY CONCEPTS QUESTION

Causes and Consequences: What were the causes and consequences of the rise of Afrikaner nationalism?

SOURCE A

The outcome of the election has been a miracle. No one expected this to happen. It exceeded our most optimistic expectations. Afrikanerdom has lived under a dark cloud and the future has been black for many years. We feared for the future of our children. But the cloud has disappeared and the sun is shining once more.

In the past we felt like strangers in our own country, but today South Africa belongs to us once more. For the first time since Union, South Africa is our own. May God grant that it always remains our own.

A statement made by D.F. Malan on 1 June 1948. He became the prime minister of the newly elected National Party government, http://v1.sahistory.org.za/pages/library-resources/onlinebooks/Luli/Place-in-the-city/Unit4/unit4.htm.

The policy of apartheid

The ideology of apartheid had been developed by Afrikaner intellectuals during the 1930s. It was supported by the Dutch Reformed Church, which taught that Afrikaners had a God-given mission to preserve the purity of the white race. It was also influenced by the ideas of **pseudo-scientific racism**, which had formed the basis of the racial theories of the Nazis in Germany. Before the 1948 election, the National Party had appointed a commission to investigate the existing segregation policies. The result of this investigation was the 1948 Sauer Report, which recommended that there should be a complete separation of the races. It proposed that the reserves should be developed into 'homelands' and that the movement of Africans from the reserves into urban areas should be strictly controlled. This was the basis of 'apartheid' that the National Party put to the electorate in 1948. But there were debates within the National Party itself about what apartheid actually meant. Some theorists believed that there should be total separation of the races, with 'white' South Africa dispensing altogether with black labour. Pragmatists, on the other hand, thought that black labour on farms, mines and industry was essential, even though white domination should be maintained.

There were three prime ministers who headed National Party governments between 1948 and 1964. D.F. Malan (1948–54) was the Cape leader of the National Party, and under him the early racial legislation was passed that established the framework for what followed later. Although he was very concerned about Afrikaner identity and culture, he was also committed to the segregation of the coloured people, most of whom lived in the Cape. He was succeeded by J.G. Strijdom (1954–8), from the Transvaal, who represented the interests of white workers and farmers, and was known to be more outspoken than Malan. Hendrik Verwoerd (1958–66), who had served as Minister of Native Affairs under both Malan and Strijdom, was the politician most closely associated with apartheid. A former academic, he tried to present apartheid in a rational and positive light, using euphemistic phrases such as 'separate development', but he was the force behind some of the most destructive legislation, such as Bantu Education, influx control and the homeland system.

The National Party strengthens its position

Although the National Party had won a majority of seats in parliament in the 1948 election, it had not actually won an overall majority of the votes cast; it received only 37 per cent against the 48 per cent polled by the United Party. One of its first concerns was to increase its support among voters, so that it would have a big enough majority in parliament to put its policies into practice. According to John Pampallis, writing in *Foundations of the New South Africa* (1997, p. 179) 'consolidating their hold on power was as much a priority for the Nationalists in the early years as their desire to restructure South African society'.

The National Party strengthened its position in a number of ways:

- In 1949, South West Africa was granted representation in the Union parliament and all six seats were won by the National Party.

- In 1956, coloured voters in the Cape Province, most of whom were supporters of the United Party, lost the right to vote.

- In 1958, the Labour Party was dissolved. Most of its supporters, who were white workers, turned to the National Party to protect their interests against black workers.

pseudo-scientific racism: the belief that some races had evolved to a higher stage than others and were therefore superior to them. It is called 'pseudo' because the ideas were not based on scientific facts but on prejudice and inaccurate theories; these ideas led to discrimination in colonial empires and, in the case of Nazi Germany, genocide against those who were seen as 'inferior'.

Historical debate:
There has been some debate about whether the National Party had a complete plan ready to put in place for implementing apartheid in 1948. But historians discount this view. William Beinart, in *Twentieth Century South Africa* (1994, p. 139), contends that the way apartheid legislation was introduced over the years was *'influenced by contending interests in the party, by contingencies, crises, and the pattern of opposition'*. Anthony Butler shares this view and suggests in *Contemporary South Africa* (2009, p. 18), that apartheid in the 1950s *'represented a series of ad hoc attempts to resolve embedded problems'*.

- In 1958, the voting age was lowered from 21 to 18, bringing the National Party more support.
- The National Party also ended the system of government-aided immigration schemes, effectively reducing the number of immigrants from Britain, most of whom would have been potential United Party supporters.

Despite these measures, the National Party still failed to gain an outright majority of the votes cast in the 1953 election. As in the 1948 election, the opposition parties received more than half the votes but, because of the way the constituency system worked, this did not translate into seats. Only in 1958 did the National Party manage to achieve a majority.

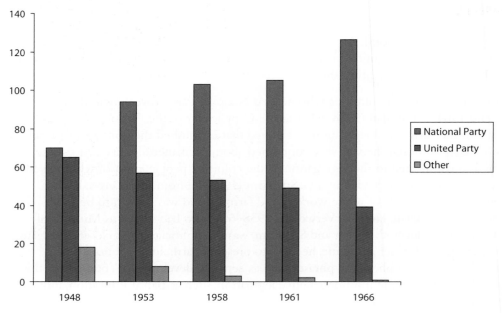

Figure 7.2 Election results, 1948–66, showing the growing number of parliamentary seats won by the National Party in each successive election

As well as increasing its parliamentary majority, the National Party also strengthened its grip in other ways. Afrikaner nationalists were appointed to top positions in the army, the civil service, the judiciary and state enterprises, such as the South African Broadcasting Corporation (SABC), which was used to influence public opinion. No independent radio stations were allowed, and the government resisted the introduction of television altogether until 1976 (many years after it was available in other countries). The government also imposed restrictions on opposition political activity. It used the Suppression of Communism Act not only to ban the Communist Party but also to restrict large numbers of activists and trade union leaders through banning orders. Two new laws enacted in 1953, the Criminal Law Amendment Act and the Public Safety Act, gave the state further powers to weaken opposition.

Support for the National Party grew steadily during the 1950s, although most English-speaking white South Africans supported the parliamentary opposition United Party. The United Party was critical of apartheid, although it supported the concept of segregation. In 1959, some politicians left it to form the more liberal Progressive Party, but it had little support from the electorate. Some whites were opposed to all forms of segregation and joined small non-racial parties such as the Liberal Party and the Congress of Democrats. Others who had been members of the banned Communist Party became actively involved in the resistance movement that developed during the 1950s.

Severing ties with Britain

As support for the National Party increased, it proceeded with growing confidence to make constitutional changes that demonstrated South Africa's sovereignty and paved the way for the establishment of a republic. In the 1949 South African Citizenship Act, the term 'Union citizen' replaced 'British citizen' on South African passports, and British citizens now had to wait for five years before being eligible to apply for Union citizenship. In 1950, the right of appeal to the Privy Council in London was abolished, making the Appeal Court in Bloemfontein the final authority in South African law. Several symbolic changes were made as well: the Union Jack was no longer flown alongside the South African flag; 'God Save the Queen' was no longer played as a national anthem; and the British-controlled naval base at Simonstown was handed over to the South African navy. In 1961, the last British symbol to be replaced was the currency – rands and cents replaced sterling.

In 1960, Verwoerd announced that a **referendum** would be held to determine voters' support for a change in South Africa's constitutional status. To gain the support of English-speaking voters, he gave the assurance that South Africa would remain in the Commonwealth. This is what India had done when its status as a republic within the Commonwealth had been recognised at the 1949 Commonwealth Conference. Despite objections from the United Party and the Progressive Party, only white people were allowed to vote in the referendum.

referendum: when the electorate is asked to vote on a particular issue.

The referendum took place in October 1960, against a backdrop of dramatic events, both national and international. These included:

- the Sharpeville shootings, the declaration of a state of emergency and the banning of the African National Congress and Pan Africanist Congress;
- an unsuccessful assassination attempt on Verwoerd by a white farmer, David Pratt;
- the outbreak of civil war in the newly independent state of Congo, which resulted in an influx of white settlers from the former Belgian Congo, serving to strengthen support for the National Party's views;
- the British Prime Minister Harold Macmillan's famous 'Wind of Change' speech in Cape Town (see Chapter 6, section 6.3, The attitude of Western governments towards apartheid), in which he expressed doubts about the policies adopted by the South African government since 1948, saying that they were contrary to the developments taking place in Africa. Afrikaners saw this as an unjustified intrusion into South Africa's domestic policies, and it hardened their resolve to break ties with Britain.

The referendum resulted in a narrow victory for Verwoerd: 52 per cent of the electorate voted in favour of a republic and 48 per cent against. In March 1961, Verwoerd attended the Commonwealth Conference in London and formally requested that South Africa's status be changed to that of a republic within the Commonwealth. But South Africa's race policies were sharply criticised at the conference, especially by the African and Asian members of the Commonwealth, supported by Canada. Verwoerd therefore withdrew South Africa's application for continued membership. This meant that South Africa was no longer a member of the Commonwealth and all constitutional ties with Britain had been broken. On 31 May 1961, the Union of South Africa formally became the Republic of South Africa.

SOURCE B

The tendency in Africa for nations to become independent, and at the same time to do justice to all, does not only mean being just to the black man of Africa, but also to be just to the white man of Africa.

We call ourselves European, but actually we represent the white men of Africa. They are the people not only in the Union but through major portions of Africa who brought civilisation here, who made the present developments of black nationalists possible. By bringing them education, by showing them this way of life, by bringing in industrial development, by bringing in the ideals which western civilisation has developed itself.

And the white man came to Africa, perhaps to trade, in some cases, perhaps to bring the gospel, has remained to stay. And particularly we in this southern most portion of Africa, have such a stake here that this is our only motherland, we have nowhere else to go.

An extract from Verwoerd's speech to the South African parliament on 3 February 1960, made in response to Macmillan's 'Wind of Change' speech, *www.sahistory.org.za/archive/hendrik-verwoerds-response-winds-change-speech*.

QUESTIONS

What is the message of the cartoon?

In what ways does it show the bias of the cartoonist?

Discuss whether political cartoons are a reliable source for historians to use.

Figure 7.3 This cartoon by the British cartoonist David Low from the UK's *Guardian* newspaper, 19 April 1961, shows Nehru and Nkrumah, the leaders of India and Ghana respectively. The small figure dressed as a messenger is Harold Macmillan, the British prime minister

There were mixed reactions to this development back in South Africa. Verwoerd returned to South Africa to a hero's welcome from republican Afrikaners. Cutting all ties with Britain, which had been the dream of Afrikaner nationalists for many decades, had been achieved. Many English-speaking whites regretted the loss of links with Britain and were concerned about South Africa's future. To the majority of black South Africans, the withdrawal from the Commonwealth represented a step towards increasing isolation and oppression.

The National Party had come to power with a tenuous majority in 1948, but in the succeeding years it strengthened its position so effectively and so ruthlessly that it was able to enforce policies that were at odds with world trends at the time and were completely rejected by the majority of the population.

End of section activities

1 Design a spider diagram to show how the National Party strengthened its political position after coming to power in 1948.

> ### KEY CONCEPTS QUESTION
>
> **Change and Continuity:** How did South Africa change between 1948 and 1964? In what ways did these changes reflect continuity in the ideals of Afrikaner nationalists?

7.2 What role did the ANC play in the protests against apartheid?

The ANC before 1939

As you read in the previous chapter, the South African Native National Congress (later renamed the African National Congress or ANC) was established in 1912, making it the oldest political organisation in South Africa. The early ANC was a conservative organisation that supported non-violent protests, such as the two unsuccessful delegations it sent to the British government in 1913 and 1919. Most of the leaders were educated men and their supporters were mainly middle-class, urban blacks. They did not pay much attention to the needs of black workers and people living in the rural reserves, although they did voice support for a municipal workers' strike in 1919 and a women's anti-pass campaign in 1920. This anti-pass campaign succeeded in getting the government to abandon its plan to force women to carry passes, and the pass laws for women were not reintroduced until the 1950s.

During the 1920s, the ANC was eclipsed by the success of the Industrial and Commercial Workers Union (ICU), which gained a substantial membership through its more dynamic approach and focus on practical issues. The ANC established some early links with the Communist Party (CPSA) when Josiah T. Gumede was president of the ANC between 1927 and 1930. He wanted the ANC to work with the CPSA to oppose new segregation legislation. But more conservative ANC leaders were strongly opposed to communism, and Gumede was forced out of office.

In the 1930s, the ANC worked with other organisations to protest against further segregation laws – once more without success. After this, people became disillusioned with the moderate approach of black political organisations and began calling for a more determined form of African nationalism and more effective forms of protest.

7

The ANC in the 1940s

During the 1940s the ANC began to change from the more cautious organisation it had been in the 1930s to the mass movement it became in the 1950s. This was partly due to changing expectations created by the war: 'African Claims in South Africa', adopted by the ANC in 1943 (see Chapter 6, section 6.12), called for political and economic rights for all. In 1944, younger members of the ANC formed the Congress Youth League (CYL), with Anton Lembede as its first president, and Nelson Mandela, Walter Sisulu and Oliver Tambo as founder members. According to John Pampallis (1997, p. 192), they represented the 'radical intelligentsia of the new generation'. They accused ANC leaders of representing the elite and being out of touch with the masses. They realised that there was a need to articulate the grievances of the urban population, such as low wages, housing shortages and poor living conditions, and in this way turn the ANC into a more effective organisation. The new approach advocated by the CYL found support among the rapidly expanding urban population, who had moved to the cities in great numbers to work in wartime production.

After the war, the CYL began to play a more active role in the ANC. They were influenced by the actions of the Indian community in the passive resistance campaign against the 'Ghetto Act' in 1946 (see Chapter 6, section 6.1, The postwar situation), and this influenced their thinking when they drew up a 'Programme of Action' that advocated the use of more confrontational forms of protest. This was adopted by the ANC in 1949, when members of the CYL were voted onto the national executive. The Programme of Action called for strikes, boycotts and other forms of civil disobedience to oppose white domination. The fact that the National Party had been voted into power the previous year added new urgency to the need for more effective action.

The ANC in the 1950s

The more assertive approach adopted by the ANC in the 1950s was partly inspired by what was happening elsewhere in the world at the time. It was the era of decolonisation and many African countries became independent during this decade. In 1955, twenty-nine newly independent countries in Asia and Africa met at Bandung in Indonesia, forming what became known as the Non-Aligned Movement. The ANC sent an observer, Moses Kotane, to this conference. These events and this contact gave the ANC the sense that their protests against apartheid were part of a worldwide struggle for freedom and rights at the time.

In 1950, the ANC allied itself with other organisations to protest against the impending Suppression of Communism Act. This resulted in the May Day strike and the subsequent National Day of Protest and Mourning, called for by the ANC after strikers in the May Day protests had been shot by police.

Even at this stage there were debates within the ANC about whether it should link up with other organisations to oppose apartheid or whether it should follow an Africanist course and reject working together with any non-African organisations. At the time of the Indian passive resistance campaign, an agreement between the ANC, the Natal Indian Congress and the Transvaal Indian Congress (often referred to as the **'Three Doctors' Pact'**) had paved the way for greater cooperation and unity between the Indian and African communities. However, the violent **Cato Manor Riots** in Durban in 1949, between Africans and Indians, in which 142 people died and more than 1,000 were injured, threatened this unity. As a result, the ANC leadership felt that it was even more crucial to demonstrate multiracial cooperation.

It was the 1952 Defiance Campaign that put into effect many of the strategies called for in the Programme of Action. The campaign was planned by a Joint Planning Council, established by the ANC and SAIC, in which the ANC played a key role. Volunteers in the campaign, acting in small disciplined groups, deliberately broke apartheid laws: Africans did not carry passes; Indian, coloured and white volunteers entered black townships without permission; 'non-whites' walked through 'whites only' entrances; and people who had been banned deliberately broke their restriction orders. Volunteers were instructed to avoid violence and to refuse to pay fines when arrested. More than 8,000 people were arrested, and many of the leaders were served with banning orders. After the government introduced harsh new legislation that provided for flogging as well as other penalties for deliberately breaking the law, the ANC called off the Defiance Campaign.

Fact: An action during the Defiance Campaign that received wide publicity was the participation of Manilal Gandhi, the son of Mohandas Gandhi, who entered an African location illegally and was given a fifty-day prison sentence as a result. Manilal Gandhi spent most of his life in South Africa, as the editor of *Indian Opinion* and running the Phoenix settlement outside Durban, both of which had been started by his father during his twenty-year stay in South Africa. Manilal Gandhi believed strongly in non-violence and supported the Natal Indian Congress in its protest actions.

Figure 7.4 Protesters carry the ANC flag on the first day of the Defiance Campaign in 1952

The Defiance Campaign had significant results. It increased political awareness inside and outside South Africa and turned the ANC, a key organiser of the campaign, into a mass movement: its membership rose from 7,000 to 100,000 paid-up members as a result, and its membership began to reflect more accurately the structure of African society. Ordinary people's perceptions of the ANC changed from that of an organisation that represented the interests of only the educated elite to one that tackled practical issues that affected the working class as well. In December 1952, Albert Luthuli, who had supported the campaign as the provincial leader in Natal, became president of the ANC. This was a clear change in direction from the previously conservative ANC leadership.

In 1953, Dr Z.K. Matthews, the Cape leader of the ANC, proposed that the ANC arrange a national meeting (a 'Congress of the People') to which all resistance groups would be invited to plan for a future democratic South Africa. A National Action Council (later called the Congress Alliance) was formed to coordinate this. It included representatives from the ANC, the SAIC, the Coloured People's Congress, the Congress of Democrats and, later, the Congress of South African Trade Unions (SACTU). The cross-racial composition of the Congress Alliance was an expression of the ANC's commitment to non-racialism. This philosophy was confirmed in its acceptance of the Freedom Charter at the Congress of the People in 1955. The Freedom Charter defined the South African nation as belonging to 'all who live in it, black and white', and it called for a democratic government for all South Africans, regardless of race. The non-racialism of the Charter became a fundamental principle of ANC policy, and it was used by the ANC as the guideline for a future non-racial South Africa.

Figure 7.5   Delegates arrive in Kliptown for the Congress of the People in 1955. The placards they hold show some of the demands of the Freedom Charter

Many ANC leaders were included among the 156 people arrested and charged with treason after the Freedom Charter was adopted. They included Albert Luthuli, Nelson Mandela, Walter Sisulu and Oliver Tambo. Although all were eventually acquitted, the long trial kept many leaders out of action for more than four years. Nevertheless, the ANC was involved in many community protests during the 1950s:

- In Sophiatown, the ANC organised a major campaign against the forced removals. It held mass public meetings and recruited volunteers to help mobilise people to resist the removals.

- When the Bantu Education Act was passed, the ANC called for a boycott of schools, but was unable to provide a viable alternative, so support for the boycott was mixed, and the ANC called off the campaign.

- The ANC Women's League was actively involved in the campaign against passes for women. It was closely linked to FEDSAW, which coordinated anti-pass protests throughout the country, culminating in the Women's March in 1956.

- In 1959, in support of the beerhall protests of women in Cato Manor (see Chapter 6, section 6.2, Women's resistance), the local branch of the ANC Women's League organised a boycott of the beerhalls.

- Also in 1959, the ANC organised a potato boycott to protest against the appalling conditions for workers on potato farms in the Eastern Transvaal.

The ANC was only partially involved in the many rural protests that took place in the late 1950s. Some of them were held in areas where the ANC had few or no organisational structures, and where the protests were sparked off by the anger of local communities at mounting government pressures.

There are debates amongst historians about how effective the ANC was in the 1950s. Paul Maylam (1986) suggests that its role was inconsistent – sometimes taking a leading role but at other times being hesitant or uninvolved. Tom Lodge (1983) believes that at this stage the ANC did not have a carefully worked out long-term strategy. **Sources C** and **D** present other views.

SOURCE C

Indeed, all the popular struggles of the 1950s failed to realize their potential fully in challenging the state. One of the reasons for this, much debated by historians, was the nature of the relationship between mass mobilization and the leadership of the national organizations, in particular the ANC. Was the ANC now converted from the elitist and essentially conservative body of the 1930s to a new and mass-based movement with more radical goals and heightened impact? Some writers have argued that this was indeed the case…

But other historians have pointed out the limitations of these arguments. Links with trade union branches were made, but the middle-class leaders of the ANC were still uneasy in a proletarian alliance and local campaigns often went beyond the calls of ANC leadership, or else were not supported at all by the organization. [Some argue that] ANC leadership was detached from any popular base, that communication and coordination of actions was at best patchy, and that many campaigns failed as a result…

Some of the debates show as much about the political sympathies and priorities of the writers in later years as they do about the nature of political mobilization in the 1950s. Clearly, the ANC failed to mobilize and coordinate widespread unified protests, as much because of its limited financial and administrative resources and heightened state repression as because of the conscious alienation of its leaders from popular or working-class interests.

N. Worden (2007) *The Making of Modern South Africa: Conquest, Apartheid, Democracy*, Oxford: Blackwell Publishing, pp. 113–14.

Theory of knowledge

History, evidence and bias: **Source C** suggests that the 'political sympathies and priorities of the writers in later years' may have influenced their interpretation of history. How does the context within which historians live affect what they write? Does this mean that all history is biased?

SOURCE D

Rural rebellions alerted African Nationalist politicians…to the potential of this neglected constituency. The new President of the ANC, Albert Luthuli, was himself rurally based. But the largely urban leadership did not always find it easy to harness localized and sometimes particularist impulses in these movements. The late 1950s had in any case been a difficult period for the ANC. Attempts to extend its political strategies through boycotts and worker stayaways were hampered by bannings and imprisonment…
The lengthy trial staged by the government, in which many Congress politicians were accused of treason, sucked in the energies of its leaders and lawyers despite their acquittals. Luthuli's balanced leadership and moral authority could not secure unity. Just as a broad political front incorporating urban women and rural rebels seemed attainable between 1958 and 1960, the Pan Africanist Congress (PAC), impatient with white and left-wing influences in the Congress alliance, broke away, dividing opposition and tearing at popular loyalties.

W. Beinart (1994) *Twentieth-Century South Africa,* Cape Town: Oxford University Press, p. 159.

ACTIVITY

Compare and contrast the views expressed in **Sources C** and **D** about the effectiveness of the ANC in the 1950s.

When Africanists within the ANC criticised the composition of the Congress Alliance and the ideology of the Freedom Charter, the main leadership defended the non-racial stance. This led to the breakaway and formation of the Pan-Africanist Congress (PAC) in 1959. Both groups planned anti-pass campaigns in 1960, which resulted in the

Figure 7.6 After Sharpeville, anti-pass protests continued. Here a woman burns her pass

Sharpeville massacre (see Chapter 6, section 6.2, The anti-pass campaigns and the Sharpeville massacre) and, in turn, a change in the nature of protest action in South Africa.

The ANC after Sharpeville

After the Sharpeville massacre, and the nationwide protests afterwards, the government declared a state of emergency and outlawed both the ANC and PAC. The state of emergency remained in force for five months, making it difficult to maintain any organisational structures. Despite this, the ANC played a key role in organising the All-In Africa Conference in Pietermaritzburg a year after Sharpeville, but the government's harsh response to its calls to negotiate led to a radical shift in policy. Up until that point the ANC had stuck to non-violent methods of protest, which had been ineffective. But now it turned to an armed struggle.

In June 1961, together with the its allies in the Congress Alliance and the SACP, the ANC established a military wing, Umkhonto we Sizwe ('Spear of the Nation' or MK), to conduct a sabotage campaign to try to force the government to negotiate. If that failed, they planned to launch a guerrilla campaign to overthrow the government. Albert Luthuli maintained his commitment to non-violence, but at the same time understood what had driven the decision. Between December 1961 and July 1963, MK conducted a sabotage campaign, and more than 200 targets were bombed, although it avoided civilian targets and loss of life. When the secret headquarters of MK in Rivonia were raided by police in July 1963, the entire leadership was arrested and subsequently sentenced to life imprisonment in the Rivonia Trial, effectively putting an end to ANC and MK operations inside South Africa for the immediate future.

Before being outlawed, the ANC had sent representatives out of the country to establish offices in exile. Among them was Oliver Tambo, who crossed over the border into Bechuanaland (now Botswana) to set up the ANC's external mission abroad. He set up offices in Dar-es-Salaam, Tanzania, and in London, but the headquarters were later moved to Lusaka in Zambia. For the next thirty years, the ANC in exile worked to mobilise international support for sanctions and to support the armed struggle in South Africa.

End of section activities

1   The African National Congress (established in 1912) and the National Party (established in 1914) represented two different forms of nationalism. Compare the two organisations, by examining the circumstances in which each was formed, its political ideology, its support base, and its interpretation of nationalism.

2   Explain whether the policies and tactics adopted by the ANC during the 1940s, 1950s and 1960s represented continuity or change.

3   Explain the significance of each of these in the development of ANC policies during the 1950s and 1960s:
    - The Programme of Action
    - The Defiance Campaign
    - The Freedom Charter
    - The banning of the ANC

7.3 What impact did the PAC have after its formation in 1959?

The ideology of Africanism

From the 1940s there had been tensions within the ANC between the 'Africanists' and those who held other views. Africanists wanted to promote African pride, assertiveness and self-reliance. This self-reliance meant that they rejected support from white liberals and also communists. In their view, Africans were the victims of racial oppression and therefore they should wage their own struggle against this oppression. This clashed with the communist view that working-class people of all races should unite against capitalist exploitation. Anton Lembede, the first leader of the Congress Youth League, was a leading proponent of Africanist views, until his premature death through illness at the age of thirty-three in 1947. Maylam (1986, p. 184) describes him as 'a charismatic figure who has taken on heroic stature in Africanist tradition'. However, until the late 1950s, the ANC held together, seemingly able to accommodate a range of viewpoints – Africanist, moderate, pragmatic and communist.

SOURCE E

The Indians should not lead the struggle… For instance, they didn't carry passes and the whites didn't carry passes, and therefore they couldn't understand anything about passes. With the whites, we say that it is not for them to say the struggle must go this way or that way, as in fact has happened. Within the ANC there has been a wave of dissatisfaction with whites in the movement.

By 1958 we decided that we couldn't take any more the policies that the ANC was carrying on. African emancipation could only be realised by the return of the land that had been taken away. The ANC had been established in 1912 in order to espouse that, with the question of the land being paramount. As Lembede said, there's a mystic connection between the soil and the soul. The economic system we inherited from our fathers, where there was no starvation, where there was no exploitation – we wanted an economic system based on these principles.

A.B. Ngcobo, a leader in the Congress Youth League in Natal, who joined the PAC in 1959, and became its first treasurer-general, explains the Africanist position. Quoted in J. Pampallis (1997) *Foundations of the New South Africa*, Cape Town: Maskew Miller Longman, p. 210. He cites J. Frederickse (1990) *The Unbreakable Thread: Non-Racialism in South Africa*, London: Zed Books, p. 73.

During the 1950s, the ANC began to work more closely with other organisations, such as the South African Indian Congress, the African People's Organisation and the Congress of Democrats in the Defiance Campaign and the Congress Alliance. But the Africanists viewed this involvement of other groups as an unwelcome intrusion into what they saw as an African liberation struggle. They were angered too by the ANC's enthusiastic adoption of the Freedom Charter, which they felt 'made dangerous concessions to multiracialism' (Maylam, 1986, p. 188). The Africanists were becoming increasingly impatient with white and left-wing influences within the Congress Alliance. Support for this view was especially strong in the Orlando branch of the ANC in Soweto, which was led by Potlako Leballo.

The formation of the PAC

In November 1958, after an unsuccessful attempt to secure control of the Transvaal executive of the ANC, the Africanists seceded from the ANC and, in April 1959, formed their own organisation, the Pan Africanist Congress, which promoted a militant Africanism. Robert Sobukwe was its first president. The choice of name for the organisation was a clear indication of its support for the ideology of **Pan-Africanism**.

Pan-Africanism: originated among black people living in America and the Caribbean who wanted to rediscover their African heritage and identity. They aimed to free Africans from colonialism and racism and wanted the political unification of Africa. The first leader of independent Ghana, Kwame Nkrumah, was a strong supporter of Pan-Africanism. After the independence of Ghana, he organised an All-African People's Conference in Accra in 1958, which was attended by representatives from South African organisations, including Walter Sisulu of the ANC and SACP.

Figure 7.7 At a stormy meeting of the ANC in 1958, Robert Sobukwe and other Africanists announced their intention of leaving the organisation to form the PAC

Historian Nigel Worden suggests that this development needs to be viewed in the wider context of the time:

SOURCE F

Africanism was aided by a number of factors. It reflected the impatience of a younger generation with the liberal style of men such as Luthuli. It was part of a wider African assertiveness in this period, marked locally by increased support for the African Independent churches, and more widely by the strength of African nationalism elsewhere, as shown by the 1958 Accra conference. Moreover, Africanists could point to the failure of the Charterists in achieving any success at halting the tide of discrimination, let alone driving it back.

N. Worden (2000) *The Making of Modern South Africa: Conquest, Apartheid, Democracy,* Oxford: Blackwell Publishing, p. 117.

Although it had hopes of attracting mass support, the PAC was never able to gain significant support in places regarded as ANC strongholds. Its main support base was in the townships of the western Cape, where influx control was more strictly applied

Historical debate:
Historians suggest that there was a certain amount of rivalry between the two organisations in organising the anti-pass campaigns. John Pampallis (1997, p. 211) contends that the PAC was deliberately trying to pre-empt the ANC campaign set for 31 March, by starting the PAC one on 21 March. According to William Beinart (1994, p.159), the PAC wanted to *'inject new urgency into campaigning and upstage the ANC in mass mobilizations'*. Other historians, however, suggest that the PAC wanted to organise a more sustained campaign rather than a series of one-day marches.

than in other parts of the country, resulting in mounting frustration and anger. It also had support in the townships around Vereeniging, south of Johannesburg, and had small pockets of support in Orlando and Alexandra townships in Johannesburg.

The anti-pass campaign

The PAC played a key role in initiating the anti-pass campaigns of 1960 through their determination to step up protest actions. They set the date of 21 March as the day on which protestors would march to police stations, burn their passes and hand themselves over for arrest. They hoped that mass arrests would affect the economy and force the government to suspend the pass laws. The response was greatest in the places that were PAC strongholds. On 21 March 1960, large crowds gathered in the townships around Vereeniging, and in Langa outside Cape Town. There was a smaller response in some other townships. Sobukwe himself led a march in Orlando.

Although the PAC existed legally in South Africa for less than a year before its banning on 7 April 1960 – which is when the Unlawful Organisations Act came into effect – it had a significant impact on events. Its determination to inject new energy into protest actions led directly to the events at Sharpeville, which had far-reaching consequences. The police response to the PAC's anti-pass protest in Sharpeville radically changed the political landscape in 1960. It led directly to the decision by the liberation movements to change from violent to non-violent protest actions.

The formation of Poqo

After it was banned, the PAC set up a military wing, Poqo, which had its strongest support base in the western Cape. Pogo planned a national uprising that was more brutal and on a larger scale their Mk's sabotage campaign. They did not try to avoid endangering human life: 'Indeed, the spilling of blood was seen as a necessary means for achieving liberation' (Maylam, 1986, p. 191). They believed that isolated acts of violence could escalate into a mass uprising that would overthrow the government and end white domination.

In November 1962, Poqo tried to start such an uprising in Paarl outside Cape Town. About 250 men armed with axes, pangas (broad, heavy knives) and various homemade weapons marched into the town and attacked the police station. After being driven off by police gunfire, they attacked and killed some random white residents before the uprising was crushed. These actions 'attracted more publicity and undermined the ANC's already uncertain strategy of using constrained violence to persuade' (Beinart, 1994, p. 212). Lodge (1983) believes that the short-lived Paarl uprising was the closest the PAC got to initiating a mass uprising.

The violence associated with the Poqo attacks did much to stir up white fears and strengthen white support for the National Party's measures to crush armed resistance.

The headquarters of Poqo were in Maseru in Basutoland, then still a British colony. In 1963, the British colonial police raided its offices and seized membership lists, enabling the South African police to identify and detain thousands of PAC and Poqo supporters. This effectively broke up the movement and ended Poqo's hopes of a mass uprising. Although the PAC survived in exile, they were isolated from events in South Africa, and attempts to organise effective incursions into the country failed, largely on account of the ring of white-controlled countries to the north of South Africa. It was only after the collapse of white rule in Angola and Mozambique in 1975, and Rhodesia in 1979, that incursions became possible.

End of section activities

1 Nelson Mandela wrote in his autobiography that 'the PAC had captured the spotlight at Sharpeville in a way that far exceeded their influence as an organisation' (Mandela, 2001, p. 94). Find out what you can about the role and influence of the PAC to determine whether you agree with this view or not.

2 Write two short newspaper editorials, one in support of and one critical of the attitude and actions of the PAC's armed wing Poqo in the armed struggle. You will need to do some additional research to answer this question.

7.4 What role did the underground Communist Party play?

The Communist Party before 1950

As you read in the last chapter, the Communist Party of South Africa (CPSA) had been formed in 1921, mainly by radical white workers and socialists from Europe, who were inspired by the success of the Bolshevik Revolution in Russia. At first most of its members were white workers, but from the mid-1920s it focused on recruiting black members and soon had a predominantly black membership, although its overall membership remained small. During the 1930s there were internal divisions within the CPSA and its membership declined as a result.

As South Africa became more industrialised during the 1930s and 1940s, the CPSA was active in organising workers in the new factories and its membership grew during the

Figure 7.8 A cartoon from the South African *Guardian*, the newspaper with links to the Communist Party, about the 1946 Mineworkers' Strike

war years. One of the unions that grew rapidly was the African Mineworkers Union, led by J.B. Marks, who was a member of the ANC and a leader in the CPSA. It was concerned about the deteriorating working and living conditions for miners. This was the union that led the 1946 Mineworkers' Strike of 75,000, which brought the gold mines to a virtual standstill (see Chapter 6, section 6.1, The postwar situation).

Brian Bunting, a member of the CPSA since 1940 and later a founder member of the SACP, claimed that the 1946 Mineworkers' Strike was led and guided by the trade union itself, but that once it had started the CPSA became involved.

sedition: inciting people to rebel against the authority of the state.

Ruth First (1925–82)

She was a journalist, academic and political activist, a member of the CPSA, founder member of the Congress of Democrats and a Treason Trialist. She and her husband, Joe Slovo, were two of the first people to be banned under the Suppression of Communism Act in 1950. After the arrest of the MK leadership at Rivonia, First was arrested and held in solitary confinement for four months. After her release she moved to London, where she continued writing and worked for the AAM. While working in Maputo, she was killed by a letter bomb sent by South African security forces. Her daughters Shawn Slovo, a screenwriter, Gillian Slovo, an acclaimed novelist, and Robyn Slovo, a producer, have referred to the unsettling experiences of their childhood in apartheid South Africa where their parents were frequent targets of police harassment.

SOURCE G

When the strike took place, the whole machinery of the Johannesburg District [of the CPSA] went into action immediately. The entire membership, black and white, was thrown into the struggle… Leaflets were printed and distributed from end to end of the Witwatersrand by Communist Party members as well as by others. Flying squads of Communist Party activists were ferried from mine to mine to give a lead to the workers and to back up the efforts of the union.

To the charge of having assisted the strike after it had broken out, the Communist Party members who were brought to court pleaded guilty with pride. They had done a good job. Without them, nothing on the scale of what was achieved would have been possible.

B. Bunting (1986) *Moses Kotane: South African Revolutionary,* London: Inkululeko, p. 130; quoted in J. Pampallis (1977) *Foundations of the New South Africa,* Cape Town: Maskew Miller Longman, p. 172.

The government blamed 'agitators', especially communists, for the strike. After the strike had been brutally crushed and the miners forced back to work, the police raided the offices of the CPSA and the *Guardian* newspaper and seized documents and party lists. Subsequently the entire CPSA committee in Johannesburg was arrested and charged with conspiracy to organise a strike, while the CPSA's central executive committee in Cape Town were all arrested and charged with **sedition**. Nevertheless, by 1948 the CPSA was in a stronger position than it had been before: its membership had grown, it was influential in a number of black trade unions, and it was slowly developing a closer understanding with other organisations such as the ANC and SAIC.

The Communist Party after 1950

When the National Party came to power in 1948, it was determined to stamp out what it saw as the dangerous ideas and activities of the CPSA, which it believed was mainly responsible for all the labour unrest among black mineworkers. Accordingly, the new government's first restriction on political activity was the Suppression of Communism Act in 1950, which outlawed the Communist Party and made it an offence to propagate communist ideas. Before the Act was passed, the CPSA, together with the ANC, SAIC and APO, planned a May Day protest for 1 May 1950 in Johannesburg to protest about plans to ban the party. Although the government banned all meetings and sent police reinforcements to the city, the May Day protests went ahead. The police attacked gatherings of protesters and eighteen strikers were killed and thirty wounded by police gunfire.

A few days before the Act was due to come into effect, the CPSA voluntarily disbanded itself. This was a controversial decision. The leadership believed that dissolving the party would protect its members from arrest and the penalty of a ten-year jail sentence once the law was in place. It would also save the assets of the party from being liquidated. But some members disagreed and felt that the CPSA should have taken a more defiant stand and that the members themselves should have been consulted. The government went one step further and, in an amendment to the Act, made it retroactive, which meant that the new law applied to anyone who had ever been a member of the Communist Party or could be considered to be a communist by his or her actions.

At the time of its banning, the CPSA claimed to have between 2,000 and 3,000 active members. Many of them remained active in opposition, as members of other political organisations, such as the SAIC, the ANC or the new Congress of Democrats (formed in 1953). Others worked in the trade union movement, especially in SACTU. However, many of them were served with banning orders, which made it difficult for them to continue any active protest actions.

Shortly after the Suppression of Communism Act was passed, the government banned the *Guardian*. It later reappeared under a succession of different names, such as *The Clarion*, *The People's World*, *Advance*, *New Age* and *Spark*, but each was banned in turn. One of the journalists who wrote for these, and was editor of the *Guardian* and later of *New Age*, was **Ruth First**. Her work as an investigative journalist exposed some of the harsh realities of labour conditions under apartheid.

Unlike the ANC, the Communist Party was briefly represented in the all-white parliament. The 1936 Representation of Voters Act, which had disenfranchised African male voters in the Cape (the only province in which anyone who was not white had any vote at all), had made provision for the election of three white 'native representatives' to represent Africans in the all-white parliament, as well as similar representation in the Cape Provincial Council. In 1948, Sam Kahn of the CPSA was elected as one of these representatives, until he was expelled from parliament in 1952. Another communist, Brian Bunting, was elected in his place until he too was expelled in 1953. Ray Alexander, a trade unionist and member of the CPSA since the age of 16, was elected in 1954, but was prevented by police from entering the parliament building to take up her seat as one of the native representatives.

In 1953, former members of the CPSA met at an underground conference and reformed the party under a new name – the South African Communist Party (SACP) – to operate in secret, with the aim of 'carrying forward and raising the banner of the Communist movement under the new and testing conditions of illegality' (quoted in www.sahistory.org.za/banned-organisation-1950-1959). Moses Kotane, who had been general secretary of the CPSA since 1939, held the same position in the new organisation, a position he retained until his death in 1978. Some SACP members helped to draft the Freedom Charter in 1955, although they could not participate openly in the Congress of the People because of their banning orders. Several members of the SACP, including Bram Fischer, Joe Slovo, Ruth First, J.B. Marks and **Yusuf Dadoo**, were among the 156 people charged with treason in 1956, although all of them were eventually acquitted.

The existence of the SACP remained unknown for several years. In 1960, during the state of emergency, the SACP issued a leaflet urging people to intensify their resistance. It also revealed that a journal called *The African Communist*, which had first appeared the previous

Yusuf Dadoo (1909–83)

He qualified as a doctor in Edinburgh and returned to South Africa, where he became involved in political activism against discrimination. He was an organiser of the Indian Passive Resistance campaign and a signatory to the pact establishing greater cooperation between Africans and Indians. He was deputy chair of the planning committee for the Defiance Campaign and served as chairperson of both the SAIC and the SACP. In spite of the Treason Trial and frequent banning orders, he continued his political work underground. After 1960, he was asked by the SACP and SAIC to go into exile to act as spokesperson for the resistance movement. He was based in London until his death. He is buried in the city's Highgate Cemetery, a few metres from the grave of Karl Marx.

Figure 7.9 Yusuf Dadoo (left) and Joe Slovo (right) participating in a protest in London organised by the Anti-Apartheid Movement in November 1963 during the Rivonia Trial

Govan Mbeki (1910–2001)

A graduate of Fort Hare University, he was a journalist, intellectual and political activist as a member of both the ANC and SACP, and was committed to socialist ideals. As editor of the *New Age* newspaper before its banning under the Suppression of Communism Act, he drew attention to the plight of people in the reserves. His most acclaimed book, *The Peasants' Revolt*, an analysis of rural struggles in Pondoland and other areas, earned him international recognition. As a member of the national high command of MK, he was arrested in the Rivonia raid and sentenced to life imprisonment. His son, Thabo Mbeki, played a leading role in the ANC in exile and succeeded Mandela as president of South Africa.

year, was the official mouthpiece of the party. After the ANC was banned, members of the SACP played a key role in setting up Umkhonto we Sizwe (MK) and in working for it. Liliesleaf Farm in Rivonia, Johannesburg, was bought by the SACP to serve as the headquarters of the national high command, and some of the Rivonia trialists who were arrested there were members of the SACP, such as **Govan Mbeki**. After 1964, many SACP members went into exile to continue the liberation struggle from abroad.

Although the numbers of people who were members of the Communist Party were never large, the party played a significant role in organising non-violent and violent protests against apartheid, even though it was banned two years after the National Party came to power. Members of the Communist Party were frequently members of other organisations as well, such as the ANC, SAIC, Congress of Democrats and MK. However, the links between the Communist Party and the ANC made Western governments wary of giving full support to the ANC in exile.

End of section activities

1 Prepare a short presentation on the role played by one of these people as members of the South African Communist Party, both before and after it was banned in 1950: Joe Slovo, Ruth First, Moses Kotane, Bram Fischer, J.B. Marks, Ray Alexander, Govan Mbeki, Yusuf Dadoo.

2 How did the CPSA try to ensure the continuity of its campaign against apartheid even after it was banned in 1950?

7.5 How effective was the armed struggle launched by Umkhonto we Sizwe (MK)?

The establishment of MK

After the banning of the ANC in April 1960 and the failure of the stayaway organised to coincide with Republic Day in May 1961, some senior members of the ANC began to consider the use of violent tactics and adopting an armed struggle. In June 1961, the executive decided that, although the ANC itself would not change its support for non-violence, those who disagreed could form a separate organisation. This was the background to the establishment of Umkhonto we Size ('Spear of the Nation' in Zulu or Xhosa), commonly referred to as MK.

However, MK was not founded solely by ANC members. The ANC's allies in the Congress Alliance (the SAIC, the Congress of Democrats, SACTU and the CPO) were also involved in the discussions leading to MK's formation. The SACP played a key role too, although not all members of the party agreed on the need for violence. Unlike the ANC (which at that stage did not have a multi-racial membership), MK was open to whites, coloureds and Indians as well as Africans. A limited number of the founder members of MK had some military experience, either as part of the South African army in North Africa during the Second World War, or (in one case) as a member of Irgun, the underground Jewish organisation that fought the British in postwar Palestine.

Structure and planning

MK was set up as a separate and autonomous organisation, which operated independently of the ANC. Nelson Mandela of the ANC and **Joe Slovo** of the SACP drafted the manifesto for MK. MK planned a sabotage campaign that would attack economic installations and public facilities, or targets which had symbolic political significance, but would avoid bloodshed. They hoped that this, together with the impact of international sanctions, would be enough to convince the National Party government to negotiate. In Beinart's words they wanted to use 'constrained violence to persuade' (1994, p. 212). However, at the same time they started planning for the second stage of the campaign which was guerrilla warfare, and sent some men to China for military training.

Historical debate:
Historians have debated the issue of whether it was the ANC or the SACP who first took the decision to embark on an armed struggle. There is a great deal of evidence to suggest that it was the SACP late in 1960, although the ANC was discussing the issue at the time but had not taken any formal decisions. Historians Irina Filatova and Apollon Davidson, in *The Hidden Thread* (2013, p. 299), contend that documents in Moscow archives confirm that the SACP were the first to make this decision.

Joe Slovo (1926–95)

He was a member of the Communist Party, a founder member of the Congress of Democrats, helped to draft the Freedom Charter, was a Treason Trialist, and one of the earliest members of MK. He left South Africa on an external mission in June 1963, one month before the raid on Liliesleaf Farm. In exile he served as chief of staff of MK, secretary general of the SACP, and was the first white member of the ANC national executive. He returned to South Africa in 1990 after the unbanning of the ANC and SACP, and played a prominent and conciliatory role in the negotiations with the National Party.

Before the actual **sabotage** campaign started, MK set up the organisational structure. The 'national high command' was situated at Liliesleaf Farm in Rivonia, on the outskirts of Johannesburg, which had been bought with funds provided by the SACP. The high command set up regional structures in different centres of the country, and they in turn set up local units to carry out the actual sabotage, normally operating in cells of four people. Where possible, people with technical or military skills were recruited, but many members had no such experience. The regional command selected the type of installation to be targeted in an area, and then selected the specific targets, independently of the national high command. Members at all levels were instructed in the use of explosives and making bombs. The organisation was done independently of the leadership of the SACP and ANC. The ANC itself continued to use traditional forms of non-violent protest, such as urging a boycott of Afrikaner-owned newspapers.

The sabotage campaign

The sabotage campaign started in December 1961, with incendiary bombings in Durban, Cape Town and Johannesburg. Targets included a post office, the Bantu Affairs Commissioner's Office in Johannesburg and the Resettlement Board Headquarters in Meadowlands (the place to which the displaced residents from Sophiatown had been forced to move). Over the next eighteen months, MK carried out 200 attacks around the country. Some of these were minor incidents, such as severing cables or setting fire to mailboxes, but others were more damaging and included bomb attacks on public buildings and a railway signals system. Most of the attacks were in Port Elizabeth, followed by Cape Town, and then Durban and Johannesburg. Although the national high command had directed that the aim was to avoid bloodshed, not all the attacks complied with this. There were instances of bombs being thrown into railway carriages and beerhalls, which threatened civilian lives, and there were also attacks on policemen and suspected collaborators.

Although there were a large number of attacks, they did not have as much impact as the organisers had hoped. Paul Maylam (1986, p. 190) suggests this was because they caused 'limited damage and gained little publicity'. Tom Lodge (1983, p. 236) attributes it to the 'considerably more frightening activities of Poqo' at the time.

The sabotage campaign was just the first stage in MK's plan to overthrow the government. The second was to organise a guerrilla campaign. They started to implement this by recruiting people to undergo military training in the Soviet Union, China and other African countries. Initially 300 were recruited and sent out of the country, but some of them were captured in what was then Northern Rhodesia by the British colonial authorities and sent back to South Africa.

Historians question whether adopting a strategy of violence was the most practical decision, given the lack of experience of those involved, and the power of the state and the measures that it was prepared to use to crush the movement. Tom Lodge (1983, p. 238) suggests that 'it is difficult not to conclude that the planning and preparations undertaken for a guerrilla insurgency were, to say the least, premature'.

The Rivonia raid

The government infiltrated MK with spies, so was able to anticipate its attacks. The law also allowed the police to detain people indefinitely without trial and this weakened the movement, as did the use of torture by the police to extract information from political prisoners. As a result of these methods, they were able to identify and arrest the leaders at the headquarters in Rivonia in July 1963. Among those captured at Rivonia were Walter Sisulu and Govan Mbeki. Other prominent MK leaders were not there: Mandela was serving a prison sentence after his arrest and conviction for leaving the country illegally, and Joe Slovo had been instructed to leave the country to brief Oliver Tambo on MK's plans a month before. Among other frequent visitors to Liliesleaf who were not there at the time of the raid was Bram Fischer, who subsequently led the defence team in the Rivonia Trial. Among the documents that were seized at the time of the raid were two copies of a document called 'Operation Mayibuye' (Operation Comeback), which contained detailed plans for a guerrilla uprising. It was based on the strategies of the Cuban Revolution.

Figure 7.10 Today Liliesleaf Farm is a museum and heritage centre where visitors can learn about the history of apartheid and resistance to it, and the part that the events at Liliesleaf played in the resistance movement

At the subsequent Rivonia Trial, the defence claimed that Operation Mayibuye was a draft document, yet to be adopted as policy by the high command of MK. However, there is some dispute as to whether this was the case. According to Hermann Giliomee

Theory of knowledge

History, ways of knowing and interpretations: The brochure in Figure 7.10 calls Liliesleaf 'a place of liberation', 'a place to reflect' and 'a place to remember'. What part do heritage sites and the way they present information influence how we interpret the past?

Fact: MK received a huge injection of new members after the Soweto uprising in 1976. This started as a protest about the quality of Bantu Education but became a nationwide uprising. Although it was brutally suppressed, it was the point at which the tide began to turn against the apartheid government. After it, thousands of students left South Africa and received training in MK camps in other African countries. As a result, MK was able to launch far bigger and more successful sabotage attacks in the late 1970s and early 1980s. Targets included the dockyards at Durban, the Sasol oil refinery, the Air Force headquarters in Pretoria and the Koeberg nuclear power station outside Cape Town.

and Bernard Mbenga, in *New History of South Africa* (2007, p. 338), Joe Slovo and Govan Mbeki thought that it had been adopted, but Nelson Mandela, Bram Fischer and several SACP officials did not.

After the arrest of the leaders in Rivonia, Bram Fischer and Wilton Mkwayi tried to revive MK. Mkwayi and others formed a new high command to continue the sabotage campaign. But the new members were arrested in September 1964. The charges included the bombing of factories, government buildings, railway signal cables and petrol depots. The accused, who included Mkwayi, the new head of MK, received sentences ranging from twelve years to life imprisonment.

End of section activities

1. Look at the 'Overcoming Apartheid' website of the University of Michigan, at http://overcomingapartheid.msu.edu/multimedia.php?id=65-259-F and listen to the interviews with activists who were involved in the armed struggle as members of MK. Also use other sources to find out more information about people involved in the armed struggle. Would you describe them as idealistic amateurs or hardened professionals? What do you learn about the impact that their involvement had on their personal lives and on their families?

2. What were the causes and consequences of the establishment of MK?

3. Explain why the establishment of MK was such a significant development in the liberation struggle in South Africa.

7.6 What was the significance of the role played by Nelson Mandela?

Early life

Rolihlahla Mandela was born in rural Transkei in 1918. As the son of a minor chief, he was brought up in the Thembu royal household after the death of his father. At primary school he was given the name 'Nelson', following the custom at the time to give all children 'Christian' names. In later life he was often referred to as 'Madiba', which was the name of the Thembu clan into which he was born. He attended Healdtown secondary school, one of the best mission schools in the Transkei, and from there went to Fort Hare, the major educational institution for blacks from all over southern Africa, where one of his fellow students was Oliver Tambo. After he was expelled from there for political activities, he left for Johannesburg in 1941, determined to train as a lawyer. There he met **Walter Sisulu** who, like Mandela, was to become a leading political figure in South Africa. Two of Mandela's fellow students at the University of the Witwatersrand were Joe Slovo and Ruth First, both of whom were members of the CPSA.

Mandela grew increasingly involved in politics; he joined the ANC and became a founder member of the Congress Youth League in 1944, together with Walter Sisulu and Oliver Tambo. He became the secretary-general of the Youth League in 1948 and from then on played an active role in the protests and resistance to apartheid. At the same time, he completed his law studies and, in 1952, he and Tambo opened the first black law firm in South Africa. During the next two years they defended hundreds of people affected by apartheid laws.

Tambo later wrote: 'Of all that group of young men, Mandela and his close friend and co-leader Walter Sisulu were perhaps the fastest to get to grips with the harsh realities of the African struggle against the most powerful adversary in Africa' (quoted in Beinart, 1994, p. 160).

Political involvement during the 1950s

Initially Mandela supported the Africanist views of Anton Lembede, believing that the ANC should stand on its own and not enter into alliances with other organisations. However, the harsh police actions during the 1950 May Day strike convinced him of the need for a broad-based non-racial alliance against the National Party and white domination. Together with Sisulu, Tambo and Moses Kotane of the CPSA, he made plans to forge what came to be known as the Congress Alliance.

During the 1952 Defiance Campaign, Mandela became one of the most influential leaders in the ANC. He was selected as the 'volunteer-in-chief'. He acted as its public spokesperson and travelled around the country enlisting volunteers. For his role in the Defiance Campaign he was arrested and charged under the Suppression of Communism Act, and given a nine-month prison sentence with hard labour, suspended for two years. At the end of 1952, he was also served with a banning order that prevented him from attending public meetings or from leaving the magisterial district of Johannesburg. His banning order was repeatedly renewed during the next nine years. Although this banning

Figure 7.12   Walter Sisulu (1912–2003)

He was a friend and mentor to Nelson Mandela and, like him, a founder member of the Congress Youth League. His strategic grasp and organisational abilities helped to transform the ANC into a mass-based organisation. He played leading roles in the Defiance Campaign and Congress Alliance, and was banned, imprisoned, placed under house arrest and charged with treason. He joined the underground SACP and was an important link in establishing a working relationship between the ANC and SACP. With Mandela and Joe Slovo, he was part of the decision to establish MK. Arrested in the raid on Liliesleaf Farm, he was sentenced to life imprisonment in the Rivonia Trial. After his release and the unbanning of the ANC in 1990, he played a key role in the negotiations that led to democratic elections in 1994.

Figure 7.11   Nelson Mandela burns his pass during the Defiance Campaign. As 'volunteer-in-chief' he played a leading role in the protests

order prevented him from playing any obvious role in ANC activities, behind the scenes he played a crucial part in planning the protest campaigns of the ANC and Congress Alliance. Unable to attend the Congress of the People, he watched the proceedings from the rooftop of a nearby Indian-owned shop.

When the ANC called off the Defiance Campaign, it formulated the 'M Plan' (Mandela Plan), so-called because Mandela was put in charge of it. This was a contingency plan in case the ANC was banned as the CPSA had been two years previously. The idea was to organise the ANC into street-based cells, so that it could communicate with its members without using public meetings or the press, both of which methods were subject to government restrictions.

In December 1956, Mandela was one of 156 people arrested and charged with treason. Over the next five years the charges against most of the accused were gradually dropped. Mandela and the final twenty-nine others were finally acquitted in March 1961.

SOURCE H

As early as 1953 he and Walter Sisulu started considering the possibility of the ANC embracing a programme of guerrilla warfare, but he remained among the more cautious figures in the ANC leadership during the 1950s, supporting the early curtailment of protests and opposing the use of picketing during strikes. Unusually among ANC leaders, he maintained contact with rural leaders, particularly in the Transkei, for he was anxious that the ANC should retain support from the chieftaincy despite the latter's incorporation into the government's 'tribal authorities'.

Mandela's moderation at this time was partly motivated by tactical circumspection, a consequence of a general recognition that he shared with communists in the movement that action needed to be supported by well-structured organisation. He was more aware than many of his fellow leaders of the weaknesses in the ANC's organisation.

Throughout the 1950s he remained optimistic that the ANC's pressure might induce liberal predispositions among whites, a conciliatory attitude that was reinforced by his more civil encounters with officials and his friendships with white activists... Until 1960 Mandela was convinced that most ANC rank-and-file supporters remained morally unready for direct and forceful confrontation with state authority.

H. Giliomee and B. Mbenga (eds.) (2007) *New History of South Africa*, Cape Town: Tafelberg, p. 332.

After Sharpeville

When the government declared a state of emergency after Sharpeville, Mandela and his co-accused in the Treason Trial were among the thousands of people detained. The subsequent banning of the ANC and PAC prompted Mandela and other activists to consider a change of tactics for the political organisations which were no longer able to operate legally.

In March 1961, a year after Sharpeville and shortly before the Treason Trial finally came to an end, Mandela made an appearance at the All-In Africa Conference in Pietermaritzburg, where he made his first public speech in nearly a decade. His banning order had expired shortly before the conference and the authorities had not yet renewed it. Other than his address in the Rivonia trial courtroom, this was to be the last public speech he made for twenty-nine years. After the conference he went underground, and spent his time travelling around the country helping to organise the planned three-day national strike for 29–31 May to coincide with the declaration of a republic. But Mandela called off the strike on the second day after harsh police reprisals against the strikers.

The banning of the ANC, followed by the suppression of the three-day strike effectively closed the door on legal political opposition and non-violent protest, and convinced Mandela that the ANC would need to look at other options. Along with other leaders in the ANC, he was influenced by displays of violence that had flared up in some protest actions around the country. He felt that it would be better to channel and control grass-roots anger than to allow random acts of terrorism that would lead to increased bitterness and hostility, and make any negotiated settlement less likely in the future. When the ANC national executive met in June 1961, Mandela put forward his view. The national executive subsequently approved the establishment of MK, and Mandela was asked to set it up, together with Joe Slovo of the SACP. In William Beinart's words, he was 'at the heart of the transformation of the ANC from a nationalist protest movement to a national liberation movement' (Beinart, 1994, p. 160).

SOURCE I

I saw non-violence in the Gandhian model not as an inviolable principle but as a tactic to be used when the situation demanded… I called for non-violent protest as long as it was effective…

[Later] I said that the time for passive resistance had ended, that non-violence was a useless strategy and could never overturn a white minority regime bent on retaining its power at any cost. At the end of the day, I said, violence was the only weapon that would destroy apartheid and we must be prepared, in the near future, to use that weapon…

Gandhi [was] dealing with a foreign power that ultimately was more realistic and farsighted. That was not the case with the Afrikaners in South Africa. Non-violent passive resistance is effective as long as your opponent adheres to the same rules as you do. But if peaceful protest is met with violence, its efficacy is at an end. For me non-violence was not a moral principle but a strategy; there is no moral goodness in using an ineffective weapon.

N. Mandela (1994) *Long Walk to Freedom,* New York: Abacus, pp. 147 and 182–3.

ACTIVITY

Compare and contrast the views expressed in Sources H and I about Nelson Mandela's attitude towards violence.

Mandela remained underground and managed to avoid arrest for seventeen months, often disguised as a driver or gardener, despite an intensive police search for him. During this time he travelled around the country encouraging and organising local groups. He also attended a Pan-African Conference in Addis Ababa, travelled around Africa meeting some of the leaders of the newly independent states, received military training with the Algerian Army of National Liberation and visited Britain, where he met leaders of opposition parties. One of his chief tasks abroad was to organise military training for MK recruits. After his return to South Africa he was finally arrested at a police roadblock between Durban and Johannesburg, on his way back from a meeting with Albert Luthuli. Many historians note that it was suspected that his arrest came after a tip-off to the police by an American CIA agent based in Durban, but this has never been confirmed.

He was charged with organising strikes and leaving the country without permission, and was given a five-year jail sentence with hard labour. He was imprisoned first in Pretoria Central Prison, where he met up with his former colleague and political rival Robert

Figure 7.13 Oliver Tambo and Nelson Mandela in Addis Ababa in 1962, where they attended a Pan-African Conference and explained to delegates why the ANC had switched from non-violent to violent forms of protest

Sobukwe, who had been sentenced and jailed after Sharpeville. Mandela was later transferred to Robben Island, and was serving his sentence there when the rest of the MK leaders were arrested in the raid on Liliesleaf Farm. Among the documents seized in the raid was Mandela's diary of his African tour.

Mandela was charged with ten others in the Rivonia Trial, where he was officially the 'first accused'. In his famous speech from the dock, he took the opportunity (so long denied because of banning orders) to detail the history of discrimination, oppression and non-violent protest, explaining why the ANC had resorted in the end to armed resistance. The speech received wide publicity both in South Africa and all over the world, and did much to create the Mandela legend over the many years he was in prison. Mandela and seven others were sentenced to life imprisonment, most of which he spent on Robben Island. For the next twenty-six years his contact with the outside world was strictly monitored and controlled, but his stature as a leader ensured that he was the political prisoner that the world did not forget.

End of section activities

1   Write an obituary for Nelson Mandela in which you try to give an objective perspective of the significance of the role he played in South African history between 1948 and 1964.

2   How does this cartoonist try to portray Mandela's significance in the struggle for rights and freedom in South Africa?

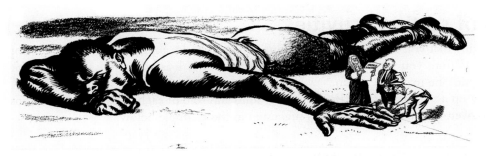

Figure 7.14   This cartoon by Leslie Illingworth was published in the *Daily Mail* on 15 June 1964 after Mandela had been sentenced to life imprisonment

7.7 What was the significance of the role played by Albert Luthuli?

Albert Luthuli was born in Bulawayo, Zimbabwe (then Rhodesia) in 1898, where his father was working as a missionary. He moved to South Africa as a child and was educated at mission schools. He worked as a teacher and lay preacher until he was elected as chief of the Groutville reserve in KwaZulu-Natal in 1935. He joined the ANC in 1945 and became the provincial leader. He was a deeply religious man and strongly supported the idea of non-violent resistance. Because of his support for the 1952 Defiance Campaign, the government ordered him to resign from the ANC or lose his position as chief. When he refused to leave the ANC, he was dismissed as a chief, and was subsequently referred to as 'ex-chief Albert Luthuli'. He played an active role in the Defiance Campaign, recruiting volunteers and addressing meetings. In December 1952 he was elected president of the ANC by a large majority.

Early in 1953, the government banned him and he was forced to stay at his home in Stanger in KwaZulu-Natal. In spite of the difficulties that this caused, he was re-elected as president of the ANC. He was one of the people arrested and charged in the Treason Trial but was released because of a lack of evidence, although he remained banned. After the Sharpeville massacre and the banning of the ANC, Luthuli was arrested and detained along with thousands of others during the state of emergency. Although Luthuli did not support violence, he accepted the decision by the ANC to adopt an armed struggle and form MK.

He was committed to non-racialism and was widely respected internationally for his resolute support for non-violence and, in 1960, was awarded the Nobel Peace Prize. His banning order was lifted for ten days to allow him to go to Oslo in Norway to receive the award. His book, *Let My People Go*, is about the struggle against apartheid. He was the first of four South Africans to receive the Nobel Peace Prize. The others were Archbishop Desmond Tutu (1984) and Nelson Mandela and F.W. de Klerk (1993). In contemporary South Africa the 'Order of Luthuli' is the highest award that can be made for contributions to democracy, human rights, justice and peace.

Luthuli remained president of the banned ANC until his death in 1967. Many people, including the US secretary of state, Robert Kennedy, visited him and consulted him at his home in rural KwaZulu-Natal. He died in 1967 when he was reportedly struck by a train while out walking near his home.

End of section activities

1 Imagine that you are a journalist working in South Africa in the 1960s. Write a list of the questions you would have liked to ask Albert Luthuli as well as the answers that you think he may have given.

2 Draw up a table to summarise the background and role of each of these organisations or movements, using the headings suggested in the example below:

Organisation	Circumstances leading to its formation	Aims/Vision	Impact
National Party			
ANC			
PAC			
SACP			
MK			

End of chapter activities

Summary

You need to be able to examine critically the role played by key groups and individuals in the struggle for rights and freedom in South Africa. You should pay particular attention to the role played by individuals such as Nelson Mandela and Albert Luthuli in the context of the broader resistance struggle. You should also be able to explain the role of the National Party in implementing apartheid.

Summary activity

Copy the diagram below. Use the information in this chapter, and from other sources, to make brief notes under each heading.

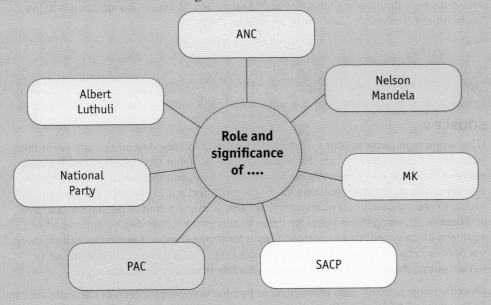

Paper 1 exam practice

Question

Compare and contrast what **Sources A** and **B** reveal about the attitudes of the British and South African governments towards decolonisation and political freedom in Africa.

[6 marks]

Skill

Cross-referencing/comparing and contrasting two sources.

7

SOURCE A

The wind of change is blowing through this continent and whether we like it or not, this growth of national consciousness is a political fact… it has been our aim in the countries for which we have borne responsibility… to create a society that respects the rights of individuals, a society in which men are given the opportunity to grow to their full stature – and that must in our view include the opportunity of an increasing share in political power and responsibility, a society finally in which individual merit and individual merit alone, is the criterion for a man's advancement, whether political or economic…

As a fellow member of the Commonwealth we always try I think and perhaps succeeded in giving to South Africa our full support and encouragement, but I hope you won't mind my saying frankly that there are some aspects of your policies which make it impossible for us to do this without being false to our own deep convictions about the political destinies of free men to which in our own territories we are trying to give effect.

An extract from British prime minister Harold Macmillan's 'Wind of Change' speech to the South African parliament, Cape Town, 3 February 1960.

SOURCE B

[T]he white man came to Africa… [and] has remained to stay. And particularly we in this southern most portion of Africa, have such a stake here that this is our only motherland, we have nowhere else to go. We set up a country bare, and the [Africans] came in this country and settled certain portions for themselves, and it is in line with the thinking of Africa, to grant those fullest rights which we also with you admit all people should have and believe providing those rights for those people in the fullest degree in that part of southern Africa which their forefathers found for themselves and settled in. But similarly, we believe in balance, we believe in allowing exactly those same full opportunities to remain within the grasp of the white man who has made all this possible.

An extract from South African prime minister Hendrik Verwoerd's speech to the South African parliament on 3 February 1960, made in response to Macmillan's 'Wind of Change' speech.

Student answer

Source A states that Britain accepts that change is happening in Africa and supports the concepts of decolonisation and political freedom. It also believes in equal rights for all individuals and a society in which individual merit is the sole criterion that should count.

Source B responds by stating that Africans should only have political rights in the parts of South Africa where their ancestors settled, but that whites who regard South Africa as their motherland should have the same rights in the rest of South Africa. He is obviously trying to justify the policy of separate development.

Examiner's comments

The answer simply paraphrases both sources without making any attempt to compare or contrast them. There is no attempt to link the sources, or to comment on them properly. The student has thus done enough to get into Band 3, and so be awarded only three marks.

Activity

Look again at the two sources, the simplified mark scheme in Chapter 8 and the student answer above. Now try to rewrite the answer, linking the two sources by pointing out similarities and differences between them, and commenting on the sources without simply paraphrasing them.

Paper 2 practice questions

1   Compare and contrast the views and tactics of the African National Congress and the Pan Africanist Congress.

2   Examine the role and importance of the South African Communist Party in resistance politics between 1950 and 1964.

3   'The African National Congress was justified in adopting a policy of armed resistance against the apartheid government.' To what extent do you agree with this statement?

4   Compare and contrast the roles played by Albert Luthuli and Nelson Mandela in the protests against apartheid between 1950 and 1964.

Exam practice

Introduction

You have now completed your study of the main aspects and events of Rights and Protest – the struggle for rights and freedoms against discrimination based on race in the United States between 1954 and 1965 and South Africa between 1948 and 1964. In the previous chapters, you have had practice at answering some of the types of source-based questions you will have to deal with in Paper 1. In this chapter, you will gain experience of dealing with:

- the longer Paper 1 question, which requires you to use both sources and your own knowledge to write a mini-essay
- the essay questions you will meet in Paper 2.

Exam skills needed for IB History

This book is designed primarily to prepare both Standard and Higher Level students for the Paper 1 Rights and Protest topic (Prescribed Subject 4), by providing the necessary historical knowledge and understanding, as well as an awareness of the key historical debates and perspectives. However, it will also help you prepare for Paper 2, by giving you the chance to practise writing essays. The skills you need for answering both Paper 1 and Paper 2 exam questions are explained in the following pages.

Paper 1 exam practice

Paper 1 skills

This section of the book is designed to give you the skills and understanding to tackle Paper 1 questions. These are based on the comprehension, critical analysis and evaluation of different types of historical sources as evidence, along with the use of appropriate historical contextual knowledge.

For example, you will need to test sources for value and limitations (i.e., their reliability and utility, especially in view of their origin, purpose and content) – a skill essential for historians. A range of sources has been provided, including extracts from official documents, tables of statistics, memoirs and speeches, as well as visual sources such as photographs and cartoons.

In order to analyse and evaluate sources as historical evidence, you will need to ask the following 'W' questions of historical sources:

- **Who** produced it? Were they in a position to know?
- **What** type of source is it? What is its nature – is it a primary or secondary source?
- **Where** and **when** was it produced? What was happening at the time?
- **Why** was it produced? Was its purpose to inform or to persuade? Is it an accurate attempt to record facts, or is it an example of propaganda?
- **Who** was the intended audience – decision-makers, or the general public?

You should then consider how the answers to these questions affect a source's value.

The example below shows you how to find the information related to the 'W' questions. You will need this information in order to evaluate sources for their value and limitations.

SOURCE A

During my lifetime I have dedicated myself to this struggle of the African people, I have fought against white domination, and I have fought against black domination. I have cherished the ideal of a democratic and free society in which all persons live together in harmony and with equal opportunities. It is an ideal which I hope to live for and to achieve. But if it needs be it is an ideal for which I am prepared to die.

The concluding words of **Nelson Mandela's address to the court** during **the Rivonia Trail**, on **20 April 1964**. He used the opportunity to explain to **South Africa and the world**, why **the ANC had adopted an armed struggle** against the apartheid government.

Who? Nelson Mandela (produced it)

What? Address to the court (type of source)

Where? The Rivonia Trial (on what occasion)

When? 20 April 1964 (date/ time of production)

Why? Explain why the ANC had adopted an armed struggle (possible purpose)

Who? South Africa and the world (intended audience)

This approach will help you become familiar with interpreting, understanding, analysing and evaluating different types of historical sources. It will also aid you in synthesising critical analysis of sources with historical knowledge when constructing an explanation or analysis of some aspect or development of the past. Remember – for Paper 1, as for Paper 2, you need to acquire, select and deploy relevant historical knowledge to explain causes and consequences, continuity and change. You also need to develop and show (where relevant) an awareness of historical debates, and different perspectives and interpretations.

Paper 1 contains four types of question:

1　Comprehension/understanding of a source (2 or 3 marks)
2　Assessing the value and limitations of a source (4 marks)
3　Cross-referencing/comparing or contrasting two sources (6 marks)
4　Using and evaluating sources and knowledge to reach a judgement (9 marks)

Comprehension/understanding of a source

Comprehension questions require you to understand a source and either extract two or three relevant points that relate to the particular question, or make one or two comments about the message of a source.

Examples of a comprehension questions can be found at the end of Chapters 2 and 5.

Origin: the 'who, what, when and where?' questions.

Purpose: reasons/what the writer or creator was trying to achieve/who the intended audience was.

Content: this is the information or explanation(s) provided by the source.

Remember: A source doesn't have to be primary to be useful. Remember, too, that content isn't the only aspect to have possible value. The context, the person who produced it and so on can be important in offering an insight.

Examiner's tips

Step 1: Read the source and highlight/underline key points.

Step 2: Write a concise answer. Just a couple of brief sentences are needed, giving the information necessary to show that you have understood the message of the source – but make sure you make three clear points for a three-mark question and two clear points for a two-mark question. If relevant, also try to make some brief overall comment about the source. Make it as easy as possible for the examiner to give you the marks by clearly distinguishing between the points.

Common mistake

Make sure you don't comment on the wrong source! (Mistakes like this are made every year. Remember – every mark is important for your final grade.)

Simplified mark scheme

For each item of relevant/correct information identified, award one mark – up to a maximum of 2 or 3 marks.

Assessing the value and limitations of a source

Value and limitations (utility/reliability) questions require you to assess one source over a range of possible issues/aspects – and to comment on its value to historians studying a particular event or period of history.

Examiner's tips

The main areas you need to consider in relation to the source and the information / view it provides are:

- **Origin**, **Purpose** and **Content**;
- value and limitations.

These areas need to be linked in your answer, showing how the value and limitations of the source to historians relates to the source's origin and purpose.

For example, a source might be useful because it is primary – the event depicted was witnessed by the person producing it. But was the person in a position to know? Is the view an untypical view of the event? What is its nature? Is it a private diary entry (therefore possibly more likely to be true), or is it a speech or piece of propaganda intended to persuade? The value of a source may be limited by some aspects, but that doesn't mean it has no value at all. For example, it may be valuable as evidence of the types of propaganda put out at the time. Similarly, a secondary – or even a tertiary source – can have more value than some primary sources: for instance, because the author might be writing at a time when new evidence has become available.

Step 1: Read the source and highlight/underline key points.

Step 2: Then draw a rough chart or spider diagram to show the origin/purpose/content of the source, and how it links to that source's value/limitation.

Step 3: Write your answer, remembering to deal with all the aspects required: origin, purpose, content, value and limitations. To do this, you will need to make explicit links between a source's origin/purpose/content and its value/limitations to an historian.

Common mistakes

Don't just comment on content and ignore the nature, origin and purpose of the source.

Don't say that a source is/isn't useful because it's primary/secondary.

Simplified mark scheme

Band		Marks
1	**Explicit/developed** consideration of **BOTH** origin, purpose and content **AND** value and limitations.	3–4
2	**Limited consideration/comments** on origin, purpose and content **AND** value and limitations. **OR** more developed comments on **EITHER** origin, purpose and content **OR** value and limitations.	0–2

Examples of value and limitations questions can be found at the end of Chapters 3 and 6.

Cross-referencing/comparing or contrasting two sources

Cross-referencing questions require you to compare and contrast the information/ content/nature of two sources, relating to a particular issue.

Examiner's tips

For cross-referencing questions, you need to provide an integrated comparison, rather than dealing with each source separately.

Step 1: Read the sources and highlight/underline key points.

Step 2: Draw a rough chart or diagram to show the similarities and the differences between the two sources. That way, you should ensure you address both elements of the question.

Step 3: Write your answer, ensuring that you write an integrated comparison. For example, you should comment on how the two sources deal with one aspect, then compare and contrast the sources on another aspect. Avoid simply describing/ paraphrasing each source in turn – you need to make clear and explicit comparisons and contrasts, using precise details from the sources.

Common mistakes

Don't just comment on one of the sources! (Such an oversight happens every year – and will lose you four of the six marks available.)

Make sure you comment on the sources identified in the question – don't select one (or two) incorrect sources!

Be careful to make explicit comparisons – do not fall into the trap of writing about the two sources separately and leaving the similarities/differences implicit.

8

Examples of cross-referencing questions can be found at the end of Chapters 4 and 7.

Band		Marks
1	**Both sources linked**, with detailed references to **BOTH** sources, identifying **BOTH** similarities and differences.	6
2	**Both sources linked**, with detailed references to **BOTH** sources, identifying **EITHER** similarities or differences.	4–5
3	Comments on **BOTH** sources, but treats **each one separately**.	3
4	Discusses/comments on **just one source**.	0–2

Using and evaluating sources and knowledge to reach a judgement

The fourth type of Paper 1 is a judgement question. Judgement questions are a synthesis of source evaluation and own knowledge.

Examiner's tips

This fourth type of Paper 1 question requires you to produce a mini-essay – with a clear/relevant argument – to address the question/statement given in the question. You should try to develop and present an argument and/or come to a balanced judgement by analysing and using these four sources and your own knowledge.

Before you write your answer to this kind of question, you may find it useful to draw a rough chart to note what the sources show in relation to the question. This will also make sure you refer to all or at least most of the sources. Note, however, that some sources may hint at more than one factor/result. When using your own knowledge, make sure it is relevant to the question.

Look carefully at the simplified mark scheme – this will help you focus on what you need to do to reach the top bands and so score the higher marks.

Common mistake

Don't just deal with sources or your own knowledge! Every year, some candidates (even good ones) do this, and so limit themselves to – at best – only five out of the nine marks available.

Simplified mark scheme

Band		Marks
1	**Consistently focused** on the question. **Developed and balanced analysis**, with precise use of **BOTH** sources **AND relevant/accurate** own knowledge. Sources and own knowledge are used **consistently and effectively** together, to support argument/judgement.	8–9
2	**Mostly focused** on the question. Developed analysis, with relevant use of **BOTH** sources **AND some** detailed own knowledge. But sources and own knowledge **not always combined** to support analysis/judgement.	6–7

Band		Marks
3	**Some focus** on the question. **Some analysis**, using some of the sources **OR** some relevant/accurate own knowledge.	4–5
4	**No/limited focus** on the question. **Limited/generalised** comments on sources **AND/OR** some **limited/inaccurate/irrelevant** own knowledge.	0–3

Student answer

The student answers below have brief examiner's comments in the margins, as well as a longer overall comment at the end. Those parts of the answers that make use of the sources are highlighted in purple. Those parts that deploy relevant own knowledge are highlighted in red. In this way, you should find it easier to follow why particular bands and marks were – or were not – awarded.

Question 1

Using the sources and your own knowledge, evaluate the success of the Freedom Summer of 1964 in advancing black civil rights in the USA. [9 marks]

SOURCE A

More than 700 college students, in the summer of 1964, under the supervision of the Student Nonviolent Coordinating Committee, risked their lives to travel to Mississippi to register black voters and open schools… Many Americans remember the names Andrew Goodman, James Cheney and Michael Schwerner, the three young volunteers who vanished that summer, their bodies later found buried under a dam. What many forget is that these three men disappeared on the very first day of the Mississippi Summer Project (Freedom Summer). Their abduction terrified the other volunteers.

Much more was to come. Some 35 black churches were burned in Mississippi that summer, and five dozen homes and safe houses were bombed. Volunteers were beaten, harassed by the police, arrested on fraudulent charges. Shotguns were fired into the houses where they slept. Pickup trucks filled with armed men followed volunteers around… The summer of 1964 in Mississippi was in some ways a failure for the volunteers. They didn't register as many voters as they had hoped. Their plans to replace Mississippi's all-white delegation at the 1964 Democratic National Convention in Atlantic City came to nothing. But their actions brought the nation's full attention to Mississippi's second-class citizens.

Dwight Garner, a journalist and book critic, writing in the article 'Mississippi Invaded by Idealism', published in *The New York Times* (2010).

SOURCE B

Outside the campaign headquarters of the MSDP in Hattiesburg, Mississippi in 1964, as they prepared for the US general election in November of that year.

SOURCE C

When the civil rights workers invaded the state [Mississippi] in the summer of 1964 to change us, presumably into their own image, they were met with a feeling of some curiosity, but mostly resentment. They spread across the state, made a great show of breaking up our customs, of challenging social practices that had been respected by people here over the years. That was the time of the hippies just coming in and they had on hippie uniforms and conducted themselves in hippie ways. They were not exactly the types of models that most people I knew wanted to copy and so the arrogance they showed in wanting to reform the whole state in the way they thought it should be, created resentment.

William J. Simmons, a spokesman for a White Citizens' Council (an organisation that openly worked to preserve segregation) in an interview for a US television documentary, *Eyes on the Prize* (1987), about the Civil Rights Movement.

SOURCE D

The murders... rocked me to the core of my very being. Lynchings were not unusual. And they were legal, as far as we could see... but I was not used to white men killing white men because of black men... So those murders in 1964 were shocking. And I felt for the mothers of the white boys. You see, the mother of a black boy knows that when he leaves home, she may never see him again, no matter where. But the white mother didn't know that. Those three young men... had the courage to go to the lion's den and try to scrub the lion's teeth... [they] are unmitigated heroes, so we have to lift them up and show them to the world.

Maya Angelou in the preface to *My Mantelpiece: A Memoir of Social Justice,* by Carolyn Goodman and Brad Herzog (New York, 2013).

Student answer

In the summer of 1964, the Civil Rights Movement made a concerted effort to step up its campaign of voter registration amongst African Americans, ahead of the November 1964 presidential election. This was to be between the Democrat incumbent Lyndon Johnson and his running-mate Hubert Humphrey — both of whom were seen as liberal and supportive of civil rights — and the far-right Republican team of Arizona Senator Barry Goldwater and his running-mate William Miller. The SNCC and CORE ran the scheme, a so-called 'Freedom Summer' of campaigning across the state of Mississippi, where levels of registration among blacks were minimal. They also wanted to organise a 'Freedom Democratic Party' to challenge the official whites-only Mississippi Democratic Party; also to set up 'freedom schools' for black children. The photograph in Source B shows the campaign headquarters of the MSDP in Hattiesburg, Mississippi in 1964, as they prepared for the US general election in November of that year, suggesting that the Freedom Summer made a significant impact. The reality, however, was different.

Source A informs us that the 'Freedom Summer' campaign was undertaken by 'more than 700 college students, under the supervision of the Student Nonviolent Coordinating Committee, [who] risked their lives to travel to Mississippi to register black voters and open schools'. These people were predominantly white and came from elite colleges and universities in the northeast and Midwest, with some well-educated African Americans from black colleges in the south. This went down badly in Mississippi, and the Freedom Summer workers were often harassed and bullied by whites. This suggests that their wish to advance the cause of civil rights was met with strong opposition, which would ultimately impact on their overall success. Indeed, to many traditionalists, they appeared to be interfering, arrogant know-alls. Source C shows that many whites in this conservative society were offended by what the interviewee saw as their attempts to unravel their customs and social practices, as held by people for many years. We must consider the bias of this source and the racism of the Deep South; Even Maya Angelou in Source D speaks of a society where 'lynchings were not unusual. And they were legal, as far as we could see.' So this shows the prejudices that the volunteers would have to try to overcome. Nonetheless, their manner of dress — it was the beginning of the Beatles era and the hippie style of fashion — and their conduct leads him to say that many in Mississippi felt that they were 'not exactly the types of models that most people I knew wanted to copy'. This suggests that these workers faced both social criticism as well as political resistance and indeed, they were impeded in their work by beatings, arson and false arrests.

But the Freedom Summer workers' voting campaign was quickly shaken when three of the activists — two of whom were white — were murdered by segregationists who were probably also members of the

EXAMINER'S COMMENT

The introduction contains good background information, setting the events of 1964 in their context; however, some of the information could be cut (US election candidates' names) or expressed more succinctly. The student makes a good reference to the sources and an evaluation; but there needs to be a sharper focus on the argument he/she intends to develop.

EXAMINER'S COMMENT

There is excellent use of information from the other three sources here, both about the arrival and the identity of the workers; their subsequent impact on the people, and the nature of the society they were working in. They are well linked by own knowledge and relevant analysis from the candidate. This is a good paragraph that now appears to be forwarding an argument and answering the question.

8

Ku Klux Klan. They were arrested on a traffic violation, and the police then told segregationists when they would be freed. Upon release, they were followed by three vehicles and subsequently disappeared. There was huge media attention and President Lyndon Johnson ordered a major investigation. FBI agents questioned hundreds of people in an operation codenamed 'Mississippi Burning'. Six weeks later, their bodies were found. They had been severely beaten and killed. This did not deter the workers of the Freedom Summer campaign. But it was the killing of two white men that made the Mississippi murders so notorious, as Source D shows, where Maya Angelou states that the mother of a black boy knows that when he leaves home, she may never see him again, no matter where. But a white mother doesn't know that.

Probably the biggest advance for black rights that summer was not in voting registration (as ultimately, due to intimidation and fear, only 1,600 were able to register to vote); but in the creation of the Mississippi Freedom Democratic Party to challenge the all-white regular Democratic Party. The Freedom Summer workers convinced 80,000 blacks to join it and they elected sixty-eight delegates to go to the 1964 Democratic National Convention in Atlantic City. But, as Source A suggests, it did not amount to much. MFDP was never officially recognised at the Convention, where they presented the assembly with two delegations claiming the same seats. A compromise was offered: their representatives could speak, but not vote; and they could have two token seats in the Mississippi delegation. They were also assured that future Democratic Party conventions would ban discrimination. All but four of the white Mississippi Democratic Party members walked out in protest, whereupon MFDP took the vacated seats, but did not officially take their place. However, Atlantic City led to racially integrated delegations at future conventions and their actions brought the nation's full attention to Mississippi's second-class citizens. It can therefore be seen as an advance in black rights and one of the indirect successes of Freedom Summer, by making the MFDP a viable alternative to Mississippi's 'Jim Crow' Democratic Party delegation.

In conclusion, although the Freedom Summer did not succeed initially in its immediate aim of increasing the black vote in Mississippi, it was important for the advancement of black civil rights because it moved the struggle to a new level, beyond the bus boycotts, Freedom Rides and sit-ins. The Freedom Summer marked the beginning of the end of exclusive white political control of Mississippi. Other Americans could see that black people were fighting for more than a seat at the lunch counter, they were now fighting for a say in the running of the country. The Voting Rights Act of 1965 was proof of this.

Overall examiner's comments

The student has made good use of the information in the sources and has linked them, although they could have been used more. However as this is a source-based paper, this is a good answer. There is also relevant contextual knowledge, showing evidence of a well-read student. But the student has not really contrasted alternative views. A more detailed link to the Voting Rights Act of 1965 would have also improved the answer. Finally there is no mention of the Freedom Schools following an initial quote from Source A. This is an important omission, overlooked perhaps, at the expense of storytelling elsewhere. The answer does develop an argument, and it is referenced throughout; but it could be expressed more crisply and could combine sources and knowledge more effectively. However it gets into Band 2 and would probably score six or possibly seven marks out of the nine available.

Question 2

Using the sources and your own knowledge, evaluate the importance of the role of Martin Luther King in securing civil rights for African Americans in the period 1957–65.

[9 marks]

EXAMINER'S COMMENT

There is excellent knowledge of the details of the murder of the three workers, but it is not all relevant as the student has drifted into storytelling. This is counterproductive when writing against the clock in a timed exam. A source is referred to, but its message is not expressed crisply. This is not as good a section as the previous one and is unnecessarily long.

EXAMINER'S COMMENT

The student has made good use of own knowledge, has used a source and has also analysed the outcome of events surrounding the MFDP and linked it to the overall question. But a contrast could have been made between the pessimism of Source A about the MDFP and the more positive side to it. Reference could also have been made to Source B showing the MDFP in electoral action later that year.

EXAMINER'S COMMENT

The conclusion shows that the student has referred back to the question and has attempted to make a judgement on the accuracy of the statement. It is, however, slightly brief and could have included a direct reference to the MFDP and been more synoptic.

SOURCE A

From 1957 to the mid-1960s, King had no major rival for overall leadership of the Civil Rights Movement… he was equally at home and equally popular with southern black and northern white audiences… but King and the SCLC did not initiate the important phase of the movement that began in 1960–61: the Sit-Ins and the Freedom Rides. But King's reputation was such that he was soon contacted about them and addressed gatherings of students… Even more significantly, his tactics forced a federal response, as happened after Birmingham…

By the time of the Washington march, leaders like King were certainly dependent on the President and Congress to see a Civil Rights Bill pass successfully and… the King approach was subject to serious criticism… Martin Luther King did not appeal to all the nation's African Americans. He was a southerner and, as a Baptist Minister, was seen as someone from the black elite. Malcolm X, by contrast, could be viewed as a role model. Many northern people could identify with him and did so.

D. Paterson, D. Willoughby and S. Willoughby (2001), *Civil Rights in the USA 1863–1980*, Oxford: Heinemann, pp. 287–9.

SOURCE B

King led by example, showing great courage and stamina in the face of opposition, assaults and threats of assassination… With his appeal to American values, such as the belief in liberty, justice and democracy, he inspired millions, both black and white. Above all, he could influence the federal government and Congress. With his preaching background, his intellectual training and his experience of life in the North, he was a brilliant communicator with white America.

M. Stacey and M. Scott-Baumann (2013), *Civil Rights and Social Movements in the Americas*, Cambridge: Cambridge University Press, p. 143.

SOURCE C

28 August 1963, Martin Luther King at the Lincoln Memorial, Washington, DC, as he prepares to speak to a crowd of more than 200,000 demonstrators who participated in the March on Washington for Jobs and Freedom

ACTIVITY

Look again at all the sources, the simplified mark scheme and the student answer above. Now try to write a sharper introduction and a better conclusion. Add material on Freedom Schools, look at bringing out more contrast between and within the sources; plus write some sentences to link the whole answer more crisply. At the same time, aim to develop a stronger argument. In this way the answer would qualify to get into Band 1 or move higher in Band 2, as it already makes good use of the information in the sources and has excellent contextual knowledge in parts.

SOURCE D

The civil rights movement's destruction of the southern caste system was a towering achievement... the foundations of this triumph were many and... although it is impossible to discount the moral and political influence of Martin Luther King, much of the spadework was undertaken by field workers and citizenship school teachers whose task was to develop a broader seam of indigenous leaders along the lines laid out by Ella Baker and others...

For most blacks and whites in the 1960s, Martin Luther King was the movement's chief figurehead. Instantly recognisable by dint of his frequent media appearances, the SCLC president symbolised more than any other leader the ongoing search for integration... yet while his high-profile visionary leadership proved invaluable to the black freedom struggle, the movement itself was far from dependent on the top-down leadership of King...

Also important were secondary and local level leaders who provided the impetus for those day-to-day civil rights activities which frequently failed to interest the national press and TV. Strong-minded, able and intelligent staff members provided the backbone for all the mainstream organisations in their headquarters and on the ground in the southern states and the urban North.

R. Cook (1998) *Sweet Land of Liberty?* Harlow: Longman, pp. 217–20.

Student answer

Martin Luther King is a controversial figure, with much written about his role in securing civil rights for African Americans in the 1960s. Contemporaries and historians have very different opinions. Some writers have argued that he was almost a communist, who incited trouble and disorder in US cities; others see him as a moderate man of peace and a pivotal figure in the African American struggle. Others such as Clayborne Carson, believe that the civil rights struggle would have evolved in the way it did, whether or not King had been a part of it. Yet the photo of King in Source C shows him addressing more than 200,000 demonstrators at the March on Washington for Jobs and Freedom. This suggests a man at the height of his power and influence. Clearly his overall influence is significant, and I am now going to evaluate the extent of that significance within the context of the period from 1957, when King became SCLC president, through to the passing of the Voting Rights Act of 1965.

King's contribution to the civil rights movement cannot be underestimated. Until the emergence of Malcolm X around 1963, King was the leading figure in the movement. As Source A notes, 'from 1957 to the mid-1960s, King had no major rival for overall leadership of the Civil Rights Movement', with Source B referring to the qualities that make him a leading figure – notably his 'preaching background... and intellectual training'. This meant that King possessed good social skills, so was equally at home and popular with both southern black and more liberal northern white audiences. Source D reinforces this by stating that, 'For most blacks and whites in the 1960s, Martin Luther King was the movement's chief figurehead. Instantly recognisable by dint of his frequent media appearances...' It is also significant that he came to symbolise 'the ongoing search for integration'.

EXAMINER'S COMMENT

This introduction provides a useful summary of how the student is going to approach the topic and indicates the argument that they intend to develop. It is immediately analytical, makes reference to historiography and incorporates a source. This is an excellent opening.

EXAMINER'S COMMENT

The student reaches the main body of the essay, writing about King's role. There is excellent use of the information from the sources here about his personality, and good linking of the three written sources, driving the argument forward and supporting the judgement and analysis. This is an excellent summary.

King maximised his SCLC leadership and his personal skills, dealing both with the White House and the disadvantaged generally. Source B supports this noting, 'With his appeal to American values, such as the belief in liberty, justice and democracy, he inspired millions, both black and white… he was a brilliant communicator with white America.' It is evident that he could approach members of Congress – and even the president – in a rational, articulate and persuasive manner; in this respect he was probably the only black leader who could 'front' the campaign before all of America. King undoubtedly kept civil rights on the political agenda and gave the movement status.

His insistence on non-violence – shown at the Greensboro sit-ins, the Freedom Rides, Birmingham and Selma – won the movement respectability and sympathy. His philosophy also brought media attention, world recognition and – as seen by the Civil Rights Act of 1964 and the Voting Rights Act of 1965 – helped invoke government intervention. King himself was awarded the 1964 Nobel Peace Prize; surely a key indicator of his status and contribution? To sum up, King was a figure of inspiration and determination – but also a figure of peace. In this respect, he was of major significance and the ideal face of the movement. But other people and factors must also be considered.

Source D calls King the 'figurehead' of the movement, and to many historians this is what he was, rather than its supremo; his profile being the result of his media-savvy appearances, his power of oratory and his growing moral and political authority. But also significant was the role of the many workers in the civil rights movement and Source D confirms that there was a continual campaign going-on by 'secondary and local level leaders who provided the impetus for those day-to-day civil rights activities that frequently failed to interest the national press and TV'.

This confirms that King and the whole movement were dependent on able staff who provided 'the backbone for all the mainstream organisations in their headquarters and on the ground in the southern states and the urban North'. Organisations like the NAACP, CORE, the SNCC and local churches all contributed to the struggle too; not just King and his SCLC.

Source A comments that by the time the Washington March (Source C) took place, leaders like King were 'dependent on the President and Congress to see a Civil Rights Bill pass successfully'. This supports the idea that there would have been no civil rights legislation without the political will to support it. King was fortunate to have the proactive Kennedy and Johnson as presidents between 1961 and 1965. They were vitally important to the success of the movement, while Eisenhower had been largely reactive.

The moderation of the movement was also highlighted by the actions of white extremists. Bull Connor in Birmingham and the Mississippi murders of the Freedom Summer workers hardened opinion and increased support for the Civil Rights Movement. Finally, by the time legislation was passed in 1964–5, Malcolm X had emerged as a prominent critic, offering an alternative to integration and non-violence. He was an inspiration to the Black Power Movement, especially those in the north who identified with his urban-ghetto background, and who had little regard for King. Source A states, 'King did not appeal to all… African Americans. He was a southerner and, as a Baptist Minister, was seen as someone from the black elite' – suggesting that, by 1964, the centre of gravity in black protest was shifting away from King and towards the north.

In conclusion, King was important in securing civil rights for African Americans between 1957 and 1965, but he was fundamentally a figurehead – albeit an influential and articulate one. The movement, not the individual was most important.

EXAMINER'S COMMENT

The case for King is further strengthened by the useful inclusion of a source and own knowledge, regarding the events taking place between 1957 and 1963. Judgement and analysis are present throughout; although the rhetorical question about the Nobel Peace Prize would be better rewritten as a statement rather than a question. The student then appears to be bringing balance to the argument by setting up the next part of the essay, where other factors are to be examined. This is a very readable and articulate section.

EXAMINER'S COMMENT

This final section shows that the student has kept the question in mind and has attempted to make a judgement on the accuracy of part of the statement. It is well-written and drawing attention to other people and events. But there is room for more critique of King, and for more content about Malcolm X. The actual conclusion itself is too brief and might suggest that the student ran out of time. It could be more synoptic, summing-up the excellent points he/she made previously, and look less 'bolted-on'.

Overall examiner's comments

The student has made good use of the information in all of the sources and has linked them well. There is also good integration of contextual knowledge to both explain and add to the sources. Sources and own knowledge are used consistently and effectively together to support argument and judgement.

The overall result is a good analytical explanation, focused on the question. However, the answer could include more information on Martin Luther King's rival Malcolm X, and lacks a stronger, slightly more synoptic conclusion. Therefore, although the answer would get into Band 1, it would not get full marks, although still scores eight marks out of the nine available.

Question 3

'Police actions at Sharpeville turned a peaceful protest into a massacre and changed the political landscape of South Africa.' Using the sources and your own knowledge, to what extent do you agree with this statement? [9 marks]

SOURCE A

We came to a large square compound in the centre, a police station surrounded by wire fences, with fields on two sides and roads on the other two. The armed vehicles went into the compound and we drove on to the waste ground beside, unobserved… I got out to see what was happening. Not much, it seemed; my guess was that there were two to three thousand there, but they were spread over a large area and with people no more than three or four deep at the fence, it didn't seem an enormous crowd. The demonstrators I talked to showed no hostility.

The cops were some distance away inside the compound, and there wasn't much to photograph… so I walked back across the waste ground to… the car. Suddenly there was shouting from the crowd.

I turned and started to walk back towards the compound. The cops were now standing on top of their armoured cars waving Sten guns, and when I was fifty yards away from the compound they opened fire into the crowd. I can't say for sure that nobody lobbed a stone at the police, but I do not believe a threatening situation had built up in the time it took me to walk the two sides of the compound and back. The cops were in no danger. I can only assume that they came out with the intention of showing the crowd, and in the process black South Africa, a dreadful lesson.

People started to run in all directions, some towards me, some away. The majority of the people who were killed were running away, around the side of the compound I had just come from. A woman was hit immediately beside me. A boy ran towards me with his coat pulled up over his head as if to protect himself from the bullets. I fell to the ground on my stomach and took pictures.

Ian Berry, a photographer with *Drum* magazine, was in Sharpeville on the day of the shooting. This is his eyewitness account of the massacre.

SOURCE B

A photograph of the crowd running away during the shootings at Sharpeville

SOURCE C

All the affidavits, he said, contradicted the government claim that the police station was besieged by 20,000 Africans. A figure supported by European witnesses to the shooting said that the crowd was no more than 4,000. The affidavits showed that the European police lined up outside the police station and fired together. All the affidavits maintain that the crowd was not armed – even with sticks. The police acted together in raising their weapons, aiming and firing. (Dr Verwoerd has said that no order was given for the police to open fire.)

The affidavits showed that the white police did not attempt to give a warning before opening fire. The only warning came from an African policeman who rushed towards the fence shouting 'Run, they are going to shoot.' At that moment the police opened fire.

The Bishop said that the overwhelming number of those being treated at the hospital had been wounded in the back.

All the affidavits insisted that the crowd was entirely good-natured and unarmed and did not converge on the police station with violent intentions.

The desperate physical condition of many of the wounded and the fact that they were in separate wards ruled out the possibility of collaboration on their stories told to the lawyers taking affidavits.

An article from *The Guardian*, 26 March 1960, reporting information gained by Ambrose Reeves, the Bishop of Johannesburg, from the sworn affidavits taken from people who were wounded at Sharpeville.

8

SOURCE D

On a sunny but chilly morning of 21 March, a crowd of black men and women began to close in on the police station in Sharpeville, a township near the industrial centre of Vereeniging. Earlier they had blocked the roads to prevent the residents from going to work. Cars had been stoned.

By lunch time the seventy-five occupants of the police station, most of them young, inexperienced Afrikaner policemen, were confronted by some 20,000 demonstrators, and their trigger fingers were itchy. Police reinforcements arrived, among them four Saracen armoured cars.

At about 1.15pm a man was arrested; scuffles broke out, missiles were thrown and police opened fire with .303 rifles and Sten guns. They continued to fire at the backs of the fleeing mob, sixty-nine of whom were killed, 186 wounded. The massacre made world headlines.

The killings were a turning point for the liberation struggle. Freedom, it was now abundantly clear would not be achieved by peaceful means. And white South Africa could no longer regard itself as a paid up member of the international community.

After March 1960, the country slid steadily into isolation.

Peter Joyce (2007) *The Making of a Nation: South Africa's Road to Freedom,* Cape Town: Zebra Press, p. 109.

Student answer

During the 1950s, the ANC and other organisations used many forms of non-violent protest against apartheid, but none of these had been effective in forcing the government to change its policies. Instead it had responded by arresting or banning their leaders. A group within the ANC became impatient with what they saw as the ineffective policies of the ANC and they broke away to form the Pan Africanist Congress (PAC). They were determined to use more effective forms of protest and decided to target the pass laws, which were one of the most hated of the apartheid laws. They planned a series of anti-pass campaigns, which were due to start on 21 March 1960.

Sharpeville was a township in which the PAC had strong support. From early in the morning on 21 March, protesters started to gather at the police station. Their intention was to burn their passes and be arrested. The PAC hoped that so many people would be arrested that the government would realise that the pass laws were unworkable. Source D hints that an element of force may have been used to get people to join the protests, because the roads out of the township had been blocked to prevent people from going to work, and cars had been stoned, but none of the other sources mention this.

By midday a large crowd had gathered. According to an eyewitness account (Source A), there were about 2,000 to 3,000 protestors. Source C says that eyewitnesses estimated the crowd at no more than 4,000. However, Source D claims that there were 20,000 protesters, which, as Source C states, is the figure that the government later claimed.

There was also conflicting evidence about the mood and actions of the crowd. The author of Source A claims that the protestors showed no hostility, when he (a photographer) spoke to them. Source C confirms this impression, saying that all eyewitness accounts described the crowd as 'entirely good-natured'. In an official statement after the shootings, however, the government claimed that the protesters had attacked the police station with a variety of weapons, including firearms, and that the police had been forced to fire in self-defence. Sources A and C challenge this view. Quoting affidavits from some of the victims of the shootings, Source C reports that the protesters were unarmed, even with sticks, and did not have any 'violent intentions'. In Source A, the photographer comments that he could not say for sure whether any stones had been thrown at the police, but that the attitude of the crowd was not threatening and that 'the cops were in no danger'. Source D, however, contradicts this view by stating that missiles were thrown at the police.

There are different accounts about the actions of the police in Sharpeville that day. Both Sources A and D mention that the police had armoured cars at the police station, and Source A says that they fired at the crowd from the top of them. This is supported by the photograph (Source C), which shows policemen with guns standing on top of armoured cars. The affidavits from eyewitnesses and victims mentioned in Source C suggested that the police actions were well coordinated because they lined up, aimed and fired together. The source also states that they gave no official warning before they started to shoot. Source D, however, suggests that the police may have panicked because they were inexperienced and 'their trigger fingers were itchy'. Source A even suggests that the police deliberately wanted to teach the black people of South Africa 'a dreadful lesson'.

The government later claimed that no order was given for the police to open fire. The prime minister, Verwoerd, even made a statement in parliament thanking the police for the courageous and efficient way that they had handled the situation and he called their actions 'exemplary'. However, the sources offer another view, and all of them show that the police shot at the protestors as they were trying to flee. Source A mentions that the majority of people were shot while running away and that the victims included women and children. Source B shows people, including women and children, running away from the police on the armoured cars. According to Source C, most of the victims being treated for injuries at the hospital had been wounded in the back, and Source D states that the police 'continued to fire at the backs of the fleeing mob'. Investigations later showed that nearly all those killed or injured had been shot in the back. The actions of the police were widely condemned around the world and brought about increasing criticism of and isolation of South Africa.

The death of sixty-nine protestors and the wounding of many more at Sharpeville on 21 March 1960 was a turning point in the resistance movement in South Africa, as Source D states. After that the government banned the ANC and PAC, effectively making peaceful protest impossible and forcing these organisations to change their tactics and adopt an armed struggle against the apartheid state. This brought the era of non-violent protest to an end. In this way, the actions of the police at Sharpeville definitely changed the political landscape in South Africa.

Overall examiner's comments

The student has made good use of the information in all of the sources and has linked them well. As this is a source-based paper, this makes it a relatively sound answer. There is also some relevant and useful own knowledge to provide a context and also to show alternative views which are not reflected in the sources. However, the answer lacks a clear introduction and, more importantly, a focus on the actual question. It is only in the concluding paragraph that the answer makes any reference to the wording of the question. The answer lacks a clear argument. Therefore, the answer would fail to get into Bands 1 and 2, which require a more consistent focus on the question, and so would probably score five marks out of the nine available.

EXAMINER'S COMMENT

Once again, the student has made good use here of the information in the sources, and has commented on how they support or contradict each other. However, there needs to be more focus on the question itself. For example, the candidate has missed an opportunity here to show how the protest became a 'massacre'.

EXAMINER'S COMMENT

The conclusion shows that the student has kept the question in mind and has attempted to make a judgement on the accuracy of part of the statement.

ACTIVITY

Look again at the all sources, the simplified mark scheme and the student answer above. Now try to write a focused introduction and add sentences to link the whole answer more appropriately to the question and at the same time develop an argument. In this way the answer would qualify to get into Band 1 or 2, as it already makes good use of the information in the sources.

Paper 2 exam practice

Paper 2 skills and questions

For Paper 2, you have to answer two essay questions – chosen from two different topics from the twelve options offered. Very often you will be asked to comment on two states from two different IB regions of the world. Although each question has a specific mark scheme, you can get a good general idea of what examiners are looking for in order to be able to put answers into the higher bands from the general 'generic' mark scheme. In particular, you will need to acquire reasonably precise historical knowledge in order to address issues such as cause and effect, or change and continuity, and to learn how to explain historical developments in a clear, coherent, well-supported and relevant way. You will also need to understand and be able to refer to aspects relating to historical debates, perspectives and interpretations.

Make sure you read the questions carefully, and select your questions wisely. It is important to produce a rough essay plan for each of your essays before you start to write an answer, and you may find it helpful to plan both your essays before you begin to write. That way, you will soon know whether you have enough own knowledge to answer them adequately.

Remember, too, to keep your answers relevant and focused on the question. For example, don't go outside the dates mentioned in the question, or answer on individuals/ states different from the ones identified in the question. Don't just describe the events or developments – sometimes, students just focus on one key word or individual, and then write down all they know about it. Instead, select your own knowledge carefully, and pin the relevant information to the key features raised by the question. Also, if the question asks for 'causes/reasons' and 'consequences/results', or two different countries/leaders, make sure you deal with all the parts of the question. Otherwise, you will limit yourself to half marks at best.

Examiner's tips

For Paper 2 answers, examiners are looking for clear/precise analysis, and a balanced argument, linked to the question, with the use of good, precise and relevant own knowledge. In order to obtain the highest marks, you should be able to refer, where appropriate, to historical debate and/or different historical perspectives/interpretations, or historians' knowledge, making sure it is both relevant to the question AND integrated into your answer.

Common mistakes

When answering Paper 2 questions, try to avoid simply describing what happened. A detailed narrative, with no explicit attempts to link the knowledge to the question, will only get you half marks at most.

If the question asks you to select examples from two different regions, make sure you don't chose two states from the same region. Every year, some candidates do this, and so limit themselves to – at best – only eight out of the fifteen marks available for each question.

Simplified mark scheme

Band		Marks
1	**Consistently clear focus** on the question, with **all** main aspects addressed. Answer is **fully analytical and well-structured/organised**. There is **sound understanding** of historical concepts. The answer also integrates **evaluation** of different historical debates/perspectives, and reaches a **clear/consistent judgement/conclusion**.	13–15
2	**Clear understanding** of the question, and **most** of its main aspects are addressed. Answer is **mostly well-structured and developed**, with supporting own knowledge **mostly relevant/accurate**. Answer is **mainly analytical**, with **attempts at a consistent conclusion**; and shows **some understanding** of historical concepts and debates/perspectives.	10–12
3	**Demands of the question are understood** but some aspects **not fully developed/addressed**. **Relevant/accurate supporting own knowledge**, but **attempts at analysis are limited/inconsistent**.	7-9
4	**Some understanding** of the question. **Some relevant own knowledge**, with some factors identified but with **limited explanation**. **Some attempts at analysis**, but answer is **mainly description/ narrative**.	4-6
5	**Limited understanding** of the question. **Short/general answer**, with very **little accurate/relevant** own knowledge. Some **unsupported assertions**, with **no real analysis**.	0-3

Student answers

Those parts of the student answer that follow will have brief examiner's comments in the margins, as well as a longer overall comment at the end. Those parts that are particularly strong and well-focused will be highlighted in red. Errors/confusions/loss of focus will be highlighted in blue. In this way, you should find it easier to follow why marks were – or were not – awarded.

Question 1

Compare and contrast the methods, and comment briefly on the achievements, of the protest movements against discrimination and segregation in the United States and South Africa between 1950 and 1964.

Skill

Analysis, argument, evaluation.

Examiner's tip

Look carefully at the wording of this question, which asks for both comparison and contrast. The main focus of the essay should be on the methods used by the

Exam practice

two protest movements, but you also need to make some comment towards the end about the relative achievements of each one. All aspects of the essay need to be addressed in order to achieve high marks. It would be a good idea to make a quick plan that you can refer to, as this question requires explicit analysis and comparison throughout.

Student answer

In both the United States and South Africa there was a long history of racism, discrimination and segregation. In the southern states of the US, Jim Crow laws discriminated against African Americans, who formed about 10 per cent of the population, and enforced the segregation of many public facilities. In South Africa, the white population, who formed less than 20 per cent of the population, enforced strict segregation laws that ensured white domination over the black majority. During the 1950s, protest movements emerged in both countries, demanding an end to segregation laws and equality for all citizens. Although there were some similarities in their methods, their achievements were very different.

In both countries, organisations had been formed before the First World War to oppose segregation. In the US, the National Association for the Advancement of Colored People (NAACP) was formed in 1909 to press for civil and political rights for all. In South Africa, the African National Congress (ANC) was formed in 1912 with the same purpose. Both organisations were essentially conservative in their approach and committed to non-confrontational forms of protest. However, the Second World War brought about dramatic changes. In the US, one million African-Americans served in the armed forces during the war and returned home determined to bring about change. In South Africa, African nationalists were inspired by the Atlantic Charter and encouraged by changing economic circumstances, where segregation laws were breaking down.

Regarding political circumstances, there were both differences and similarities between the two countries after the war. In the US, the Truman administration made some tentative steps towards recognising the civil rights of African Americans; for example, by outlawing segregation in the armed forces. By contrast, in South Africa, the predominantly white electorate voted the National Party into power in 1948, and it was determined to introduce and harshly enforce a much stricter form of segregation called apartheid. In the early 1950s, one similarity between the governments of both countries was their hostile attitude towards communism. In both cases they regarded calls for racial equality as being linked to subversive communist ideology. In the US, Senator McCarthy's House Committee on Un-American Activities investigated the activities of suspected communists in government departments and trade unions, while in South Africa, the Suppression of Communism Act banned the Communist Party altogether.

The first method used to challenge segregation laws in the US in the early 1950s was through the courts. This was the method favoured by the NAACP, which did not support direct protest actions. It won a significant victory in 1954 when the Supreme Court ruled that segregation in the public school system was unconstitutional. This was the famous Brown v. Topeka Board of Education case. After this, the NAACP supported efforts to register black students in previously all-white schools. In 1957, in Little Rock, Arkansas, there were violent clashes when white racists, backed by the state governor, tried to prevent this from happening. It was only resolved after the federal government sent troops to protect the black students and enforce the law. In spite of this, most schools in the south remained segregated.

In South Africa, protesters also used the legal system, but in a more limited way. When the government disenfranchised coloured voters in the Cape using methods that violated the constitution, a group of voters successfully challenged this move in the courts, which ruled on two occasions that the government's actions were unconstitutional. However, using devious means the government sidestepped the issue and proceeded with its plans to ensure that only whites had voting rights.

The main form of protest in both countries was non-violent civil disobedience. The ANC in South Africa and the main civil rights organisations in the US supported non-violence and their leaders were both awarded the Nobel Peace Prize in recognition of this – Albert Luthuli in 1960 and Martin Luther King in 1964.

Throughout the 1950s, there were mass non-violent forms of protest in South Africa. In 1952, the ANC and other groups organised a Defiance Campaign in which protesters deliberately broke the law; for example, by using 'whites only' entrances. Although it did not succeed in getting the government to change its policies, the campaign increased political awareness inside and outside South Africa and turned the ANC into a mass-based organisation. Opposition groups also organised a mass rally, the 'Congress of the People', and adopted a 'Freedom Charter' as a blueprint for a future non-racial democracy. Another example of mass protest was a Women's March to Pretoria to protest against the pass laws. There were also protests organised by communities about specific aspects of apartheid, such as Bantu Education, forced removals and conditions in the reserves. In 1960, mass demonstrations were planned by the ANC and the newly formed Pan Africanist Congress to protest against the pass laws, one of the most hated of all apartheid laws. It was at one of these protests, at Sharpeville, that the police responded by killing sixty-nine protesters, ending a decade of non-violent protest.

There were also grass-roots community protests in the US. In Montgomery, Alabama, a year-long boycott of the public transport system by 50,000 black inhabitants of the city, resulted in the Supreme Court outlawing segregation on buses in 1956. This was after the Rosa Parks incident. As a result of the boycott, a young African American minister, Martin Luther King, emerged as the leader of the Civil Rights Movement. He supported non-violent resistance, or civil disobedience.

Despite the success of the Bus Boycott in ending segregation on the buses in Montgomery, this success did not spread to other parts of the south, where segregation remained in force. But the Civil Rights Movement gained momentum in the 1960s. In January 1960, black students at a college in North Carolina staged a 'sit-in' at a lunch counter in a shop that refused to serve black customers. Their example was followed by other students, who held similar protests in other segregated facilities. They organised 'kneel-ins' in churches, 'read-ins' in public libraries, 'play-ins' in city parks and 'wade-ins' on beaches. Their courage encouraged others to become involved in the struggle. Soon thousands more, black and white, joined in a massive campaign of non-violent civil disobedience to demand the desegregation of public facilities. They persisted despite violence and intimidation by southern authorities and white supremacists.

Other protesters became 'Freedom Riders', travelling on inter-state buses to force the integration of buses and bus stations all over the south. Although the protesters still supported the concept of non-violent protest, they urged more proactive direct action to provoke reactions from the authorities and segregationists. Many of them were savagely attacked by angry white mobs, but they succeeded in the end in getting federal support.

An important step in the civil rights campaign was a massive demonstration in the capital, Washington, DC, in 1963. At the Lincoln Memorial, 250,000 people, from all religious and ethnic backgrounds, joined together to demand full racial equality. Although many critics had

EXAMINER'S COMMENT

The student has made an attempt here to contrast the use of legal action in both countries, but there is no real analysis of these developments. For example, the answer does not show an understanding of the significance of the *Brown* ruling. Nor does it suggest reasons why legal challenges weren't really an option in South Africa. The answer is a bit vague in places too.

EXAMINER'S COMMENT

This section is a bit disjointed. There is a good attempt initially to draw parallels between the two movements, but this point isn't developed fully. The answer then proceeds to give a narrative account of protest actions, firstly in South Africa and then in the US, without showing any links or making any analytical comments. In each case it is more like a descriptive list than an analysis, and there are no attempts to compare or contrast.

EXAMINER'S COMMENT

In the last two paragraphs, the student has made some valid analytical comments about the relative success of the protest actions in the US compared to those in SA. But, importantly, the answer lacks a concluding paragraph to tie up the argument and link the essay to the question.

predicted violence, the huge crowd remained peaceful, listening to protest songs and speeches, such as Martin Luther King's 'I Have a Dream' speech.

In the Freedom Summer of 1964, black and white civil rights campaigners from the more liberal northern states went to Mississippi to open Freedom Schools and to encourage blacks to register as voters. The Freedom Schools taught basic literacy and black history, and stressed black pride and achievements. But there was a violent reaction to their efforts: black churches were bombed, hundreds of Freedom Summer workers were beaten and arrested, and some were murdered.

Despite the violent reactions to their protests, the Civil Rights Movement in the US maintained its support for non-violence. In South Africa, however, the situation was different. After the Sharpeville massacre, the government banned the ANC and PAC. As they were no longer able to operate legally, they formed underground wings to conduct an armed struggle against the apartheid government. The ANC's armed wing, MK, conducted a sabotage campaign against government installations. The PAC's armed wing planned an armed uprising. Neither was successful as the authorities uncovered their plans and arrested their leaders, who were subsequently sentenced to life imprisonment.

As a result of the efforts of the Civil Rights Movement, the US Congress passed the Civil Rights Act in 1964. This law barred segregation and discrimination in employment and in all public facilities, including schools, hotels and restaurants. This was a major achievement for the Civil Rights Movement, although in practice racism, prejudice and discrimination, as well as serious economic inequalities, remained. The Civil Rights Movement had achieved this success by 1964 because it had the backing of the Supreme Court (which ruled that segregation was illegal), the federal government in Washington (which sent troops to enforce the integration of schools) and Congress (which passed the Civil Rights Act).

This was in contrast to the situation in South Africa at the time, where the resistance movement had no official support. Instead, the government used legislation, the police and the army to enforce an even stricter system of segregation and oppression. By the end of 1964, it seemed as if the government had crushed all protest. The protest movements had been banned and their leaders (such as Nelson Mandela, who was serving a life sentence on Robben Island) were in prison or in exile.

Overall examiner comments

This answer starts off promisingly with a balanced introductory paragraph that focuses on the question. There are also attempts in parts of the essay to point out similarities and differences between the two situations. However, the student has not maintained this comparative focus and much of this answer consists of a narrative of events in each country. There is plenty of correct own knowledge, but its relevance and significance are not always demonstrated. The essay also lacks any reference to different historical interpretations.

Consequently, this answer is not good enough to go higher than Band 3 – probably getting seven marks. To reach the higher bands, there needs to be more explicit comparison and contrast of the two case studies, as well as a sustained analytical rather than narrative or descriptive approach. The student clearly has good knowledge, and some of the information needed to produce a good answer is already present.

ACTIVITY

Look again at the simplified mark scheme and the student answer above. Now try to write a few extra paragraphs to push the answer up into Band 1, and so obtain the full fifteen marks. As well as making sure you explicitly compare and contrast the two case studies, try to integrate some references to relevant historians/historical interpretations.

Further information

Case Study 1: Civil Rights in the US, 1956–65

Blum, J.M. (1991) *Years of Discord: American Politics and Society 1961–74*, New York: Norton.

Bottaro J. and Stanley J. (2011) *Democratic States*, Cambridge: Cambridge University Press.

Boyer P., Clark C., Kett, J., Salisbury N., Sitkoff H. and Woloch N. (2008) *The Enduring Vision*, 2008 Houghton Mifflin p868.

Chafe, W. (1981) *Civilities and Civil Rights*, New York: Oxford University Press.

Chafe, W. (1999) *The Unfinished Journey*, Oxford: Oxford University Press.

Cook, R. (1998) *Sweet Land of Liberty*, Harlow: Longman.

Fairclough, A. (1987) *To Redeem the Soul of America: The Southern Christian Leadership Conference and Martin Luther King Jr.*, Atlanta: University of Georgia Press.

Farber, D. and Bailey B. (2001) *The Columbia Guide to America in the 1960s*, New York: Columbia University Press.

Gilbert, J. (1981) *Another Chance, Postwar America 1945–68*, New York: Alfred A. Knopf.

Heale, M.J. (2001) *The Sixties in America: History, Politics and Protest*, Edinburgh: Edinburgh University Press.

King, R.H. (1992) *Civil Rights and the Idea of Freedom*, Athens, GA: University of Georgia Press.

Levine, P. and Papasotiriou, H. (2005) *America Since 1945*, Basingstoke: Palgrave Macmillan.

Marable, M. (1991) *Race, Reform and Religion*, Jackson, MS: University Press of Mississippi

Morris, A.D. (1984) *The Origins of the Civil Rights Movements*, New York: The Free Press.

Paterson, D., Willoughby, D. and Willoughby, S. (2001) *Civil Rights in the USA 1863–1980*, Oxford: Heinemann.

Rieder, J. (2013) *Gospel of Freedom*, New York: Bloomsbury Press.

Sanders, V. (2006) *Race Relations In the USA 1863–1980*, London: Hodder Murray.

Stacey, M. and Scott-Baumann, M. (2013) *Civil Rights and Social Movements in the Americas*, Cambridge: Cambridge University Press.

Steigerwald, D. (1995) *The Sixties and the End of Modern America*, New York: St. Martin's Press.

Traynor, J. (2001) *Modern United States History*, Basingstoke: Palgrave.

8

Case Study 2: Apartheid in South Africa, 1948–64

Beinart, W. (1994) *Twentieth-Century South Africa*, Cape Town: Oxford University Press.

Butler, A. (2009) *Contemporary South Africa*, Basingstoke: Palgrave Macmillan.

Dubow, S. (2000) *The African National Congress*, Johannesburg: Jonathan Ball Publishers.

Filatova, I. and Davidson, A. (2013) *The Hidden Thread: Russia and South Africa in the Soviet Era*, Cape Town: Jonathan Ball Publishers.

Giliomee, H. and Mbenga, B. (2007) *New History of South Africa*, Cape Town: Tafelberg Publishers.

Joyce, P. (2007) *The Making of a Nation: South Africa's Road to Freedom*, Cape Town: Zebra Press.

Lodge, T. (1983) *Black Politics in South Africa since 1945*, Johannesburg: Ravan Press.

Mandela, N. (2003) *The Illustrated Long Walk to Freedom*, London: Little Brown/ Abacus.

Maylam, P. (1986) *A History of the African People of South Africa: From the Early Iron Age to the 1970s*, Cape Town: David Philip.

Nasson, B. (ed.) (2004) *Turning Points in History: Industrialisation, Rural Change and Nationalism*, Cape Town: STE Publishers for the Institute of Justice and Reconciliation and the South African History Project.

Oates, D. (ed.) (1988) *Illustrated History of South Africa*, Cape Town: Reader's Digest Association.

Pampallis, J. (1997) *Foundations of the New South Africa*, Cape Town: Maskew Miller Longman.

Ross, R. (1999) *A Concise History of South Africa*, Cambridge: Cambridge University Press.

Sheehan, S. (2002) *South Africa Since Apartheid*, London: Hodder Wayland.

Thompson, L. (2006) *A History of South Africa*, Johannesburg: Jonathan Ball Publishers.

Welsh, D. (2010) *The Rise and Fall of Apartheid: From Racial Domination to Majority Rule*, Johannesburg: Jonathan Ball Publishers.

Wilson, F. (2009) *Dinosaurs, Diamonds and Democracy: A Short, Short History of South Africa*, Cape Town: UMUZI.

Worden, N. (2007) *The Making of Modern South Africa: Conquest, Apartheid, Democracy*, 4th edition, Oxford: Blackwell.

Index

African Americans *see also* employment, African
  Americans
  enslavement of 7–8
  Freemasons, Ohio 99
  postwar conditions 20–2, 24–5
  and Second World War 8, 15, 18, 19–20
African Mineworkers Union 149, 202
African National Congress
  Freedom Charter 153, 159, 194, 198
African National Congress (ANC) *see also* MK
  (Umkhonto we Sizwe)
  anti-pass campaigns 160–1
  banning orders and 11, 12, 137, 142, 172,
    193, 203
  charterism 153, 159, 194
  and community protests 194–6
  and the Congress Youth League (CYL) 149,
    151, 192
  formation of 146, 191
  links with CPSA 135, 151, 191
  mass action and 151–2, 192
  multiracial policies 153, 159, 192, 194,
    198, 205
  and other organizations 192, 198
  Programme of Action 149, 151, 192, 193
  tensions with Africanists 159, 198
  Women's League 147, 156, 195
African People's Organization (APO) 151, 202
African Resistance Movement (ARM) 174–5
Africanism 147, 149, 159, 192, 198 *see also* Pan
  Africanist Congress
Afrikaners 9–11, 118, 185–7
Alabama Christian Movement for Human
  Rights (ACMHR) 102
Albany Movement 90–1, 102
All-African Convention (AAC) 146
Anti-Apartheid Movement (AAM) 164–6
apartheid
  and forced removals 128–33, 187, 194
  Group Areas Act 125–6, 129–30
  Immorality Act 124
  introduction of 9, 122–3
  legal enforcement of 124–5, 137–8, 175
  segregation policies 12, 125–8, 187
  Western governments and 169–70
armed resistance/struggle 11 *see also* MK
  (Umkhonto we Sizwe)
  against apartheid 172–5
  arrests of resistance leaders 175–6, 179
  Poqo (Pan Africanist Congress) 174, 175, 200
Atlantic Charter 146, 147

Baker, Ella 90, 101, 106
Bandung Conference 192
Bantu Education Act 127–8, 157, 195

Bantustans 12, 131–2
Birmingham campaign (1963) 97–8, 102–4,
  110–11
black churches 88, 89, 96–9
Black Panther Party 93
Black Power movement 24, 107
Black Sash 155–6
Boers 9–11
Botha, Louis 123, 185
Boycott Committee 164
Brown II (desegregation plan) 28, 30
Brown v. Topeka Board of Education 1954 17, 21,
  24, 26–8, 30, 32, 36, 85

Cape Town 130, 131, 157
Cape Town March 162–3, 171
Carmichael, Stokely 93, 106
Cato Manor Riots 192
civil disobedience, USA 73–7
civil rights 11, 16, 17
Civil Rights Act (1964) 21, 66–9, 75–6, 105
Civil Rights Acts (1957/1960) 37–8
Civil Rights Movement, USA
  Eisenhower's lack of interest in 24, 30, 38–9
  emergence of 15, 25, 31–2
  FBI surveillance of 29
  impact of Little Rock, Arkansas 36–7
  and the Montgomery Bus Boycott 47–8
  and non-violent resistance 47–8, 50–1
  race relations, 1950s 24
  strategies and tactics 58, 82–4, 85
  tensions within 65, 94–6
  white support for 1, 56, 58, 59, 92, 93–4
Clark, Jim 69, 72
Cold War 22–3, 136, 171
colonialism 6–7, 9, 118, 120
colour bar 120
communism 23, 29
Communist Party of South Africa (CPSA)
  links with the ANC 135, 151, 191
  Suppression of Communism Act 136, 137,
    138, 187, 202–3
  and workers' rights 135–6, 201–2
Congress Alliance 138, 153, 172, 194
Congress of Racial Equality (CORE)
  Mississippi Freedom Summer, 1964 52, 56,
    58, 59, 63
  and other civil rights groups 94–6
  overview of 24, 83–4, 86–8
Congress of the People 153, 154, 194, 203, 210
Congress Youth League (CYL) 147, 149, 151,
  192, 198, 208
Congressional Committee on Civil
  Rights 21
Connor, Theophilus Eugene 'Bull' 52, 56, 102

Council of Federated Organizations (COFO)
  59, 87
Criminal Law Amendment Act (1953) 137

Dadoo, Yusuf 192, 203, 204
Deacons for Defence and Justice 87–8
Deep South, USA 18, 19, 24, 29, 30, 86
Defiance Campaign 137, 151–2, 193, 209
desegregation of schools, USA *see also* education
  segregation
  1954 Supreme Court ruling 15
  Brown II (desegregation plan) 28, 30
  federal intervention 34–6
  legal enforcement of 35
  Little Rock, Arkansas 32–4
  media coverage of 107
  opposition to 29, 30, 33–5
  Southern Manifesto and 29
Du Bois, W.E.B. 21, 84

Eckford, Elizabeth 32, 33
education segregation *see also* desegregation of
  schools, USA
  Brown v. Topeka Board of Education 1954 17,
    21, 24, 26–8, 30, 32, 36, 85
  march against 16
  in South Africa 127–8, 129
Eisenhower, Dwight D.
  appointment of Earl Warren 26, 28–9, 31
  career 23–4
  Civil Rights Acts 37–8, 86
  lack of action over civil rights 24, 30, 38–9
  response to Little Rock 33, 34–6
employment, African Americans
  black employment, USA 19, 24–5, 68, 74,
    104
  and the Civil Rights Act, USA 66, 67, 68
  Fair Employment Practices Commission
    (FEPC) 21, 22
  Operation Breadbasket 88

Farmer, James 87, 88
Faubus, Orval 33, 35–6
FBI (Federal Bureau of Investigation) 29, 61
Federation of South African Women 143, 152,
  155, 195
Fellowship of Reconciliation (FOR) 86–7
filibuster 68
First, Ruth 202, 208
Fischer, Bram 175–6, 207, 208
forced removals 128–33, 187, 194
Fort Hare 128, 208
Freedom Charter 153, 159, 194, 198
Freedom Rides 52–5, 56, 58, 84, 90
Freedom Schools 62–3

241

Acknowledgements

The author and publishers acknowledge the following sources of copyright material and are grateful for the permissions granted. While every effort has been made, it has not always been possible to identify the sources of all the material used, or to trace all copyright holders. If any omissions are brought to our notice, we will be happy to include the appropriate acknowledgements on reprinting.

Images

Cover © Steve Schapiro/Corbis; 1.1 MPI/Getty Images; 1.3 © Corbis; 2.1 © Wally McNamee/CORBIS; 2.2 Afro American Newspapers/Gado/Getty Images; 2.3 ullstein bild/ullstein bild via Getty Images; 2.4 Popperfoto/Getty Images; 2.5 © World History Archive/Alamy; 2.7 © Everett Collection Historical/; 2.8 Francis Miller/The LIFE Picture Collection/Getty Images; 3.1 © Pictorial Press Ltd/Alamy; 3.2 Don Cravens/The LIFE Images Collection/ Getty Images; CH3 Source B © Jack Moebes/CORBIS; 3.3 © Everett Collection Historical/Alamy; 3.4 kschlot1 CC by 2.0; 3.5 AFP/Getty Images; 3.6 MPI/Getty Images; 3.7 © Bettmann/CORBIS; 3.8 © Bettmann/CORBIS; 3.9 Universal History Archive/Getty Images; 3.10 Morton Broffman/Getty Images; 3.11 © Everett Collection Historical/; 3.12 J. R. Eyerman/Time & Life Pictures/Getty Images; CH3 Source A © Bettmann/CORBIS; 4.1 Pictorial Parade/Hulton Archive/Getty Images; 4,2 Patrick A. Burns/New York Times Co./Getty Images; 4.3 Afro American Newspapers/Gado/Getty Images; 4.4 © Bettmann/CORBIS; 4.5 © Everett Collection Historical/Alamy; 4.6 Robert W. Kelley/The LIFE Picture Collection/Getty Images; 4.7 Don Cravens/The LIFE Images Collection/ Getty Images; 4.9 BILL HUDSON/AP/Press Association Images; 4.10 Transdiffusion; 4.11 Michael Ochs Archives/Getty Images; 4.12 MPI/Getty Images; 5.1 Ernest Cole; 5.3 Central Press/Getty Images; 5.4 © Hulton-Deutsch/Hulton-Deutsch Collection/Corbis; 5.5 The Granger Collection/Topfoto; 5.7 Terrence Spencer/The LIFE Images Collection/ Getty Images; 5.8 © Drum Social Histories/Baileys African History Archive/Africa Media Online; 5.10 © Drum Social Histories/Baileys African History Archive/Africa Media Online; 5.11 © Charles O. Cecil/Alamy; 5.13 © Gille de Vlieg/South Photos/Africa Media Online; 5.14 Stellenbosch University, Library and Information Service, Special Collections, DF Malan collection.; 6.1 Jurgen Schadeberg/Getty Images; 6.2 (c) 1995-2015 Zapiro; 6.3 © Drum Social Histories/Baileys African History Archive/Africa Media Online; 6.4 Keystone-France/Gamma-Keystone via Getty Images; 6.5 © Cedric Nunn/Africa Media Online; 6.6 Jurgen Schadeberg/Getty Images; 6.7 Jurgen Schadeberg/Getty Images; 6.8 Universal History Archive/UIG via Getty images; 6.10 © Drum Social Histories/Baileys African History Archive/Africa Media Online; 6.11 National library of South Africa/Photo © PVDE/Bridgeman Images; 6.12 (c) Henry Grant Collection/Museum of London; 6.13 STF/AFP/Getty Images; 6.14 © Keystone Pictures USA/Alamy; 6.15 © Punch Limited; 6.16 AP/AP/Press Association Images; 7.1 © CSI Productions/Alamy; 7.3 solosyndication; 7.4 © Drum Social Histories/Baileys African History Archive/Africa Media Online; 7.6 © Drum Social Histories/ Baileys African History Archive/Africa Media Online; 7.7 © Drum Social Histories/Baileys African History Archive/ Africa Media Online; 7.10 Liliesleaf Trust and Historical Papers; 7.11 © Rob Crandall/Alamy; 7.12 © World History Archive/Alamy; 7.13 ADN-Bildarchiv/ullstein bild via Getty Images; 7.14 Associated Newspapers Ltd./Solo Syndication; 8.1 © Bettmann/CORBIS; 8.2 AFP/Getty Images; 8.3 Universal History Archive/UIG via Getty Images.